Journal of Wetland Archaeology 9, 2009

Managing Editor: Bryony Coles, University of Exeter, UK

Contents

Sunken Village, Sauvie Island, Oregon, USA
A Report on the 2006–2007 Investigations
of National Historic Landmark Wet Site 35MU4

By Dale R. Croes, John L. Fagan and Maureen Newman Zehendner

With contributions by (in order of first contribution)
Akira Matsui, Robert Kentta, Pat Courtney Gold, Eirik Thorsgard, Melanie Diedrich,
Michele Punke, Kathleen Hawes, Bethany Mathews, James Goebel, Jr., Tressa Pagel,
R. Todd Baker, Virginia Butler, Rebecca Wigen, Philip Pedack, Michael Martin,
Jason Channel, Tyler Graham, Olivia Ness, Bud Lane, Nola Nahirnick,
Germán Löffler, Mark Collard, Carolyn Dennler

Authors' Dedication

In Memory

To **Bruce M. Crespin (1953–2008),** Juaneno Band of California Mission
Indians, Acjachemem Nation
Archaeologist and Cultural Resources Specialist
Oregon State Office, Bureau of Land Management
Who loved our work at wet sites of Sunken Village and Qwu?gwes because
of the excellent preservation of wood and fiber, and especially basketry,
that he knew showed identity
We will miss his help and visits

To **George Douglas (1924–2008)**, highly supportive property owner of the Sunken
Village site. George and his wife Mary, always enjoyed our visits and learning about
the work and discoveries at their site. They always made sure we were welcomed
and able to record the National Historic Landmark on their property.
Thank you George.

*Frontispiece. Cedar root cross-warp basket from Sunken Village, Sauvie Island,
Oregon, USA.*

Personal registration and subscription activation on Ingenta Connect

In order to access your personal subscriptions online, you must complete a one time simple 2-step process.

1. Register

   Go to: www.ingentaconnect.com/register/personal
   Enter your information in the fields provided
   Choose a username and password
   (username/password must be at least 5 characters)
   Click on the 'Register' button at the bottom of the page.

You will receive an email from Ingenta thanking you for registering on Ingenta Connect.

2. Activate Subscriptions

   Click the 'Activating Personal subscriptions' link.
   Click the 'Add' tab.
   Search for or browse to the journal title(s) you subscribe to.
   Enter your publisher subscription number in the box provided to the right and tick the box to the left of the journal title.
   Click the 'add' link at the top or bottom of the journal list.

You will then receive an on-screen confirmation message that your request has been received. Once access has been verified, the journal title will appear in your current subscriptions list.

   To request access to additional titles just sign in with your username and password, and select the 'Personal subscriptions' option under 'Manage My Ingenta'. You can then view the titles to which you currently have access, or activate new ones on the 'Add' tab.

Institutional registration and subscription activation on Ingenta Connect

To register and activate your Institutional journal subscriptions go to:
https://www.ingentaconnect.com/register/institutional

The whole process involves 5 simple steps and should take you no more than 5 minutes. Please have ready the following information:

Contact details:
- As administrator, your basic contact details
- Your library/institution's name and address
- If articles are to be received via fax or Ariel, a default fax number or the IP number of your Ariel machine (optional).

Authentication:
Access to IngentaConnect can be set up in two ways. You may choose one or both methods of authentication.
- IP address/range (users accessing from computers within an IP range defined by the site administrator) – You may need to consult your network administrator for this information.
- Username and password.

Step 1 – Institutional and administrator contact details
Step 2 – Authentication
Step 3 – Article delivery information
Step 4 – Admin sign in
Step 5 – Confirmation of Registration

The confirmation screen will provide you with your Ingenta customer ID number. Please provide this number whenever you contact Ingenta as this will allow us to bring up your registration details immediately. After reading about the benefits of IngentaConnect Premium, you can click 'continue'. You can now click on the link 'set up subscriptions' to set up your institutional subscriptions.

At a later date, to request access to additional titles just sign in with your Administrator username and password and select the link for 'subscriptions' on the right navigation. You can then view the titles to which you currently have access to, or set up new ones.

WIND*gather*
P R E S S

an imprint of

OXBOW
BOOKS

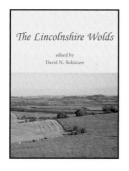

The Lincolnshire Wolds   *edited by David Robinson*

The Lincolnshire Wolds are a range of hills in the county of Lincolnshire. They are a designated Area of Outstanding Natural Beauty (AONB), and the highest area of land in eastern England between Yorkshire and Kent. This book is a collection of papers on the landscape history and regional geography of the Lincolnshire Wolds, bringing together the important known historical, natural and cultural information about the area. The volume particularly focuses on the Area of Outstanding Natural Beauty in its regional setting, making it the first of its kind to be published. *160p, col illus throughout (2009) 9781905119264.* PB £20.00

Poisonous Plants: A Cultural and Social History

by Robert Bevan-Jones

In this book, which is richly illustrated with modern colour photographs and illustrations from herbals, Robert Bevan-Jones brings together a wealth of documentary and archaeo-botanical sources to discuss the cultural, social role of the fifty most significant species of poisonous plants and fungi found in Britain. An introductory essay puts into context the development of British society's knowledge of toxic plants: the 'cultural botany' applied in Britain today has evolved over thousands of years. This is an essential book not only for botanists and historical ecologists, but also for anyone interested in the toxic plant traditions of Britain and Europe.
220p, illustrated with colour throughout (2009) 9781905119219 PB. £25.00

POISONOUS PLANTS
Poisonous Plants in North-Western European Society: A Study

Robert Bevan-Jones

10 Hythe Bridge Street, Oxford, OX1 2EW
Tel: 01865 241249 Fax: 01865 794449 Email: orders@oxbowbooks.com
WEB: WWW.OXBOWBOOKS.COM

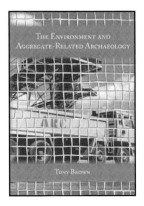
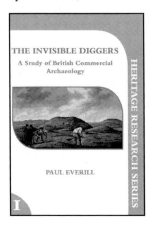

1 Introduction

1.1 Introduction to the Project

The Lower Columbia River section of the Northwest Coast of North America is thought to have had one of the highest population densities north of Mexico during aboriginal times (Darby 2005; Pettigrew 1977, 1990; Silverstein 1990), yet it has only been in recent years that Chinookan sites and culture have been the focus of concentrated research efforts by professionals. Archaeological studies in the Portland Basin, U.S.A. from the mid-1980's to the present under the direction of Dr. Kenneth M. Ames of Portland State University (PSU) have provided substantive new data for interpreting the region. Much of the research has focused on household archaeology at the large village sites of Meier (35CO5; Ames 1994; Ames and Maschner 1999) and Cathlapotle (45CL1; Ames *et al.* 1998, 1999). Just south of these major village sites, on the southern end of Sauvie Island, Portland, Oregon, U.S.A. is the well-preserved wet site of Sunken Village (35MU4), placed on the National Historic Landmark registration by Dr. Ames and Maureen Newman Zehendner (Newman 1991). Only about 250 archaeological sites in the U.S.A. are given National Historic Landmark status, and Sunken Village site achieved this status from over 50 years of erosion and collecting at the site, not systematic excavation or professional investigations.

In September of 2006 and 2007 the first systematic testing and recording of this waterlogged wetland site finally happened as a cooperative U.S. and Tribal and international archaeological effort. The mapping of 60 acorn leaching pits and well-preserved basketry in 2006 caught the interest of Japanese researchers working with similar wet sites from ancient Jomon Japan, and they offered and sponsored the extended field work in 2007. With combined limited resources, and the typically resulting abundant wood and fiber artifacts from well-preserved wet sites, we felt it important to promptly report this initial and exciting first look at one of the most significant wetland sites on the Northwest Coast of North America, and fortunately we can share this comprehensive work with an international audience through the *Journal of Wetland Archaeology*.

Sunken Village (35MU4) represents the largest known acorn leaching pit site in North America. During the low waters of September 2007, the international team of Japanese, U.S. and Tribal archaeologists mapped over 110 hemlock bough lined pits containing remnants of numerous waterlogged acorns, as well as basketry fragments, wooden wedges and abundant wood and fiber debitage. We estimate that, if all pits recorded were used, over 2.5 million acorns could be leached in a season at this site.

One fragile and ancient diamond-plaited soft flat bag recovered has drawn attention from regional basketry experts in the desert west of the U.S.A. Great Basin, through Jomon period wet site specialists in Japan. This distinct basketry type is recorded for up to 9,000 years in cave sites in the state of Nevada, U.S.A through Klamath and Puget Sound Native American modern collects in Northwestern U.S.A. In Japan these diamond-plaited soft bags are seen associated with acorn pit waterlogged sites from 7,000 years ago through Ainu modern collections. We have used cladistic analyses to associate ancient Northwest Coast basketry through over 2,800 museum baskets collections, and plan to expand that sample into the contact and ancient U.S.A. Great Basin and Japanese Jomon basketry. We hope this will demonstrate the first concrete evidence of a broad Pacific and very ancient cultural sharing, where ideas moved rapidly throughout the North Pacific Basin, as demonstrated through the use of acorn pit processing/storage, and with the sharing of distinct styles of basketry around at least the North Pacific.

1.2 Forewords

1.2.1 2007 Sponsor: Dr. Akira Matsui, Chief Archaeologist, National Institute for Cultural Heritage, Nara, Japan and Pacific Representative, *Wetland Archaeological Research Project* (WARP).

Last September, five fellow researchers and I went to Oregon in the United States of America to participate in an excavation. It all started when my old friend Professor Dale Croes from the South Puget Sound Community College emailed me saying: "I found some pits packed with acorns in an ancient Columbia River intertidal beach site called Sunken Village. Would you like to do a collaborative project there?"

We knew that in the fall, the ancient Japanese Jomon people would store large amounts of acorns in storage pits so that during the passing winter they would have food. However, there is a difference between how Eastern and Western Japan went about this. Eastern Japan Jomon put their storage pits on top of a hill, and the West puts it at the bottom of a hill in a muddy, wet place. We didn't know the reason for this. When I asked Dale about the acorn pits, we hoped that we could get some ideas through this Oregon work.

I've been part of the Higashimyo wet site research advisory board, Saga City Board of Education, coordinating the excavations and research since 2004. On the Ariake Sea, with the Kose River running along it, the early Jomon people lived there 7000 years ago. We found six shell middens, and around their bases we found 200 acorn storage pits. What surprised me was how many of the baskets were still preserved. By the time the excavation was over, the total number had risen to 730 basketry examples.

With the formation of these ancient Jomon communities, even more than now, global warming was a problem, and as a result the land went under the water and people were forced from their homes. The sites were covered in thick clay, similar to the initial deposition, and now once more, with excavation, the shape of these sites are visible again.

The Sunken Village wet site is approximately one hour North of Portland in the silty intertidal banks of the Columbia and Willamette River slough, located on the west side of Sauvie Island. The Columbia River empties into the Pacific Ocean about 70 km west of the site location, but even so, during high tide the site is submerged. When the water is pumped through garden hoses and fine adjust nozzles, you spray water to clean off the surface, and you can see the outline of frequent and overlapping acorn pits, so I'm sure you can imagine how long it would take to excavate this site where we located 114 acorn pits in a week of work. Through the center of the site runs an underground aquifer that comes from fresh, spring water. Perhaps this is one of the reasons why they are so concentrated in only this one area. We realized that the construction of the storage pits was adjacent to the water. First, they were 0.5–1 meter from the river bank. Lining the acorn pits were hemlock boughs, then they were concealed by woven basketry. The acorns here are in the white oak family so they are deciduous and have tannic acids in them. Before you eat them you have to crack and soak them in moving ground waters. Dale is doing an experiment where he made a model acorn pit in an aquarium and runs water through it, experimenting with methods to make the acorns edible. Last year, the storage pits we mapped had radio-carbon dates from 130 to 700 years old (as best as we can tell). I am sure if we dug deeper, we'd find even older materials, since our coring at the site revealed cultural layers to 3.5 meters deep!

The people of the Northwest made coiled baskets, wooden bent-wood boxes, and/or skin bags in pits to put water in, and used white-hot rocks to boil the water. It seems like they did not have any trouble cooking using these hot stones. On the American Northwest Coast, they can capture abundant fish and shellfish, depositing huge piles of shell midden sites. Inland, they would have acorns and upriver migrating salmon. As hunters and gatherers, these Columbia River people had an extremely rich economic prosperity. They had a high population density (the Portland Basin, where Sunken Village is located, has been considered the largest population north of Mexico), a highly stratified class system (nobles, commoners and slaves), and their quality of life, making a living by hunting, fishing and gathering, was well known, and no other tribes in recent times can be compared with these rich cultures. I'd like to point out that there was a similarity between the ancient Jomon's prosperous years and those seen on the American Northwest Coast.

To me, being able to directly compare the separated American Northwest Coast and ancient Japanese cultures has been a dream of mine since my student days, and I look forward to continuing this collaborative effort into the future.

1.2.2 Robert Kentta, Cultural Resources Director, Confederated Tribes of Siletz Indians; also an elected member of the Siletz Tribal Council.
Much already has been, and much more still can be, said about the Lower Columbia River, traditional homelands of the Chinookan people, and about Sauvie Island (I believe the largest freshwater island in the United States, once criss-crossed with sloughs and ponds and much of it flooded during freshets – now surrounded by a levy, ditched and drained). Sunken Village site has suffered many long decades of intentional and unintentional destruction and neglect. Systematic and relentless looting of site contents by surface collection, digging, prop washing, etc has left relatively little of the once deeply stacked layers of Multnomah Band of Chinook history and cultural remains. Wave action erosion from passing pleasure craft and working vessels has taken its toll

as well. Most other sites in the area have fared not much better or even worse impact. Large stone sculptures and ornately carved mortars, and small zoomorphic figures of the classic Columbia River style have been found and removed to museums and private collections. Sunken Village had the added attraction of having preserved wood and fiber artifacts to draw collectors.

While it is easy to lament the losses, it is important to recognize the recent efforts and successes. It took some kicking, screaming, and arm twisting (of permitting/regulatory agencies), but several phases of work have now been completed including an inventory of private and institutional collections from Sunken Village and the surrounding area; and important testing was conducted to guide the placement of a considerable rip-rap armor that was needed to stabilize the levy directly at the site; and the most recent work presented here has added so much to document the persistence, diversity and yet continuity of local weaving traditions and subsistence practices. Sauvie Island was a cultural cross-roads, having the rigid and durable cedar root coiled work, cedar bark plaited matting, openwork split root twining and soft rush (tule, cattail, sedge, dogbane bark) plaiting, twining and sewn basketry represented. Anyone familiar with basketry will recognize that this covers pretty much all of the basic divisions of techniques (coiling, plaiting, twining, and sewn flat work). I don't know that this kind of technique diversity is known to exist at any other single site.

Having Dr Akira Matsui and his team come and sponsor and conduct their work also emphasizes the importance of this place and its ongoing power to bring diverse people together – as in the days when the Chinooks (Trade Masters of the Pacific Northwest) conducted trade with the many visitors drawn to their immense plank villages and the wealth [prosperity] accumulated/passing through there. The similarities to the ancient Jomon culture sites and the technologies/techniques represented are amazing and provoke speculation. But theories of connections (or at least striking similarities) can be found the world-over, just as we found with our Maori friends of New Zealand…some of who visited the project while in Oregon.

Many thanks go to Dale Croes and his associates from South Puget Sound Community College and Archeological Investigations Northwest (AINW), for putting a dream team together to accomplish the many tasks while battling tides and other challenges. The Native American Rehabilitation Association (NARA), an inpatient addictions treatment facility located in close proximity to the site, provided camp space, showers, meals, and moral support. Their continued willingness to have the crews move in on them is much appreciated. Rhonda Foster and the Squaxin Island Tribe's Cultural Resources Program's openness and willingness to share their considerable experience in this type of work and invitations to participate in their trainings are also encouraging signs of good things to come. Finally, it was good to have cooperation and coordination between the three Tribal governments (Grand Ronde, Siletz and Warm Springs) on this project to promote protection, guide the processes, and accomplish more together than we could singly…Kloshe Kahkwa (good that way).

1.2.3 Pat Courtney Gold, Wasco Nation of the Confederated Tribes of Warms Springs Reservation, Master Basket Weaver, P.O. Box 981, Scappoose, OR., U.S.A. 97056
Touching the Ancestors: I had a very emotional and spiritual experience touching a basket remnant dating to 700 years old, approximately. I looked at the basket with awe; at the beauty of the basket as if it were woven just a weeks ago. The cedar warps were approximately ¼ inch wide, the basket was a cross-warp, twined with ⅛ inch wide cedar bark [see Frontispiece *in situ* photograph]. This technique is exactly the same that I use in my cattail cross-warp baskets. As I touched the basket, handling the warps and wefts, I felt that I was touching the hands of the weaver while she twined and crossed each warp. Her spirit and my spirit connected. I was blessed by an ancient weaver.

I am a Native basket weaver living in Scappoose, Oregon, a Chinook town, though it is now an Americanized town. In Lewis and Clark's journals, the Scappoose area was known as 'Clakstar'. Scappoose is a Chinook word meaning 'easy shore for canoe landing'. For twelve thousand years Chinook people lived along the Columbia River from the coast upriver to the central area around The Dalles, Oregon, area. The Wasco tribe (my tribe) is the upriver sub-tribe of the Chinook Nation. There were many Chinook towns on Wapato Island (now Sauvie Island, location of the Sunken Village Site), and in the Multnomah Slough area near Scappoose.

The Chinook Nation was known for commerce (trade). An important Chinook trade center was the Wapato Island area. Wapato and acorns grew abundantly on the island. Historically, there were hundreds of Chinook villages in this area. The Chinook were a wealthy Nation trading internationally and inter-Tribally. The River provided salmon and steelhead that was processed for consumption and trade. Some goods that were traded included European beads, cloth, metal objects such as hammers, fish hooks and cooking pots. Other food sources included dried sea food (clams), dried sea vegetables, deer, elk, wapato, acorns, hazelnuts, root crops, berries, and baskets. Baskets were used as containers and often traded along with the contents.

Unfortunately, in the late 1700s, and again in the 1830s, small pox and malaria epidemics spread along the Columbia River. It is estimated that 85 to 90 per cent of the population died. The descendents of the survivors continue to live along the Columbia River. Much of our traditional knowledge was lost forever.

In 2006 Professor Dale Croes and assistants were excavating along the Multnomah Channel, Wapato Island, at a site called Sunken Village. To me it looks like the farmers on the Island built a canal there and plowed extra earth on top of the existing Chinook village. It was there that Professor Croes unearthed the basket remnants. Professor Croes phoned me, and invited me to study the basket. I took some of my weaving fibers with me to compare plant fibers. My red cedar bark, split cedar limbs, and split cedar roots matched the old basket fibers. This was the exciting moment that I described earlier.

In 2007 Professor Croes, sponsored by Japanese archeologist Dr. Akira Matsui, and U.S., Tribal, Canadian, and Japanese assistants returned to do more mapping and recording. An exciting find was another basket! This basket was a wicker plaited, over two stand strings soft basket, woven and string warps made with sturdy cattail leaves or a sedge grass. At that time, I was in Washington DC, receiving a National Endowment for the Arts award, and was unable to see and handle this basket. In looking at Professor Croes photos, I thought the fibers looked more like sedge grass, and the researchers have identified it as sedge grass from the cell structure (see below).

I am a basket weaver continuing the tradition of Chinook-Wasco basket weaving, with their unique twined geometric designs. These baskets all have unique designs created by the full turn twine technique ('Z' twine). Some plant fibers that I use include red cedar bark (*Thuja plicata*), cedar roots, tule (*Scirpus acutus*), various sedge grasses (*Carex obnupta*), cattail leaves (*Typha latifolia*), and dogbane bark (*Apocynum cannabinum*).

Red cedar trees are sacred to the Chinook People. Cedar logs are used for canoes, plankhouses, and carvings (see the wooden wedges for splitting cedar from Sunken Village, below). Cedar bark, limbs, and roots are used in baskets, and for making cordage as found at the site. Cordage is used for wrapping and tying large bundles, and sometimes for the assembling the planks in plank houses. This way, the house can be dissembled and moved. Cedar clothing is made from the pounded cedar bark as found at Sunken Village. Baskets are also made with cedar bark, split cedar roots and split cedar limbs – see the pictures of these below. Baskets made with cedar are bug repellent, important for storing food.

In this area sedge grass and tule are common plant fibers used in weaving. I work with sedge grasses, which are wonderful plant materials for weaving. The sedge stem is long, and has 3 sides, like a long prism, and they usually grow in estuaries, marshes, or wet areas. I think that the edges are like a ship's prow, standing tall as the sea or river rises and falls. Other plants with leaves would be pulled along with the tide/currents and be weakened or damaged. The triangular shape is also one of the strongest of all shapes.

In the harvest baskets that I make, the weft is twined around the crossed warps. Twining strengthens the weft fiber as it is twisted (spun) around the warps. The cross warps also are stronger than the straight warps. The cedar root acorn basket is made with the cross warp technique and the sedge soft bag is close wicker plaited over strong 2–strand strings, made from this sedge grass. When harvesting bulbs, roots, acorns or nuts, and the basket is full, it is straight forward to dip the basket and contents together into a stream to clean the contents. The plant fibers in the basket can withstand this 'in and out' of water, and be reused again and again.

It is so encouraging for me to see these beautiful old baskets made by my ancestors, and to know that my weaving techniques and knowledge have been handed down throughout these many generations. It's a wonderful feeling for me.

1.2.4 Eirik Thorsgard MAIS, Cultural Protection Coordinator, Confederated Tribes of the Grand Ronde Community of Oregon

The site known as Sunken Village (35MU4) has been one of the fascinating archaeological sites in Oregon since its discovery. The site sits along the Multnomah Channel on Sauvie Island and is part of the Willamette and Columbia River drainages. It has been systematically looted for at least 50 years by a variety of amateur archaeologists and professional collectors, making this site that much more important to understand because of the earlier damage. The other aspect that makes this area specifically important to the Tribe is that it is within the ceded lands of the Confederated Tribes of the Grand Ronde Community of Oregon. Ceded lands are defined as lands that tribes have agreed with the United States federal government to cease to own or occupy in exchange for monies, goods, and services as agreed upon in treaty. The exception is the reservation where the land is held in trust by the federal government for the tribe. This trust was created for tribes to occupy and otherwise inhabit (Wilkins 2007). So this specific region is vitally important to the Tribe's history and protection and stewardship of it furthers our cultural values and worldview.

The age of the site has been established through radiocarbon dating at about the past 700 years and displays the material culture of the MuLtnoMah people that inhabited the area and were eventually relocated to the Grand Ronde Agency. The archaeology of the Portland Basin was fairly well understood, but it became immediately obvious that there were some gaps when the investigations at this site began. No information from previous excavations in the Portland Basin have recovered the same level of basketry and none have displayed the technology about the acorn leaching pits that are quite abundant at this site. Additionally, very little oral traditions about this particular practice have been maintained in the Tribe today. While the Tribe can boast a very robust Oral Tradition, the population loss just prior to this entry of Euro-American settlers, including epidemic diseases of smallpox, tuberculosis, influenza, and malaria and among others, were devastating to the Ancestral people of the Columbia River (Mackey 2004). These 'virgin soil epidemics' were catastrophic for the indigenous Tribes of the Columbia River (Crosby 1994).

It has been estimated that the population loss from these diseases ranged between 50–90%. The exact numbers are unknown, but through comparing data from the Clackamas Tribes an estimate can be established. Lewis and Clark estimated that the population of the tribe in 1805 was around 3,500 people. By 1855 the population had dropped to 77, and by 1877 the number stood at 55 (Suttles 1990), placing the population loss at about 64%. It should be noted that the estimates of population by the Lewis and Clark expedition were most likely under representative of the actual population numbers and that the epidemics may have killed off as much as 99% of the population. Some evidence indicates that the population of the Kalapuya prior to contact may have been between 10,000 and 20,000 people with only 8,831 surviving in 1831 and by 1840 a mere 600 surviving the population losses from disease (Boyd 1995). This population loss accounts for up to a 97% mortality rate from diseases. These impacts from disease and subsequent relocation of Tribes and the curtailing of traditional life practices and language loss have left holes, one of which is being filled by the discoveries at the Sunken Village Site.

In addition to the unique food preparation practices discovered at the Sunken Village a basketry fragment was located that is made in a distinct technique called 'diamond plaiting.' This practice according to a basketry expert that the Tribe regularly consults with (Margaret Mathewson, personal communications 2008) is very limited in its use. The best examples are from Spirit Cave, Roaring Springs Cave; an example has been located in the Museum of Natural History from the Wilkes Expedition, and one from the Summers Collection at the British National Museum, as well as one from the Klamath Lake area located in the Grace Nicholsan Collection at the Peabody Museum. The Burke Museum in Seattle has several examples of a technique known as 'warp twining' which is a related technique and has a wide distribution in other museums. This technique superficially resembles the 'diamond plaiting' technique but its construction methodology is completely different. In addition to these there are some from the Great Lakes region, and are associated with the Sauk and Fox and Winnebago Tribes. This broad range of locations in the Americas circumscribes into a few regional areas: the Great Lakes, Great Basin, Northern California, Willamette Valley, Puget Sound (similar appearance but different technique), and now the Columbia River. For a more detailed analysis of the technique and examples of this analysis, the best reference would be a text called *Beyond Cloth and Cordage: Archaeological Textile Research in the Americas* (2000; also available as a digital text by the University of Utah Press at: http://content.lib.utah. edu/cdm4/document.php?CISOROOT=/UU-pressandCISOPTR=709).

The Sunken Village site, located within the ancestral and ceded lands of the Confederated Tribes of the Grand Ronde Community of Oregon, is also important in a spiritual sense. The location of cultural material from ancestors is often believed to be just as important as the remains of ancestors. This place at Sauvie Island is one such place, and damage has been done in the past, but the limited testing that has been conducted was planned, managed and conducted through consultation with the Tribes in a way to lessen the spiritual damage that could have occurred with unrestrained scientific excavation and analysis of the site. The level of consultation and involvement of Tribes as co-managers has created a unique situation where the desires of State and Federal agencies for testing could occur, without the inherent damage to the spiritual connections of the descendants of the MuLtnoMah people.

Even with involvement from three federally recognized Tribes, the Oregon State Historic Preservation Office, the Army Corps of Engineers, one University, a private contracting firm, the local Drainage District, and many interested individuals the research at Sunken Village after the first round of testing left some of the questions we had unanswered. Dr. Akira Matsui along with several of his colleagues from Japan not only assisted in funding additional research, but also flew out to assist with the excavation and initial analysis. This international support was unexpected by the Tribe, but quickly and overwhelmingly accepted. Dr. Matsui along with his colleagues as well as those involved from the beginning ensured that the work done at Sunken Village not only is unique in its cooperation from so many different groups, but is also been one of the most fruitful investigations within the ceded lands of the Confederated Tribes of the Grand Ronde Community of Oregon.

Overall the interaction with the research team from the South Puget Sound Community College and the team from Archaeological Investigations Northwest, Inc with regards to the excavation and analysis of the recovered archaeological material has provided a benefit for more than just the local community at Sauvie Island. The research and new knowledge has brought new information about the Tribe's rich past cultural practices, has provided a new look at a well known, but damaged, site, and allowed the Tribe to work toward stewardship of its archaeological and cultural sites throughout their ceded lands.

1.3 Acknowledgements

South Puget Sound Community College (SPSCC) and Archaeological Investigations Northwest, Inc. (AINW), conducted the testing and reporting of the Sunken Village National Historic Landmark (NHL) site (35MU4), which was made possible through financial support from the Sauvie Island Drainage Improvement Company (SIDIC), the Oregon Heritage Commission, the Confederated Tribes of the Siletz Indians, an international grant through Nara National Cultural Properties, National Institute for Cultural Heritage (NIFCH), Nara, Japan, SPSCC Anthropology Club, an SPSCC Exceptional Faculty grant and Jean and Ray Auel. Numerous researchers, Tribal community members, field personnel, and students contributed to the project's fieldwork, analysis and reporting. Though this volume owes its existence to these and many previous and current researchers, the summary and conclusions remain the responsibility of the authors.

In an attempt to acknowledge the many individuals involved in this project, we wish to name the persons who have been most instrumental in the testing efforts at Sunken Village. Realizing someone will be missed in this long list, we apologize in advance for any unintentional oversights.

1.3.1 Tribal Members and Officials

The Confederated Tribes of the Grand Ronde (CTOGR), Confederated Tribes of Siletz Indians (CTOSI), and The Confederated Tribes of Warm Springs (CTOWS) actively helped through consultation during the planning, testing and follow-up work. Even before the hydraulic excavations at Sunken Village, both Robert Kentta, Cultural Resources Director and Councilman, and Bud Lane, Language and Traditional Arts Instructor, and Vice Chair of Council, CTOSI, visited with Rhonda Foster, Director, Cultural Resources Department, Squaxin Island Tribe (SIT), toured the Squaxin Island Tribe Museum, and participated in the Qwu?gwes wet site on Mud Bay. Bud brought two members to train with our wet site excavation field school at Qwu?gwes the summer before we tested Sunken Village in 2006.

At the Sunken Village site testing, representatives of the Tribes were present daily and assisted as co-managers in the actual survey and testing. Contributing members include CTOGR, Site Protection Specialist, Eirik Thorsgard, who continues to contribute to the research process and provides a Forward introduction; Mel Schultz, who provided appreciated suggestions about logistics; and Daniel Haug, who helped with the careful survey, mapping and flagging. Robert Kentta, Cultural Resources Department Director and Councilman, CTOSI, visited frequently, helping with the initial survey and screening, and communicated daily by phone or e-mail. Robert also contributed a Forward introduction and to our comparison of the ancient Sunken Village basketry and current collections and as co-author of the basketry report below.

Other Tribal members who contributed through visits and phone contact include Khani Schultz, Cultural Protection Specialist, CTOGR. Bud Lane, Vice-Chair and Language and Traditional Arts Instructor, CTOSI, visited the site, bringing Maori artists Rose and her husband Rangitihi Tahuparae, who is also kaumatua to the House of

Representatives in the New Zealand Parliament. Bud helped us analyze the ancient basketry from the site, and is a co-author of the basketry report below. Pat Courtney Gold, Wasco master basket-weaver and member, CTOWS, generously visited and analyzed the ancient Sunken Village basketry and is co-author of our basketry paper below and provides a Forward introduction. Karen Quigley, Executive Director, Legislative Commission on Indian Services visited the site and she appreciated the coordination between the Tribes and the archaeologists.

Robert Kentta, CTOSI, also kindly arranged our facilities and meals through an agreement with the Native American Rehabilitation Association (NARA) residence, five miles from the site. In 2006 and 2007 our crew members were able to set up their tent camp in the NARA baseball field and contracted for three hot meals a day and shower facilities. Our stay at NARA made our project financially feasible, since we had limited support, and could not afford traditional per diem costs for the volunteer crew. NARA personnel were excellent hosts, including us in several of their events, including graduations of clients, and the clients and their families were interested and supportive of our protective efforts at the Sunken Village heritage site. They were able to visit the site in NARA vans and see the work for themselves. The meals were outstanding, and instrumental to our crew's well-being and moral. The NARA staff and clients also hosted us in weekly sweats in their sweat-houses to help protect and clean us. We appreciate the opportunity to live at and with this successful program, staff and clients for the 2006 and 2007 seasons of excavations.

1.3.2 2007 Japanese Sponsorship

The 2007 project was grant-aided by the Japan Society for the Promotion of Science (No. 19200058) under the administration of Dr. Akira Matsui, Chief Archaeologist, NIFCH, Nara, Japan. Dr. Matsui brought four Japanese associates to participate in the field work: Dr. Naoto Yamamoto, Dr. Toru Miyao, Dr. Atsushi Iwasaki, and Dr. Tomonori Kanno. Dr. Matsui is a wet site expert and Pacific representative (along with Dr. Croes) of the Wetland Archaeology Research Project (WARP) out of Exeter, England. Dr. Matsui personally recognized the value of this waterlogged site on the Northwest Coast and especially the similarity of this site to a number of Jomon period wet sites that contain preserved acorn pits and basketry throughout Japan. His team had worked at a number of these Jomon wet sites.

1.3.3 Local Community Supporters

Josh Townsley and the Board of the SIDIC provided us with logistical support to make sure the project could be completed as planned. Josh and others provided the upstairs of the Sauvie Island Fire Station to process all the trays of Sunken Village artifacts, debitage, fauna, macro-flora, and 100% samples. We were allowed to use their fax machine to send catalogs of daily finds to the Confederated Tribes of Grand Ronde and their wireless computer network allowed our staff and crew to stay in touch through e-mail contacts. Josh also provided daily logistical support as needed, including a porta-potty, pump equipment, back-fill materials, a tractor for back-fill, an all-terrain vehicle (ATV) to help bring our coring equipment to the site in 2007, and often brought much-needed ice cream and treats. Josh also arranged local residents tours of the site and a 2007 public talk by Drs. Akira Matsui and Dale Croes at the Sauvie Island Fire Station.

Oregon Archaeological Society (OAS) member, Dennis Torresdal (and island resident) and Cindy Ede, volunteered to help us screen, draw artifacts and excavate, visiting throughout the program. Dennis has continued to assist us in finding private collections from the Sunken Village site, so we can expand our data base.

1.3.4 Agency Support

Gail Celmer, Regional Archaeologist and Jennifer Richman, Asst. Division Counsel, U.S. Army Corps of Engineers (USACE) helped guide the required 2006 testing to assess the potential affects of the proposed rip rap on the Sunken Village site. They coordinated the required work, and visited during the testing phases of the work. Roger Roper, State Historic Preservation Officer, Dennis Griffin, Lead Archaeologist, State Historic Preservation Office, and Susan White, Assistant State Archaeologist, visited and assisted in the fieldwork. Dennis provided additional assistance in arranging the donation of three 50 gallon barrels of preservative polyethylene glycol 400 molecular weight from a friend of his, Dr. Lucille (Lucy) Johnson, Professor, Anthropology, Vassar College, Poughkeepsie, NY. Until that could be arranged, the Squaxin Island Tribe generously allowed us to use preservative they have purchased for the Qwu?gwes archaeological site. Kristie Haertel, National Park Service Archaeologist, Northwest Region provided guidance and input and joined Gail Celmer, Eirik Thorsgard and Dr. Ken Ames on a Panel Discussion following our symposium at the 60th Annual NW Anthropological Conference, on March 14–17, 2007, WSU, Pullman Washington. Kristie continues to help guide our work at this NHL site into the future, providing the major part of the subsidy needed to produce this timely report of the professional work on this National Historic Landmark wet site.

1.3.5 Academic Support

Scholars and academics of considerable acclaim helped lead the way in the Sunken Village investigations. Dr. Kenneth Ames and Dr. Virginia Butler, Professors, Anthropology, Portland State University (PSU) visited the testing and offered suggestions and input. Dr. Bulter generously analyzed and identified our fish remains for this report. Dr. Ames provided laboratory space at PSU and the collections from the Sunken Village site for our researchers to record and report. Dr. Curt Peterson, Geologist, PSU, and students also conducted north-south remote sensing tests, using a portable, digital pulseEKKO 100 Ground Penetrating Radar (GPR) system, and provided a full report describing their results, adding greatly to our understanding and reporting of Sunken Village in this volume. Elizabeth Callison, a PSU graduate student also volunteered her time to help excavate, draw artifacts and record the Sunken Village site in 2007. Victor Shaul, Washington State Department of Agriculture, preliminarily identified our seeds from the 100% samples taken from the centers of the acorn leaching pits. Melissa Darby, Lower Columbia Research and Archaeology, helped us overview the macro-flora analysis and review the question of why no wapato at Sunken Village, including re-visiting the 1987 cores from the site, located at PSU, to see if we could identify reported wapato-like tubers.

Patrick T. Pringle, Centralia College and Alex Bourdeau, U.S. Fish and Wildlife Service carefully reviewed our paper on the Sunken Village site setting and geomorphology. They reviewed and edited the text for this section, providing a more comprehensive synthesis. Ann Trieu, Ph.D candidate, SIU, has been always available to help us with cellular analysis of the plant and charcoal materials at the site. Dr. Dana Lepofsky, Professor, Anthropology, Simon Fraser University and Dr. Nancy Turner, Professor, School of Environmental Studies, University of Victoria, provided valuable information about plant food uses in the Northwest and continues to comment on our research and reports.

College administrators, and especially SPSCC President, Dr. Gerald Pumphrey, Vice President of Instruction, Dorna Bullpitt, and Social Sciences Dean, Dr. Deborah Teed provided the lab space, administrative leadership and personnel necessary to conduct the research on campus. Lynnette Rushton, Professor, Biology, SPSCC, provided us with guidance and equipment to do the seed identification and cellular analysis of artifacts made of wood and fiber. Professor Michael Martin, Computer Aided Drafting Department, SPSCC provided his special talents in mapping and drafting the maps seen in this report. SPSCC Welding Department provided state-of-the art metal 3-layer screens and a special intake valve for our pump. SPSCC Maintenance provided a needed fire hose extension for our pump.

1.3.6 Field Crew 2006

Twelve wet-site trained crew members provided outstanding professional work, mostly as volunteers for room and board, in order to assure that this NHL site received as thorough a testing as possible. The three field excavation and lab supervisors were Carolyn Dennler, German Loffler, and Phil Pedack. Their leadership was required for the overall success of the project. The excavation crews worked all day and then after dinner until dark at the site and included: Jason Channel, Maria Densley, Elana Dobson, Lenore Harper, Kathleen Hawes, Leroy Keener, Josh Martin, Bethany Mathews and Olivia Ness. The success of this field project is directly due to these individuals dedicating a focused and intensive 2006 testing effort – it would have not been possible without their professional skills and true dedication.

1.3.7 Field Crew 2007

Fourteen wet-site trained crew members provided outstanding professional work, mostly as volunteers for room and board, during the low waters of 2007 to assure that this NHL site was well mapped and recorded, especially the remaining *in situ* acorn leaching pits and stakes and all surface finds. The four field excavation and lab supervisors were Kathleen Hawes, Olivia Ness, Leroy Keener, and Bethany Mathews. The SPSCC CAD mapping crew was lead by Professor Michael Martin with assistance from Roy Griggs and Jason Channel. Their leadership was required for the overall success of the project. The excavation crews worked all day and then after dinner until dark at the site and

included: Vanessa Chang (SFU), Tyler Graham, Heather Haigh, Morgan Lee, Tressa Pagel, with set up help by Philip Pedack, James W. Goebel, Jr., Melanie Diedrich. The success of this field project is directly due to these individuals dedicating a focused and intensive 2007 mapping and recording effort – this second effort would have not been possible without their professional skills and true dedication to a very important site.

1.3.8 Student Researchers

Many of the students that participated in the field testing and others who joined the research team contributed the time and effort needed to properly evaluate the huge amount of data recovered during the testing phase of this project. Most of the papers in this report were presented by these researchers at either (a) the 60th Annual Northwest Anthropological Conference, March 14–17, 2007, at Washington State University, Pullman, Washington, (b) the Society for American Archaeology symposium, organized and chaired by Drs. Akira Matsui and Dale Croes, during their 73rd Annual Meeting, March 26–30, 2008, Vancouver, British Columbia, Canada, and/or (c) the 61st Annual Northwest Anthropological Conference, April 23–26, 2008, Victoria, British Columbia, Canada. They are recognized as the authors in the following reports. Their dedication to conducting professional research and presenting their results at a professional conference through these papers and illustrated presentations, makes the detailed results of our work available through this volume.

1.3.9 Research Leads

The teaming up of our SPSCC and AINW programs allowed this project to go forward with the field and research facilities needed. Dr. John Fagan, Jo Reese and Maureen Zehendner provided a full research team from their company (with special contributions here by Dr. Michele Punke, David Cox, R. Todd Baker, and Terry Lee Ozbun). Dale Croes has had the pleasure of working with these three leads for decades and recognized the need to team up to assure the professional background needed to explore the Sunken Village Site. Our ongoing relationship has expanded through the trials and tribulations created in reaching the goals we all set.

The professional talents of Professor Michael Martin, and his assistant Roy Griggs, from the SPSCC Computer Aided Drafting Department, allow for the main 2007 objective – to professionally and accurately map and record the entire remaining NHL site of Sunken Village.

1.3.10 Journal of Wetland Archaeology Editors and Staff

We would like to thank Bryony Coles and her associates with the Wetland Archaeology Research Project (WARP), Exeter, England, for encouraging the review and timely release of our international and inter-tribal work at the Sunken Village wet site, Portland, Oregon, U.S.A. Professor Coles directed us through a re-organization of our original synthesis report, making this a much better and more effective presentation of our large data base. Mike J. Rouillard compiled the large numbers of illustrations and figures for this special issue. Dale Croes has had the pleasure of working for about two decades with Mr. Rouillard on projects, and would like to express the pleasure of working with him once again – he makes things magically work. And copy-editor Adam Wainwright was in touch with all the authors, making sure their text was in order, and providing invaluable comments and revisions, and his work has enhanced the overall content of the presentations. This WARP team has once again pulled together a well-crafted volume.

Through the years Bryony Coles and John Coles have endeavored to create an interacting world community of wetland archaeologists, through WARP conferences, newsletters and publications. Through these WARP programs Dr Akira Matsui, of Nara, Japan, and Dale Croes met and began sharing their research, and now collaborate on this Sunken Village research. When WARP and Oxbow established this professional and international journal, they provided the proper format for us to share this unique wetland archaeology data with the world researchers. We owe them a great deal of recognition for their ongoing pioneering work and helping to make research available in the timeliest of manners. The publishers at Oxbow have provided the window of opportunity to produce this international journal for archaeologists throughout the world.

To all the above people this volume owes its existence, we know others helped too. The final conclusions, however, remain solely the responsibility of the authors.

1.4 Structure of Volume and Related Websites

The Sunken Village report is set up in six synthetic sections, starting with the above Section 1 general introduction, forward and listing of the contributors that made this examination possible on a very limited budget. Section 2 introduces the physical setting of this pivotal location, at the junction of the Willamette and Columbia rivers, and how this unique location contributes to the cultural importance of this historic Chinookan trade center on the Northwest Coast of North America. The historic developments in the Sunken Village area are discussed, affecting the archaeological wet site and originally revealing its uniqueness through over fifty years of vandalism and collecting. The archaeological sequence setting is set forth as well. Section 3 outlines the 2006 and 2007 first systematic archaeological investigations of the Sunken Village NHL wet site, followed by the overall geoarchaeological interpretation of the wet site from test excavations, ground penetrating radar and deep-coring. Section 4 considers the floral and faunal remains, and especially the focus of the site use, the leaching of millions of acorns in pits. Section 5 details the rich wood, fiber, lithic and bone artifacts, especially the sensitive basketry artifacts. And Section 6 synthesizes the array of data considered and summarizes the ecological, artifactual, and functional context of this newly investigated and much better understood local, regional and Pacific-wide bridging wet archaeological site.

A number of web sites have been established to make the entire data base available to the readers without a large appendix here with the data spreadsheets. Also previous permit reports (Croes *et al.* 2006, 2007a) are in these web sites to make information of tangential importance to this synthesis still available to researchers. The data base appendices and past reports web site can be reached at: http://www.library.spscc.ctc. edu/crm/JWA9.pdf, and are referenced throughout this text when they apply to the data being discussed.

Journal of Wetland Archaeology 9, 2009, 15–38

2 The Physical and Cultural Background

2.1 Introduction to the Site

The Sunken Village wet site (35MU4) is on one of the most important river junctures on the Northwest Coast of North America – where the Columbia River drainage of British Columbia, Canada and Washington State, U.S.A. is joined by the Willamette River flowing through much of western Oregon State, U.S.A. (Figure 2.1). The site is on Sauvie Island, where a major aquifer pumps under the natural levee into Multnomah Channel, providing a unique 125 m wide beach area where acorns placed in shallow hemlock bough-lined pits were leached in huge numbers by ancient Multnomah Peoples (Figure 2.2).

2.2 Location and Setting

By Melanie Diedrich

2.2.1 Introduction

The Portland Basin of the lower Columbia River (the current location of the largest city in Oregon State, USA: Portland) exhibits a widening floodplain containing several alluvial islands, Sauvie Island being the largest at more than 24,000 acres (Figure 2.2). This floodplain is rich in resources, both natural and agricultural; not only is the land attractive for its resources, the Columbia and its tributaries have provided a huge transportation network to Natives and, later, to European/American settlers. Human settlements have occupied the Lower Columbia River Basin for thousands of years, adapting to changes caused by geologic, catastrophic, seasonal and climactic events.

Developing a regional survey of the geology, hydrology, climate, and Basin ecology provides a platform from which to view the formation of Sauvie Island as a whole, and more particularly the streamside resources available at the Sunken Village Archaeology Site (35MU4). From this we hope to build a better picture of the ancient peoples and cultures that called this area home.

2.2.2 Location

Sauvie Island is part of and just northwest of the major city of Portland, Oregon, U.S.A. (Figure 2.1). At the southern tip of the island the Willamette River divides, forming

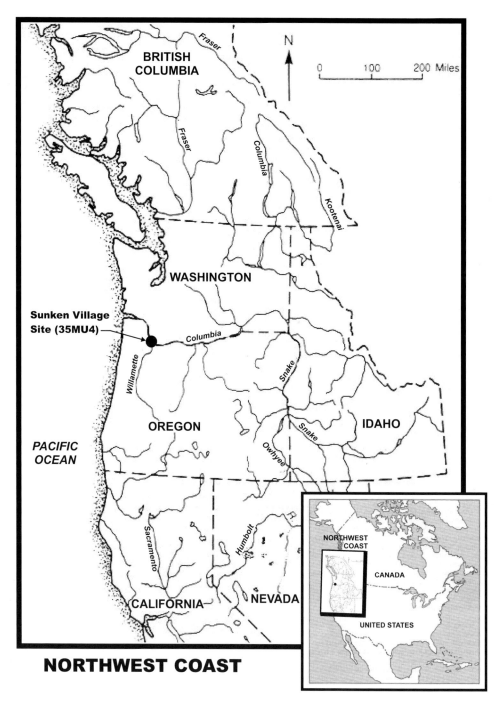

Figure 2.1. Location of the Sunken Village Site (35MU4) in the Northwest Region of the U.S.A, strategically placed at the juncture of the Columbia and Willamette Rivers.

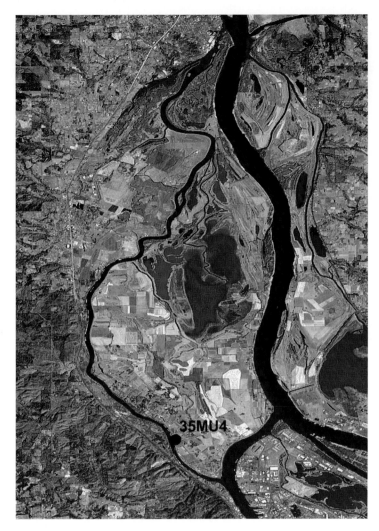

Figure 2.2. Aerial photograph of Sauvie Island, between the Columbia River (right) and the Multnomah Channel (left) on the northwest edge of Portland, Oregon, USA. Sunken Village, Site 35MU4, is on the southwest shore of Sauvie Island, and the rivers flow northwards round the island (i.e., from bottom to top of the photo).

the Multnomah Channel to the west, and flowing into the massive Columbia River to the east (Figure 2.2). This island was formed in the floodplain of the Columbia River where the river makes a nearly 90° bend to the north. At the downstream end of the Island is a rocky outcrop, which stretches across the Multnomah Channel and into the Columbia River. It has been suggested that sediment accumulated at this outcrop and grew from there, as the river's bend caused the flow of the water to decrease. The island also contains many ridges, lakes, and drainage streams; some are the result of recent flood control, some are ancient channels or ridges (Figure 2.2). Yearly winter and spring floods, occasional extreme flood events and various upstream and downstream catastrophic events, have combined to deposit layer on layer of sediment, forming Sauvie Island (Bourdeau 2003; Hajda 1984; Spencer 1950).

The Sunken Village Wet Site, 35MU4 is located on the Southwestern portion of

Sauvie Island, on the east bank of Multnomah channel, Section 46, Township 2 North, Range 1 West, Willamette Meridian (Croes *et al.* 2006). During limited excavations in September of 2006, more than 60 acorn-leaching pits were located and mapped. It has been demonstrated that groundwater from a large freshwater aquifer continually moves through this particular 125 m section of the beach, perpendicular or oblique to the Multnomah Channel. This type of flowing aquifer, just below the water table would be necessary, regardless of the river level, in order to remove the tannins from the acorns buried in the hemlock bough lined pits (Mathews 2007, below).

2.2.3 *Physiography and Hydrography*

The combined Columbia and Willamette river basins comprise an area that covers approximately 258,000 square miles in four USA states and British Columbia, Canada (Figure 2.3). Many of these river basins were modified during the Missoula Floods, which were the result of several periodic sudden ruptures of a lobe of ice in northern Idaho State, USA, that blocked drainage of Glacial Lake Missoula. The glaciers of the last Ice Age peaked about 16,000 years ago, the ruptures and flooding occurred between 15,000 and 13,000 yr BP. These massive floods formed the Channeled Scablands of Eastern Washington State, USA, (Alt and Hyndman 1984). The sedimentation they carried also affected the floodplain and delta of the Lower Portland Basin. Because of Sauvie Island's location, the rivers of primary interest here are the Willamette and the Columbia itself, and to a lesser degree, the Sandy River, east of Portland (EPA 2006).

The Willamette River originates 450 feet above sea level, 187 miles south of the city of Portland, and flows north between two mountain ranges; the waters of the Willamette contain ancient volcanic material originating in the Cascade Mountains to the east, as well as Coastal Range marine sediment and littoral sedimentary rock to the west. There are eleven flood-control dams on the Willamette River today; these reservoirs also provide irrigation for a large agricultural industry that runs the length of the fertile Willamette Valley (USACE 2003).

The Sandy River issues from Reid Glacier on Mount Hood and carries a variety of primarily volcanic material as it flows northwest past the towns of Sandy and Troutdale where it joins the Columbia River approximately 14 miles east of the city of Portland. The Sandy River Delta was formed by volcanic eruptions that triggered lahars and sediment-rich flows from Mt. Hood. These sediments were further washed down the Columbia to the Lower Portland Basin. A significant volume of deposits within the delta are from "eruptions of about the year 500" and the more recent "'Old Maid' eruption probably started in the winter of 1781–1782" (Cameron and Pringle 1986, 1987; Crandell 1980; O'Connor, 2004; Pringle *et al.* 2002). The first American overland expedition by Lewis and Clark crossed the Sandy through this delta less than 25 years later. William Clark's detailed descriptions and map indicate active sand deposition that has subsequently aggraded downstream areas of the Columbia River floodplain (Bretz 1913; O'Connor 2004).

The Columbia River totals more than 1,230 miles in length, and begins in British Columbia, Canada 2,657 ft above sea level (Figure 2.3). There are more than forty tributaries that contribute to the river. The twelve largest range from 2,930 to 56,900

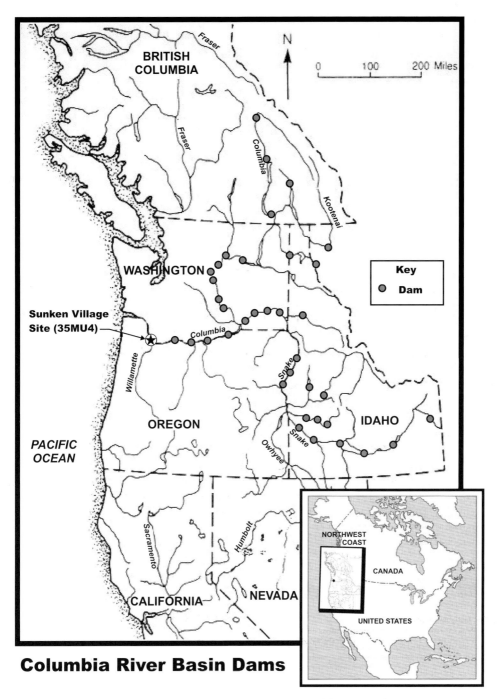

Columbia River Basin Dams

Figure 2.3. Columbia River Drainage, dams and location of 35MU4

cubic feet per second average discharge. The Columbia's sediment load is "enriched with materials eroded from the northern Rocky Mountains and volcaniclastic materials derived from the Columbia Plateau and the eastern... [and] western slopes of the Cascades" (Bourdeau 2003). Development of the Grand Coulee dam began in the 1930s; there are now six federal, five non-federal and three Canadian dams along its main-stem, many others both large and small, are on its tributaries. These dams are not only used for production of hydroelectric power, but also flood control and irrigation reservoirs (Figure 2.3). Unfortunately, they have also resulted in the dramatic decline and in some cases eradication of once abundant salmon runs within the Columbia basin.

Since discharge data collection began only a few years prior to dam construction, obtaining accurate data that reflects pre-dam/reservoir seasonal flows has been difficult and complex. River flow in the Portland area is strongly affected by daily tidal fluctuations, especially during low river flow months in late summer and early fall. The river levels can rise and fall as much as two feet twice a day. The USGS has official Portland stage data, adjusted for tidal effects on the Columbia and Willamette Rivers from as early as 1879. The Vancouver station began stage data measurements, as opposed to simple discharge data, in 1973 (USACE 2004).

A 1968 Department of the Interior publication, *Discharge in the Lower Columbia River Basin, 1928–1965*, not only has early- to mid-twentieth century river flow data, but also provides 'adjusted' data giving somewhat more accurate pre-reservoir discharge rates (see Appendix B:205, website: http:www.library.spscc.ctc.edu/crm/JWA9.pdf). The adjusted data was developed from two methods, the summation method and the correlation method. The summation method combined gauged flows with precipitation and, when monthly flow at the beginning of a month was different than at the end of the month, a travel-time adjustment was added. When travel-time adjustments were necessary, the difference between the two flows was used in the equation: flow difference (cf/s) × travel time (days)/# of days in month = adjustment amount (cf/s). When gauging stations data was missing, the correlation method was used. This method used the available summation method data correlated with the sum of flows, adjusted for seasonal changes and upstream storage adjustments. Further adjustments were made for precipitation, evaporation and time-of-travel in the same way as the adjustments in the summation method. All of the above travel times and adjustment were based on information from the National Weather Bureau, Corps of Engineers, and USGS personnel (Orem 1968).

For the purposes of this report, the 1928–1965 adjusted rates for each month during a given year were entered into a spreadsheet, where mean-monthly-discharge rates were tabulated. More recent unadjusted rates from 1970 to present were also tabulated to represent mean-monthly-discharge. These were then put into bar graphs for comparison (Figures 2.4 and 2.5; see data, Appendix B, 205, website: http:www.library.spscc.ctc.edu/crm/JWA9.pdf). It must be remembered that in geologic terms, the river discharge data that is available in general is only a very small period of time and may not reflect anything but the most recent period. What these graphs show us is, first of all, the difference between present discharge rates with the flood control management and what the naturally occurring discharge rates may have been. In general, these graphs illustrate the natural flows of the rivers to have had higher highs and lower lows. A

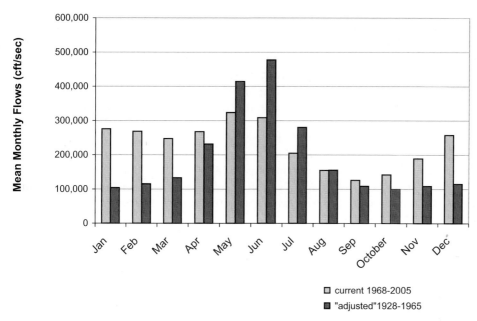

Figure 2.4. Mean monthly discharge rates (cft/sec) of the Columbia River.

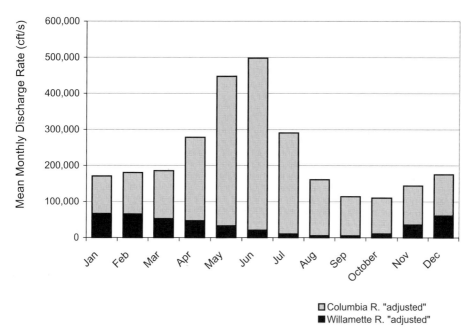

Figure 2.5. Comparison of mean monthly discharge rates (cft/sec) of the Willamette and Columbia Rivers (1928–1965).

comparison graph was also constructed to illustrate the differences and similarities of the Columbia River Discharge rates to the Willamette (Figure 2.5). Though the Willamette flows are much smaller, the graphs do provide a visual picture of the affects of winter rains and rain-on-snow events vs. the spring snowmelt. The most relevant point is the low discharge rates shown for both rivers in August, September, and October. Significantly, the graphs also illustrate a slight drop in discharge rate in February and March. These illustrate seasonal highs and lows, especially significant at the site at Sauvie Island.

Another issue, which directly affected the area, is the sedimentation rate that occurred during seasonal flooding. Unfortunately, the construction of the aforementioned dams within the Columbia River Basin has drastically reduced the quantity of sediment that actually reaches the lower basin area. Nationwide, many dams built 30 to 60 years ago are dealing with reduced reservoir capacity due to a build-up of sediment behind the dams; sediment that in natural conditions of flow would have been carried to wider floodplains or even to the river deltas. Additionally, the changes in land use, drastically changing the surface flows into the basin, increased channelization of the Willamette and the Columbia (Postel and Richter 2003). At the Sunken Village Site it appears what has been buried since before European contact is now being degraded and each year more of the site may disappear, due in part to the lack of regular sediment deposition.

2.2.4 Formation and Change: Catastrophic Events

A number of catastrophic events such as the massive glacial Lake Missoula Floods, volcanic eruptions, with resulting lahars and ash flows, and major landslides and seismic events have played an important role in forming the current lower Columbia River floodplain.

J. Harlan Bretz described the Missoula Flood "flow rate to have been 70 million cubic feet per second, more than fifty times the largest historic Columbia River flood of 1894" (O'Connor 2004). Comprising a series of enormous flood events from about 15,000 to 13,000 yr BP, this size of flood not only explains the formation of the Washington State scablands and gravel deposits, but also clarifies the formation of the current wide floodplain of the Portland Basin, and the deposition of what is known as the Portland Delta gravels. As the glacial ice caps melted the sea level began to change, ultimately rising about 100 meters between 10,000 to 3,500 years B.P. (Newman 1991). It is generally recognized that this rise in sea level accounts for the fact that, although the Portland Basin has been inhabited for about 11,000 years, no cultural site has been found on the floodplain dating earlier than about 2,000 years BP (Newman 1991; Bourdeau 2003).

Although evidence of volcanic activity in the Cascades vicinity extends back more than four billion years, more recent Holocene period eruptions at Mount Hood and Mount St. Helens have produced mudflows composed of pyroclastic material and water, called lahars, that have affected river flow both upstream and downstream (Bourdeau 2003; Pringle, et al. 2002).

Upstream about fourteen miles east of Portland, the Sandy River delta has received lahars from Mt. Hood that have aggraded the Columbia and contributed to the natural sediment build-up at Sauvie Island. At 11,239 ft., Mt. Hood is the highest peak in

Oregon State and has had intermittent periods of eruptive activity during the past 30,000 years.

Mt. St Helens has had an approximately 40,000 year eruptive history, and though the direct influences of any pyroclastic material or lahars occurring on these rivers downstream from Sauvie Island would be slight, if any, the indirect influences may have been very significant. It has been theorized that some of the Mt St. Helens induced large flowage deposits temporarily dammed the Columbia River below Sauvie Island, slowing the flow and thereby causing the Columbia's sediment load to drop, forming additional base layers within the floodplain. When this dam was breached a short time later, deep channeling would have scoured the main river channel of sediment and debris, leaving sediment on upland and slack-water areas (Bourdeau 2003, personal communication 2007; Pringle, personal communication 2007; for more examples, see Croes *et al.* 2006, 2007a).

Another catastrophic event that left its mark on the Lower Columbia River Basin is the Bonneville Landslide. Lewis and Clark made note of the Cascade Rapids and a submerged forest, both believed to be related to the Bonneville Landslide. This submerged forest was still evident in 1934 when Donald B. Lawrence began trying to date the event that buried it (O'Connor 2004). Lawrence's work dated the Bonneville Landslide to about 1250 AD, while more recent radiocarbon dating by Alex Bourdeau, Jim O'Connor, Patrick T. Pringle, and Nathan Reynolds has tentatively placed the event at somewhere between 1430 and 1450 AD, though more field and research work is needed to come to a definitive date (O'Connor 2004).

This landslide originated on Table Mountain, north of the Columbia, and geological investigations prior to the construction of the Bonneville Dam "concluded the slide had dammed the river to a height of at least 250 feet (over three times higher than Bonneville Dam)" (Bourdeau 2003). It is estimated that this blockage of the river would be overtopped in three to eight months, at which time a breach might have caused a cataclysmic flood event that carried sediment far downstream. "Subsequent [studies have] established that Bonneville was the most recent of four major slides and numerous minor slides that have occurred along the stretch of river north and west of Stevenson, Washington" (Palmer 1977; Bourdeau 2003).

All of the volcanic and landslide events most likely contributed to the formation of the wide floodplain and islands of the Lower Portland Basin. Ancient river channels have been filled with sand and debris, fine sediment from annual floods overtopped; the only evidence of these old riverbanks may be the ridges and swales that run through the area, a large one runs the length of Sauvie Island (Bourdeau 2003). There may be more, smaller versions throughout the Island, former basin drainage that is now filled with sand. This may account for relatively late dates for cultural materials at the Sunken Village, where approximately 700 years ago the massive flow of the Bonneville Landslide release may have sheared away sites throughout the Portland Basin (see below; Croes *et al.* 2007a).

2.2.5 Climatic History

Ten thousand years ago signaled the end of the last ice age and the beginning of an extensive warming period, dated by pollen record "from approximately 7000 BC to approximately 600 BC" referred to as the Hypsithermal Interval (Deevey and Flint 1957; Pringle 2002). A gradual decline in temperatures then began approximately 2,000 B.P., and triggered two Neoglacial Advances. "The first of these episodes peaked between 2,800 and 2,600 yr B.P." (Pringle 2002). A second episode, termed the Little-Ice-Age, lasted from AD 1250 to about the middle of the nineteenth century, peaking approximately 600–700 years ago (about the estimated radiocarbon date of the Sunken Village excavations). During this time, localized alpine glaciers were larger, leaving evidence of moraines extending nearly a kilometer further down Mount St. Helens than pre-1980 glaciers (Pringle 2002).

Current climate of the Sauvie Island/Portland Basin area is relatively mild-maritime. Average temperatures are about 40 degrees F, winter temperature ~34 degrees, summer temperature ~75–78 degrees (USDA 1983). As Clinton Rockey describes on the NOAA website, the Coastal range shields the inland area from storms off the Pacific while the higher Cascade mountains "offer a steep slope for orographic lift of moisture-laden westerly winds, resulting in moderate rainfall for the region" (Rockey 2007). Stating reasons of accuracy, the National Weather Service limits their minimum and maximum extreme temperatures to data gathered between 1941 and 1999. The agency lists the extreme maximum temperature (1941–1999) of 107 degrees F occurred in 1981, extreme minimum temperature (1941–1999) of -3 degrees F occurred in 1950. Historically, this may not be the most extreme minimum temperature, however, as there are written records documenting that during the winters of 1862 and 1888, "the Columbia froze over so that teams of horses and wagons were driven across the river on the ice. (Spencer 1950). Average Precipitation is from 36 to 37 inches per year, the highest precipitation occurring November thru March, peaking in December with an average of about 6 inches (NOAA) (Figure 2.6).

These temperature and precipitation figures represent data from only the last one hundred years. As current worldwide glacial melting indicates, this data may reflect a dramatic warming trend. Although the floral remains recovered from the site are not drastically different from present day vegetation, climate conditions at the Sunken Village Site may have been much cooler, making winter conditions more difficult 600 years ago, especially in the upland areas surrounding the rivers.

2.2.6 Resources

Ames et al. (1999), Boyd and Hajda (1987) and Newman (1991) refer to the Seven Habitat Types developed by Saleeby (1983) to describe the fresh water and terrestrial habitats of the floodplain in and around the Sauvie Island vicinity. These are listed as Riverine, Lacustrine, Palustrine, Riparian, Oak Woodland, Grassland (prairie), and Conifer Forest. As Ken Ames points out, six of these habitats are "on the floodplain proper" (Ames et al. 1999), and all six exist on Sauvie Island. The seventh, Conifer Forest, is within a day's journey by foot and canoe. This means that within this local area there were remarkably variable and seasonally plentiful resources.

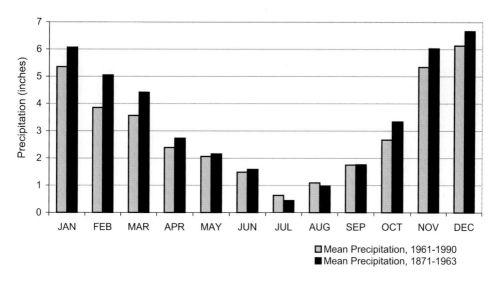

Figure 2.6. Mean monthly precipitation, Portland, Oregon, U.S.A.

2.2.7 Flora

The Soil Conservation Service 1983 Report lists Oregon ash (*Fraxinus latifolia*), Oregon white oak (*Quercus garryana*), black cottonwood (*Populus balsamifera*), and willow (*Salix spp.*) as the primary trees native to the floodplain (USDA 1983). Within close proximity on the adjoining upland slopes are Douglas fir (*Pseudotsuga menziesii*), Western Hemlock (*Tsuga heterophylla*), and Western Red Cedar (*Thuja plicata*) forests. In general, the stands of Oregon white oak (*Q. garryana*) dominated the highest ridges on the floodplain; on Sauvie Island the highest ridges do not exceed 50 feet above sea level. Richard Pettigrew cites a particular oak tree at the Merrybell site (35MU9) with a trunk "about 2 m in diameter, indicating the tree is nearly the maximum age for the species (about 500 years)" (Pettigrew 1981). Interestingly, very little mention is made of acorns as food in the majority of ethnobotanical sources. Pojar and MacKinnon (1994) indicates acorn use by the Salish people of the Puget Sound area; Dan Moerman (2003) lists *Quercus* spp. use by the Iroquois of New York and the Cahuilla, and other tribes, of California; neither indicates these were widely eaten in the study area (see Mathews, below).

Among the oak trees grew native blackberry (*Rubus vitifolius*), as well as various undergrowth species such as hazelnut (*Corylus cornuta*), serviceberry (*Amelianchier alnifolia*), and snowberry (*Symphoricarpos albus*) (Ames et al. 1999; Pettigrew 1981). Bracken fern (*Pteridium aquilinum*) proliferated in the open prairies adjacent to the oak groves and into the lower marshlands. This is in part because of its widespread habitat, and also because the Native practice of burning encouraged its growth; the rhizomes were harvested and eaten in late summer (Boyd 1987; Pojar 1994; White 1980). Prior to non-Native settlement and agricultural development, lowland areas of the Lower

Columbia Floodplain, especially marshy wetland soils, were noted for wapato (*Sagittaria latifolia*) and camas (*Camassia quamash*), particularly on Sauvie Island, previously known as Wapato Island (Boyd 1987; Hajda 1984; Newman 1991). Both of these were highly prized by local inhabitants; Boyd (1987) lists both wapato and camas as 'Class Two' resources, that is, those cited as food 6 to 15 times among their large database of researchers, literature and ethnobotanists studying the area. Other wetland plants native to the area, and used as food plants, are bracken fern (*Pteridium aquilinum*), horsetail (*Equisetum telmateia*), cattails (*Typha latifolia*), cow parsnip (*Heracleum lanatum*), Indian plum or osoberry (*Oemleria cerasiformis*), salal (*Gaultheria shallon*), thimbleberry (*Rubus parviflorus*), dewberry (*Rubus ursinus*), and salmonberry (*Rubus spectabilis*) (Ames *et al.* 1999; Hajda 1984; Pojar 1994).

2.2.8 Fauna

Due to the remarkable variability of habitat, the Lower Columbia Basin floodplain was home to a wide range of animals. Some were predators such as the black bear, bobcat, red fox, puma, and hawk. In forested areas there were elk and deer. The raccoon, river otter, and beaver populated four of the six habitat types near a source of water; the rivers and lakes abounded with freshwater mussels, freshwater turtles, and seasonally available salmon, steelhead, sturgeon, eulachon, and cyprinids. Non-migratory birds, kingfishers, and various waterfowl lived throughout the area (Ames *et al.* 1999).

In developing their thesis regarding regional population movement to and from the Columbia, Robert Boyd and Yvonne Hajda (1987) highlighted the regional human preference for fish over larger game animals for food, and outlined the seasonal availability of various fish species. The eulachon (*Thaleichthys pacificus*) appear in February and March; the white sturgeon (*Acipenser transmontanus*), which feed upon the eulachon, appear in March and again in August; and finally spring Chinook salmon (*Onchorhynchus tschawytscha*) come up the lower Columbia in March and April. "Spring Chinook salmon appear in the lower Columbia … running in essentially the same tributaries as do the eulachon… The bulk of the Willamette River run passes through the Multnomah Channel by Sauvie Island." The summer salmon runs begin in June with Sockeye (*O. nerka*), the summer runs of Chinook (*O. tschawytsha*), and then Chum Salmon (*O. keta*) in October (Boyd 1987).

2.2.9 Summary and Conclusions

The Sunken Village Archaeology Site is situated in an area known to have been inhabited by humans for thousands of years. It is rich in natural resources, providing food, materials for utilitarian use and trade, as well as transportation. The Columbia and Willamette rivers' seasonal flows, nearby volcanic eruptions on both sides of the Columbia and affecting both upstream and downstream river sedimentation, and landslides at Bonneville and the Cascades have all contributed to the formation of the Portland Basin floodplain in general and Sauvie Island in particular, filling or covering lowland or ancient channels with tephra, sand, and sediment. This, in turn, may have contributed to the flow of groundwater from upland marshes through the

35MU4 archaeology site and into the Multnomah Channel, providing ideal conditions for acorn leaching.

The climate, availability of water, and variation in habitats on and near Sauvie Island provided resources for more than just the people who lived there year around; many people from inland locations migrated to the river at various times of year to partake of available resources. Since no other archaeology site in the Western U.S.A. is known to have used passive acorn leaching in such great quantity, questions regarding the source of this technology, the extent of its use, and its success over time within the culture and its potential influence on cultures to the north, and especially south, remain.

The seasonal flooding and catastrophic events also created hazards for inhabitants. Village sites had to be carefully chosen in regard to high water and sediment deposition. Food storage and trading locations close to the river ran the risk of inundation. Proximity to the river transportation system, however, offset the risks, drawing large populations to take part in food harvesting, fishing and processing, and providing great wealth to those who controlled its waters.

2.3 Portland Basin Cultural Sequence and Ethnographic and Post-contact Background of Sauvie Island

By Maureen Newman Zehendner

2.3.1 Introduction

As seen in the environmental section above, the Portland Basin has been formed and transformed by numerous geological events, no doubt influencing the resources and the cultural history of the juncture point of the Willamette and Columbia rivers. Now we will discuss what is known about the cultural history of the region, mostly established using projectile point typologies, explore the local archaeological and ethnographic record and review the post-contact effect of non-Indian occupation in the Sauvie Island region.

2.3.2 Pre-contact Cultural Sequence

The earliest proposed prehistoric cultural sequence of the Portland Basin developed by Richard M. Pettigrew outlines two main phases: the Merrybell, 600 BC to 200 AD; and the Multnomah, 200 AD to contact. The Multnomah contains a series of sub-phases (Pettigrew 1977; 1981; 1990). The sequence is based primarily on projectile point types and stone implements including net-weights. Pettigrew developed the chronology after sub-surface testing at seven sites, surface collecting at three others in the Sauvie Island-Scappoose area, and studying private collections. He defines two types of archeological sites in the Portland Basin, upland (more than 1 kilometer from the river) and floodplain (less than 1 kilometer from the river) (Pettigrew 1990). Due to post-pleistocene sea level rise and depositional patterns on the floodplain of the Columbia, he suggests that evidence of the earliest occupations of the area has been inundated with water and alluvial deposits on the floodplain. Most of the sites investigated in the Portland

Basin are floodplain sites. The Portland Basin, including Sauvie Island and the north and south shores of the Columbia River, is rich in archaeological sites (Dunnell *et al.* 1974; Hibbs 1972, 1987; Jermann and Hollenbeck 1976; Kongas 1979; Munsell 1973; Newman and Starkey 1977; Reese *et al.* 1990; Strong 1959; and others). Some sites have been excavated by an avocational group, the Oregon Archaeological Society. Pettigrew's work in the late 1970's was the first intensive testing work done by any professional archaeologists. These test excavations were the basis for his chronology.

Recent research, directed by Kenneth M. Ames, has been conducted at the Meier Site (35C05) in Scappoose, Oregon (Ames *et al.* 1998) and the Cathlapotle Site (45CL1) near Ridgefield, Washington (Ames and Maschner 1999; Ames *et al.* 1998). As a part of the Wapato Valley Archaeological Project based at Portland State University a series of summer field school excavations at both the Meier and Cathlapotle sites have revealed large house structures, hearths, and storage pits. Study at these sites is the first long-term, intensive professional research of an archeological site in this area. Based on these investigations, Ames developed a Portland Basin Chronology with Paleo Indian, Early and Late Archaic phases not designated in the Pettigrew sequence, and a Pacific phase beginning 5,500 years before present comprised of three time periods and a late modern period (Ames 1994). The later Pacific and modern periods correspond chronologically with the Merrybell (3,500 to 1500 BP) and Multnomah (1500 BP to present) phases of Pettigrew's chronology.

Pettigrew argues that the Bonneville Flood, a geological event that took place upstream from the Portland Basin in the Columbia River Gorge (see Diedrich, above), had a major impact on archaeological sites in the Portland Basin. He dates the flood at *ca.* 1250 AD (Pettigrew 1990, 523). When the flood entered the Portland Basin, it:

> .....appears to have changed the floodplain topography and may have destroyed many, if not most, settlements in the Portland Basin and downstream. None of the prehistoric sites dated in the vicinity of the Bonneville Dam-Cascades area of the Columbia Gorge predates the landslide, ...Furthermore, in the Portland Basin, sites that were occupied both just before and after the landslide are extremely rare or nonexistent. It would appear that settlement destruction and landform changes were so severe that virtually all subsequent floodplain sites were relocated (Pettigrew 1990).

While Pettigrew makes a strong case for the impact of the Bonneville landslide/flood on archaeology of the area, the flood remains to be clearly defined in the archaeological and geological record of the Portland Basin (see Diedrich, above).

2.3.3 Ethnographic background

As mentioned in the Introduction, the Lower Columbia River section of the Northwest Coast Culture area is thought to have been one of the highest Native population densities in North America (Pettigrew 1981), yet it has only been in recent years that Chinookan sites and culture have been the focus of concentrated research efforts by professional archaeologists.

In 1804–06 journal accounts of the Lewis and Clark expedition the population estimates for the Lower Columbia indicate more than 17,000 individuals occupied the area from The Dalles to the mouth of the Columbia River. Nearly 6,000 individuals lived on Sauvie Island alone (Boyd 1985). However, the Chinookan populations in the Portland Basin (including Sauvie Island) were essentially gone by 1836, dying from "introduced diseases, particularly smallpox and malaria" (Boyd 1985). Between The Dalles and the coast, two Chinookan dialects were spoken. The Upper Chinookan dialect was spoken in the Portland Basin and up-river to The Dalles, while down river the Lower Chinook dialect was used. A substantial trade network flourished on the Lower Columbia and Chinook 'jargon' developed and was widely used as a trade language among speakers of various native languages as well as non-Indian fur traders.

The area of Sauvie Island is included in Silverstein's Chinookan sub-group of Multnomah (1990). He describes this portion of the Lower Columbia as a densely populated area with villages found from Government Island to the mouth of the Lewis River, a stretch of river which includes the Multnomah Channel and Sauvie (Wapato) Island as well as the mouth of the Willamette River. Groups in the area including the Cathlapotle with villages above the Lewis River, the Shoto at Lake Vancouver, and the Multnomah of Sauvie Island, spoke an Upper Chinookan dialect (Silverstein 1990).

Social organization and various aspects of the culture during the historical period have been discussed by Hajda (1984) based on available ethnographic and historical accounts from 1792–1840. From what is known about the Chinook, at that time, it appears that they typically located their villages at or near the mouths of major rivers and streams and conducted extensive trade up and down the river. During the winter they occupied semi-permanent villages, using plank house construction typical of other areas of the Northwest Coast. Temporary seasonal locations were occupied during the remainder of the year where various activities involved with foraging, fishing, and hunting took place.

Using evidence from archaeological excavations Saleeby (1983) has proposed a model which suggests that some permanent villages occurred aboriginally in the Portland Basin. She divides the Lower Columbia area into three sections: the Coast, Portland Basin, and Cascades. While aboriginal populations in all three areas were basically hunters and gatherers, she suggests that the abundance of resources in the Portland Basin provided the economic and food base for permanent villages. Added to this was the seasonal influx of outside groups which increased the population size during the fishing and harvesting months. Saleeby's model differs from the earlier work done by Dunnell et al. (1974) which suggests that none of the villages were occupied year round and that all the groups in the area occupied temporary locations during the fishing and harvesting periods, and semi-permanent villages during the winter months.

2.3.4 Cultural affinity

While there remain a substantial number of unanswered questions about the aboriginal populations of the Lower Columbia, there seems to be well accepted evidence that the groups, at least from The Dalles to the coast, can be clearly linked in terms of their cultural patterns to the Northwest Coast. As a part of the Northwest Coast (NWC) culture area there are many shared traits, but with regional variation in style and perhaps emphasis in regard to the importance of some practices and material objects. Ames and Maschner (1999) included extensive discussions of the Lower Columbia River Chinookan peoples in their comprehensive work on the archaeology and prehistory of the Northwest Coast. While there are some variations on house construction, art and the complex relationships among groups throughout there are vast similarities and cultural patterns linking these groups to the Northwest coastal groups. Ray (1938) describes their social patterns as having class and rank systems but not as rigid as was seen with Northern groups in the NWC culture area. Slavery, warfare and the practice of head flattening were all part of the Lower Chinook culture area. In addition, a highly developed system of trade was conducted along the Columbia River and the main mode of transportation was by canoe or on foot over-land. Permanent or winter village dwellings were cedar plank houses, while simpler cattail mat structures were built during warmer seasons. Ray (1938) notes: "...they made use of sweat lodges of two types, a plank structure" and a "typical Plains hemispherical hut."

2.3.5 Material Culture

Aboriginal populations occupying cedar plant houses made use of a wide array of objects that were produced from wood, cedar bark, spruce root, bone and shell. These served both utilitarian and ornamental functions. Stone was less prominent being used mainly for net-weights, and 'heat radiators' for cooking (Silverstein 1990).

Specific items made from these materials included in Silverstein's text are: (made from wood) carved boxes, troughs, carved and painted spirit-power figurines and reliefs on the house framework; bowls; serving pieces; canoe shaped trenchers. Baskets of several twined varieties; sewn cattail mats up to six or seven feet long; hemlock and crabapple wood wedges for splitting wood; needles of bone and wood; clothing made from cedar bark; robes and capes of fur, sea otter, beaver, raccoon and wood rat (1990). Many of the artifacts from this area are produced from wood and plant fibers and are quite perishable in a moist, mild climate. As will be discussed below, wet-sites provide an excellent opportunity to recover these types of perishables, and 35MU4 has been shown to contain substantial deposits of undisturbed organic remains and some of these items.

The Northwest Coast is also known to have had a highly developed art tradition. The aboriginal populations used wood, bone, antler, and perishable plant fibers for much of the art work. An extensive report on stone art from the Lower Columbia/ Portland Basin was done by Petersen (1978). Clay figurines are also known from sites in this area. Butler discusses the importance and the potential of the Portland Basin in the development of art styles in the region, suggesting the once densely populated Sauvie Island area may hold evidence that could provide substantial information on the origins and development of the aboriginal art styles of the Lower Columbia River Valley (Butler 1965).

When earlier investigations were undertaken on Sauvie Island, an examination of extant collections revealed that the Sunken Village site had already yielded a number of art objects from the wet deposits (Newman 1991, Appendix C, 208), and it was expected other such artifacts would be recovered during future excavations. The 2006 and 2007 excavations reported on below show that the prediction was accurate, and the results significant for our understanding of material culture from the island.

2.3.6 Introduction to Sauvie Island Contact Period History

In late December 2007 a massive 365 foot long steel framed bridge span was floated by barge down the Willamette River and into Multnomah Channel just north of Portland, Oregon, U.S.A. (Tucker 2007). At its new location the arching structure serves as the center span for a new bridge connecting Sauvie Island to the mainland replacing the existing 1950s era bridge. The two-mile trip down stream took several hours and once lifted into place the modern span took three days for construction crews to complete the work required to fit it securely into place. The replacement bridge opened in the summer of 2008 and now accommodates the ever increasing traffic traveling to and from the island. Activity on the island is booming on weekends from early spring bird watchers through a busy summer of bicyclists, and the fall harvest with pumpkin patches and corn mazes attracting families to the island. While a bit more peaceful in the winter there are still the dedicated bicyclists, hikers, runners, dog trainers, hunters and fishing enthusiasts who continue the activity year round. Before the 1950s bridge was constructed transportation between the island and the mainland was usually by ferry boat. The earliest travelers likely reached the island by canoes or fording the waters of Multnomah Channel. Sauvie Island has been inhabited for centuries first by Native American Chinookan speakers, then farmers for the Hudson's Bay Company, and donation land claim settlers, some of whose descendents still occupy the rural properties on the island.

The 1950s bridge brought more visitors to the island, making access easier for residents as well, but the island has managed to maintain its rural lifestyles despite ever increasing development pressure form the surrounding Portland metropolitan area. In recent years the desirability of the island and its rural lifestyle so close to the urban amenities of Portland has pushed land prices to premium levels. The resistance to development, preservation of farming properties and large areas of public Oregon State Fish and Wildlife lands has the added benefit of preserving the abundance of archaeological sites on the island including 35MU4. Despite decades of artifact collecting and digging at many of the island's sites many such as the Sunken Village, 35MU4, still provide the potential for research.

The archaeological and historical evidence suggests that the island has been an attractive place to live for the past 3,000 years. The rich resource base, indicated by the range of biotic habitats listed above, not only sustained the dense Chinookan populations, but also seasonally drew other Indians to the area. During the historic period, it was attractive to early Euro-American settlers. In 1850, the Donation Land Law, distributed land grants of 320 acres for single men and 640 for a man and wife. The law required that claimants occupy and cultivate the land (Carey 1971). After the act several parcels of land on Sauvie Island were claimed by early settlers (Cleaver 1986).

2.3.7 Post-contact Early Period Chronology

During their expedition to the Pacific, the American overland exploration of Americans Lewis and Clark mapped the location of Sauvie Island and called it 'Wappato Island' (Figure 2.7). Following that the island was named Wyeth's Island after the first white settler and later was given the name Sauvies Island (McArthur 1974), (the 's' appears in early maps) for the Hudson's Bay Company (HBC) employee, Laurent Sauve'. Sauvie Island is in use today. While its historic uses have varied, the island remains relatively undeveloped considering its proximity to the City of Portland, Oregon, U.S.A., and its rapidly expanding, particularly west and southwest, suburban areas.

When British Captain George Vancouver sent Lt. William R. Broughton on a mapping and exploration expedition of the Columbia River in 1792, Broughton named several locations which still retain those designations. He named Warrior Point, the downstream tip of Sauvie Island, Belle Vue Point at the southern end of the island, Mt. Hood, and Mt. St. Helens. In 1805–1806 Lewis and Clark mapped a number of locations of villages (Figure 2.7) and named it Wappato Island because of the abundance of Wapato (*Sagittaria latifolia*). Their maps show villages located on both the Columbia River side of the island and along Multnomah Channel. Hajda has suggested that 35MU4 could be the Cathlahcommatup village identified by Lewis and Clark.

William McKay said that a village of 500 was one mile from the head of the island, on the Howell place, and that all inhabitants were found dead during the 1830–34 epidemic. This points to a spot near 35MU4, and it may or may not have been Cathlacommatup. The 'Indian Camp Field' 2/3 miles south of the Benjamin Howell house was being used by Indians (doubtless another group) in the 1880s–1890s according to John Lampher (1881) (Hajda, Part III, in Hibbs 1987).

Other traders and explorers describe the island, including Gabriel Franchere in 1811, and David Thompson in the same year. However, it wasn't until 1834 that the first white settlement took place on the island. Nathaniel J. Wyeth established Fort William on high ground above Multnomah Channel on the west side of the island (Spencer 1950). By 1835, Wyeth's venture in trade had failed and Fort William was dismantled. The site of Fort William on the Multnomah Channel side of the island, is down stream from the Sunken Village site. A later venture at that location, in 1838, by the Hudson's Bay Company proved more successful. The company not interested in the location for a trading post, established a dairy farm on the site of Fort William. Eventually, the HBC operated three dairies on Sauvie Island (Spencer 1950). It was from the HBC employee Laurent Sauve', who was in charge of the dairy operation, that the island received its name. Following Sauve's retirement in 1844, James and Isabelle Logie took on operation of the dairy. They eventually filed a donation land claim including the site of the dairy. After the area was claimed by the United States, the British HBC had evacuated (Spencer 1950).

Following passage of the 1850 Donation Land Law by the U.S. Congress a number of DLC's were established along the southern end of the island. Included in these were the Bybee and the Howell DLC's. At the SW tip of the island is the Menzies DLC. Eventually, the Howell family acquired both the Bybee and Menzies DLC lands forming the Howell Bros. Farms.

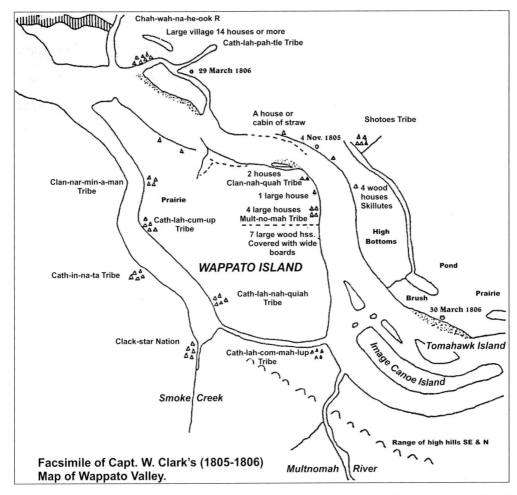

Chah-wah-na-he-ook R
Large village 14 houses or more
Cath-lah-pah-tle Tribe

o 29 March 1806

A house or
cabin of straw   Shotoes Tribe

4 Nov. 1805

Clan-nar-min-a-man
Tribe

Prairie

2 houses
Clan-nah-quah Tribe

1 large house

4 large houses
Mult-no-mah Tribe

4 wood
houses
Skillutes

Cath-lah-cum-up
Tribe

7 large wood hss.
Covered with wide
boards

High
Bottoms

Cath-in-na-ta Tribe

WAPPATO ISLAND

Pond

Cath-lah-nah-quiah
Tribe

Brush

Prairie

30 March 1806

Clack-star Nation

Cath-lah-com-mah-lup
Tribe

Tomahawk Island

Image Canoe Island

Smoke Creek

Range of high hills SE & N

Facsimile of Capt. W. Clark's (1805-1806)
Map of Wappato Valley.

Multnomah River

Figure 2.7. Facsimile of William Clark's map (1805–1806) indicating villages on Sauvie Island
(from Oregon Archaeological Society's Screenings).

When the Howells bought out the DLC lands of James Bybee they also acquired what is now the historical monument the Bybee-Howell House, owned by the Portland area Metro Regional Government, The house was owned by the Howells until 1962 when it was donated to Multnomah County and was operated by the Oregon Historical Society for several years. Three sisters who are descendants of the Howells, lived in the house as children and the later years of there lives on Sauvie Island properties near the original homestead. The Howell Brothers Farm also included the property where 35MU4 is located. That portion of the land, however, was acquired by the Douglas Brothers Farms in the 1940s, the present day owners of the property.

2.3.8 The Twentieth Century and Change

Along with the modern conveniences made possible when electricity came to the island in the 1930s and vast improvements in communication when the telephone arrived in the late 1940s, two major construction projects have taken place on the island since 1900 that have brought significant changes to Sauvie Island. The first was construction of the Sauvie Island Dike from 1938–40. The Dike allowed a shift from a predominantly cattle grazing economy to farming. In 1949–1950, the Sauvie Island Bridge was constructed. The bridge made the island easily accessible from the mainland increasing its use for recreation including artifact collecting. Emory Strong published an article in the Oregonian in 1952 about the wealth of archaeological materials available at the major sites on the island and gives some specific locations for those interested in collecting. He regales his readers with reports of successful artifacts hunts but also informs them that the finds are now mostly arrow points since the 'large stuff' has been previously 'carried away' (Strong 1952).

Prior to construction of the Dike in 1938–1940, annual floods, or spring freshets made growing crops nearly impossible on the island. In extreme floods, most of the island would be inundated except for some high areas with elevations around 50 ft. along Multnomah Channel (Spencer 1950). Before the bridge, transportation to and from the island, as well as on the island itself was extremely limited. Steamboats and later a succession of ferry boats connected the island with the mainland and the City of Portland. On the island itself there were no official roads until after 1910 when a ferry landing was constructed on the Multnomah Channel side of the Island connecting with the area called Burlington on the mainland. Following this, a section of county road was constructed running southward along Multnomah Channel and a stretch heading eastward across the island. The road was eventually extended to form what is now Reeder Road and Gilihan Loop Road. These sections of county road are shown on the 1918 and 1920 topographic maps.

The section of county road constructed along Multnomah Channel appears to have been constructed through or adjacent to the Sunken Village Archaeological site. According to Marjorie Taber (personal communication 1987), the eastern edge of the site consisted of a series of burial mounds. During construction of the county road these mounds were destroyed. Her father removed the disturbed burials and reburied them at another location on the island. Mrs. Taber said she knew where the Indian remains were reinterred, but in order to protect them she would never disclose the location.

The remainder of 35MU4 seems to have been undisturbed until later construction of the dike. Leon Taber began visiting the Howells at Sauvie Island about 1917–18 and during this time he began to search various locations for artifacts. At that time 35MU4 was on the Howell's property and he remembers visiting the site quite frequently. After his marriage to Marjorie Howell, Taber moved to Sauvie Island to the property he named Arrowhead Acres, adjacent to the Bybee Howell house. When the Taber's home burned in 1986 most of the collection accumulated from 1917–1980s was destroyed (Taber 1987).

2.3.8.1 CONSTRUCTION OF THE DIKE

Following passage of the federal Flood Control Act of 1936, island residents decided to request federal funds to construct a dike along the southern tip of the island. The proposed dike was to be approximately 32 ft high and would protect some 12,000 acres on the upper end of the island. Construction of the dike was started in 1938 and finished in 1941. The project was undertaken by the U.S. Army Corps of Engineers and cost was shared by the Federal Government and the island landowners (Spencer 1950). Requirements under the federal act directed the establishment of the Sauvie Island Drainage District with power to assess and collect taxes. The drainage district still continues in operation today as the Sauvie Island Drainage Improvement Company and is one of the agencies that has jurisdiction regarding activities at 35MU4. During construction of the dike much of the fill material used was dredged from the adjacent waterways. A report in the Oregonian describes this:

> Material for the long dike will be dredged from the channels of the Willamette and Columbia rivers and Multnomah channel, work usually done solely in the interest of navigation (McClure 1938).

Along the western end of the island dredge material was pulled up from Multnomah Channel and deposited on the river bank to gradually build the dike to a height of about 32 ft. Archaeological site 35MU4 is located well within the project area and both field observations, and accounts from island residents indicate that parts of the site were actually scooped out of Multnomah Channel and deposited over other areas of the site. This impact to the site is discussed in both Newman's 'Site Description' and "Management Plan" sections (1991, 97–134). The county road was also buried by the dike in areas and those portions of the road were later rebuilt on top of the dike.

Following construction of the dike the acreage protected by the dike could then be use for farming. Another factor which Spencer points out in his 1950 book (nine years after the dike was completed):

> With improved land use and increased food production and therefore income, have come increased costs and expenses. An illustration is in taxes, which have risen from approximately one dollar per acre per year to five dollars per acre per year (1950).

Following construction of the dike a major portion of the Howell Brothers property, including the area where 35MU4 is located, was purchased by the present owners the Douglas Brothers Farms (personal communication, M. Taber 1987; personal communication, G. and M. Douglas 1988).

Spencer continues:

> The Big Dike has also brought changes other than crops. Roads have been graded, rocked and hard surfaced. The Island now has forty miles of roads with but six dead ends. While electric service from Portland General Electric Company was extended to the Island in the year 1936, since the building of the Big Dike that service has been improved and is maintained at a high state of efficiency. Telephone service came to the Island when The Pacific Telephone and Telegraph Company

installed its plant and facilities and began furnishing its excellent rural service during 1948 – a service comparable to that in any large city (1950).

From Spencer's description, it is evident that along with the dike came the types of public services needed to serve the developing farming community.

2.3.8.2 SAUVIE ISLAND BRIDGE

The second significant development came in 1950 when construction of the Sauvie Island Bridge, begun in 1949, was completed. Now directly connected to the mainland, the island was easily accessible. Spencer expresses his own concern for the potential development of the island:

> As to those who see in the bridge a chance to plat land into small tracts which they would sell at great profit with inevitable shacks and an uncertain and transient population let their speculative real estate ventures be lost in the fogs of the island (1950).

Spencer's concerns, expressed as a resident of the island and chronicler of its history, have not yet become a reality, although the bridge has made the island accessible for many purposes including recreation. During the 1970s, one attempt was made by some property owners to use several acres for subdivisions. This proposal was opposed by large numbers of island residents, and the environmental organization 1000 Friends of Oregon. The project was never approved by the county planning commission. In the 1980s a portion of the Douglas Brothers Farm was to have been sold for development of a golf course under a special community service designation which can be allowed for farm lands. However, the land sale was never completed when Multnomah County failed to approve the land use applications that would be needed to satisfy conditions set forth by the prospective buyer (personal communication G. Douglas 1987). Under Oregon's Land Conservation and Development Commission regulations, most of Sauvie Island is designated as farm land. In the northern section of the island a large area was established a number of years ago as Oregon Game Commission Land (Department of Fish and Wildlife).

Other development pressures along the waterways such as Multnomah Channel include boat marinas and houseboat moorages as well as increased recreational use of the waterways. At one time a marina was proposed for a section of the bank of Multnomah channel that would come within a few hundred meters of the southern boundary of the Sunken Village.

2.4 Previous Archaeological Research and National Historic Landmark Status

By John Fagan

For such an important and well known archaeological site that has been listed in the National Register of Historic Places and that has been given the status of a National Historic Landmark, it is surprising that so little scientific research has been done. While the water-saturated deposits at 35MU4 have been known to yield rare organic artifacts to collectors for well over 50 years (Strong 1959, 24–31), only a few professional studies until now have been conducted at the site, and controlled scientific excavations have been previously limited to only a few auger tests that were excavated into the saturated deposits below the water line (Croes 1987; Pettigrew and Lebow 1987), and into the upland deposits within the natural levee (Hibbs and Ellis 1988).

Site 35MU4 was formally recorded by Richard Pettigrew in 1973 while conducting his dissertation fieldwork on the Lower Columbia River. The 1973 site form referred to the saturated deposits, twig or basket-lined basins, and to the numerous perishable materials that local collectors had found. Pettigrew also mentioned that shell lenses and burnt areas were visible in the cutbank at the site (Pettigrew 1973). In 1977, Thomas M. Newman, Bob Campbell, and Maureen McNassar, of Portland State University (PSU) documented their observations on a site form for 35MU4. The PSU team described two organically stained strata that were visible in the cutbank at the site, and noted that the bank extended 50 centimeters (20 inches) above the beach and contained charcoal fragments within the two strata. The PSU researchers noted that the upper stratum was horizontal but discontinuous, while the lower stratum was undulating and discontinuous. They also noted that there was evidence of some digging in the bank, particularly in an area that contained a large amount of fresh water mussel shell.

The first formal archaeological testing work at 35MU4 was conducted in 1987 during a survey for a natural gas pipeline (Hibbs and Ellis 1988). During the survey, 25 auger tests were excavated within and adjacent to the recorded boundaries of 35MU4. Map NCF-07 (Hibbs and Ellis 1988) shows that eight of the augers, numbers 2, 4, 5, 11, 13, 14, 20, and 23 contained cultural materials, and the auger record forms in Section A of the 1988 report indicate that augers 19 and 25 also contained cultural materials, but their locations are not indicated on the site map. The excavations conducted for the pipeline survey were all located on the upland portion of the site to determine site boundaries and the presence or absence of cultural deposits beneath the constructed levee within the proposed pipeline corridor (Hibbs and Ellis 1988 Part 1, 92–94).

The subsurface testing work conducted in 1987, documented intact stratified deposits beneath the constructed levee and confirmed the northern, eastern, and southern boundaries of site 35MU4 (Hibbs and Ellis 1988 Part 1, 92–94). The auger tests documented cultural deposits beneath 1.5 to 2 meters (m) (5 to 7 feet[ft]) of levee fill as evidenced by the presence of charcoal, ash, fire-cracked rock, debitage, and bone fragments (Hibbs and Ellis 1988 Part 1, 92).

Formal testing of the saturated deposit at 35MU4 was conducted in November of 1987 by Richard Pettigrew and Clayton Lebow, assisted by Dale Croes and Kenneth Ames. The testing work included the excavation of auger probes in the saturated deposits at the edge of Multnomah Channel. Of the eight 25 cm (10 in) diameter auger probes excavated within the saturated deposits in 1987, six contained cultural material including perishable organic items (Pettigrew and Lebow 1987, 20). The total volume of deposits excavated during 1987 amounted to only 0.61 cubic meter (less than 1 cubic yard compared to approximately 4–5 cubic meters (yards) excavated in our limited evaluation here) (Pettigrew and Lebow 1987, 11; Croes 1987). None of the auger test locations were evident along the beach during the 2003 AINW fieldwork;

however, several of the twig-lined acorn leaching pit features were visible at and just below the water line.

In 1991, Maureen M. Newman completed her Master Thesis at PSU that summarized previous research at 35MU4, reviewed the distribution and significance of saturated sites, particularly in the Pacific Northwest, completed a National Register Nomination form for the site, and provided management recommendations for the protection and preservation of the unique site and its valuable cultural deposits (Newman 1991). The thesis was a culmination of several years of research that included Ms. Newman's participation in the only two previous professional archaeological studies conducted at the site, as well as numerous volunteer efforts to monitor and protect the site during periods of low water when the saturated deposits were exposed and vulnerable to damage from artifact collectors. In her 1991 thesis, Ms. Newman recommended site stabilization as an immediate need for the protection of the resource, and offered several detailed approaches for implementing site protection measures.

The Sunken Village site was accepted to the U.S.A. National Register of Historic Places in 1989, and, in an attempt to provide additional status to the well-preserved wet site, Maureen M. Newman and her thesis chair, Kenneth Ames, proposed its nomination to the U.S.A. National Park Service as a National Historic Landmark (NHL). Only one other archaeological site in Oregon state, the Paleo-Indian Fort Rock Cave (an arid cave site producing 75 woven sagebrush sandals dating to approximately 10,000 years ago), has been afforded NHL status, and only approximately 250 archaeological sites have been given NHL status in all of the U.S.A. Ames and Newman felt that the Sunken Village wet site was unique in its preservation and demonstrated that wood and fiber artifacts reported by collectors through the years, and also hoped, if accepted, that this would provide avenues for raising support to better manage and explore the site. They were right on the archaeological significance of Sunken Village, and it was accepted as a NHL in 1989 as well, however, and unfortunately, this status did not seem to lead to additional support for management or professional investigations. The potential failure of the dike along the site in 2005, largely through tunneling into the dike by collectors, lead to our 2006 evaluation of potential detrimental effects of placing rip-rap along the cutback at this NHL wet site, then, following the 2006 report, the results lead to international interest and support from Japan to further document and compare this site in a northern Pacific rim context.

3 The 2006 and 2007 Field Seasons at Sunken Village

3.1 Introduction

As mentioned, the 2005 erosion of the dike placed on the natural levee facing the intertidal waterlogged portion of the Sunken Village site had threatened the residents of the island, initiating a proposal by the Sauvie Island Drainage Improvement Company (SIDIC) to place protective rip-rap rock along the face of the bank. Since the site is on navigational waters under the authority of the U.S. Army Corps of Engineers, field evaluation of this National Historic Landmark archaeological wet site was required to assess the potential effects of placing protective rip rap rock on the channel bank in order to comply with U.S. Section 106 of the National Historic Preservation Act (Croes *et al.* 2006).

A call for proposals was initiated by the SIDIC in the late summer of 2006 and a South Puget Sound Community College (SPSCC) proposal in partnership with the Archaeological Investigations Northwest, Inc. (AINW) was awarded (Croes *et al.* 2006).

3.2 Archaeological Investigations

3.2.1 2006

From September 5–20, 2006 the limited evaluation through excavation, coring and surface mapping was conducted by specialist and field excavators from SPSCC and AINW. The main field excavators were seasoned wet site archaeologist who had served as supervisors or demonstrated exceptional skills as field school students during training at the 2006 SPSCC Qwu?gwes archaeological wet site at Mud Bay, Olympia, Washington – a project being co-managed by SPSCC and the Squaxin Island Tribe (Croes *et al.* 2007b). Wet sites require an understanding of hydraulic excavation techniques, not commonly learned at other sites, so these additional skills served the Sunken Village crew well. Wet (waterlogged) archaeological sites have excellent preservation of wood and fiber cultural materials, including debitage: wood chips, split wood and basketry waste elements, and discrete artifacts, such as basketry, cordage, wooden wedges, boxes, arrow shafts, etc., all found at the Sunken Village site. Once the aquifer waterlogged levels are reached in a wet site, a lack of oxygen prevents typical decay organisms, such as bacteria and fungi, from operating, and you encounter well-preserved wood and fiber artifacts, often

70–90% of the artifacts found from Northwest Coast wet sites (versus the more common stone, bone and shell artifacts on the Northwest Coast; Croes 1995, 79–80).

Due to the fragile nature of these wood and fiber material culture items, a technique of hydraulic excavation is best, use of spray from fine adjust garden nozzles, and use of pumps to pressurize the water, work best for excavating and recovering delicate wood and fiber artifacts. Using water also requires drainage, so it is common to excavate drainage trenches systematically from a beach surface Test Unit (TU), following the prescribed 1 m trench length and 10 cm excavation levels to form the trench from the TU. This carefully excavated drainage trench also provided a 10 cm wide transect exposure from the TU to the edge of the intertidal zone, adding significantly to the understanding of the perpendicular cross-section of the bank to the tidal shoreline of the site that might be impacted by the rip-rap deposit. Since drainage trenches are not common in dry site TU excavations, but required in hydraulic excavation, it was discussed at meetings, but not specifically outlined in the original Scope of Work (see in Appendices on website: http://www.library.spscc.ctc.edu/crm/JWA9.pdf), though the procedure is part of this kind of wet site approach and its logistical value was recognized during site evaluation (Figure 3.1; see Figure 4.15 example of 10 cm wide trench cross-sectioning an acorn leaching pit, below).

The subsurface testing at site 35MU4 was initiated with trowels in Test Units (TU) 1–3 in separate transects (Transects in this case mean 25 m wide areas, running from the levee cutbank to the water's edge, forming manageable bank to water units for testing and surface collecting; the TUs were placed in the least disturbed Transects IV-VI, or in three transects along 75 m of intertidal beach). The hydraulic surface washing revealed that the main site cultural deposits were limited to five transects or 125 M (transects II–VI). Three of the 1 × 1 M test units were placed in the three least disturbed transects (transects IV–VI), with the two to the north end of the site (II–III) having a large irrigation/drainage pipe dug through them in the 1980s. These three initial test units (1–3) were placed close to the bank where the rip-rap rock was to be placed (Figure 3.2; Croes et al. 2006). The visually densest area of this wet site was determined by flagging surface in situ features (pink flags for acorn leaching pits, lime flags for wooden stakes) and surface debitage, fauna/flora, and tools (red-orange flags). These highly significant in situ features/stakes and all discrete debitage, fauna/flora, and tools were also carefully mapped as an important part of data collecting.

In summary, with time and funding limitations, and following the provisions of the scope of work, the 2006 wet site work at 35MU4 consisted of:

- excavation of 4 1 × 1 meter test units, with drainage trenches 10 cm wide extending from three of the test units to the intertidal limits (dug in 10cm levels; Figures 3.1–3.4),
- the cross-sectioning of 5 round acorn pit features in these drainage trenches, cross-sectioning and bulk sampling of one fairly complete acorn pit feature (Figures 3.1 and 4.15),
- excavation of a half-test unit (HTU) 50 cm into the bank (Figure 3.1) where AINW's testing in the winter of 2003 indicated in situ features (Fagan 2004, Figures 3–6),

Figure 3.1 (left) On beach a 10 cm wide drainage trench transect leads downslope from Test Unit 2 (TU2); in foreground, the Half Test Unit (HTU) being excavated into the upper cut bank; (right) Test Unit 3 with 10 cm wide drainage trench transect into the intertidal beach. Each trench cross-sections at least one acorn leaching pit, seen as TAR/FCR(thermally altered rock/fire-cracked rock) clusters in the intertidal zone.

- surface mapping of (a) the *in situ* wooden stakes, (b) *in situ* and numerous acorn pit features (following hydraulic surface cleaning and retaining any encountered cultural surface debris on these pits; 60 mapped in 2006), and (c) surface cultural materials, including lithics, animal bone, wood chips, basketry strips, and split wood,
- coring to a depth of 25 feet across the natural levee in line with the HTU, TU-2 and the TU-2 drainage trench to best observe a perpendicular cross-section through the site (Figure 3.2).

To expand our perpendicular exposure and evaluation of the beach to the bank deposition, a 1 Meter wide by 50 cm deep exposure was excavated into the bank (called the Half Test Unit (HTU)) in line with TU2 and the TU2 drainage trench in 10 cm levels (Figures 3.1–3.3 and 3.4c). Also in line with this exposure and Test Unit 2, a series of 4 cores were taken to a maximum depth of 25 feet on top of the levee using a Geoprobe 6620 DT, which is a direct push corer mounted on the back of a small, track mounted rig (Figures 3.2–3.4c). These 2006 cores are approximately 2 inches in diameter, providing enough sediment for litho-and bio-stratigraphic studies (see Punke, below).

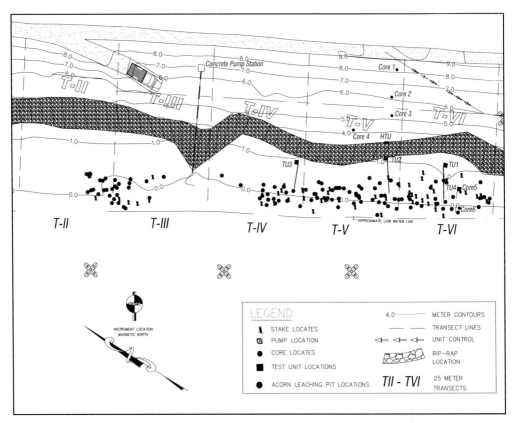

Figure 3.2. Map of main transects with in situ acorn leaching pits and wooden stakes, Test Units with drainage trenches, and deep cores (Map by Michael Martin, CAD, SPSCC, 2008).

After staff and tribal deliberations our final and fourth Test Unit (TU4) was initiated in the second week of limited excavation, when a distinct area of vegetal mat preservation was seen along the exposed bank in Transect VI. Aquifers flowing through these deposits vary in rate of discharge, and, in this area of the site, it was obvious that this was a location of considerable water flow and preservation. This exposure required hydraulic excavation because of the density of vegetal mat (wood and fiber) layers. We also initiated a cross-section of a pedestaled acorn pit, Pit P, Transect VI, found *in situ* in this well preserved area of the site (Figures 3.2, 3.3, 3.4c, 3.12).

The excavation units, the 10cm wide drainage trench excavations, and the bank half test unit (HTU) were excavated in 10–cm levels, by the use of trowel, shovel, and/or water spray from fine adjustable nozzles. All excavated soils were water screened through nested ½, ¼ and ⅛ inch metal screens. Measurements, observations, and collected items were recorded on standardized level forms, specialized *in situ* acorn pit forms, *in situ* wooden stake forms, feature forms, and unit summary forms.

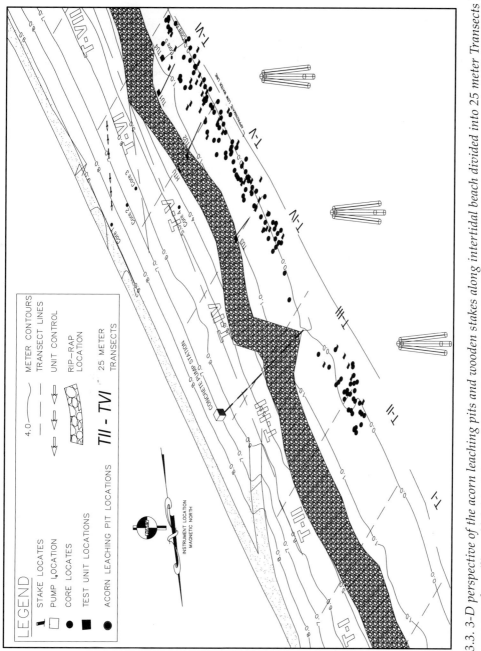

Figure 3.3. 3-D perspective of the acorn leaching pits and wooden stakes along intertidal beach divided into 25 meter Transects I–VI. Map shows wooden pilings (dolphins) for log rafts and the rip rap placed on steep bank of site (Map by Michael Martin, CAD, SPSCC, 2008.

The main features encountered were on the exposed surface of the beach, and included both (a) *in situ* circular pits averaging 80 cm. in diameter and containing whole acorn remnants and (b) *in situ* wooden stakes averaging 5 cm in diameter and driven into the beach surface. Approximately sixty pits were mapped in transects II through VI in 2006 (Figures 3.2, 3.3 and 3.4a–c). These pit features were hydraulically surface cleaned, photographed and sampled. One half of one of the dissected acorn pits was excavated revealing a western hemlock bough lined basin, and remnants of whole acorns.

The other *in situ* features were the wooden stakes, of which 32 were recorded in 2006. After the consideration of staff and tribal representatives, two stakes were hydraulically excavated showing that they are long (approximately 1 meter), adze sharpened at their ends, and one had its bark still adhering to the pole (see Figure 5.13). Many of the acorn pits had a stake on their south edge, no doubt marking the location of the pit.

In the bank half test unit (HTU) a fire-cracked rock feature was found, mapped, and recovered for analysis. A charcoal sample from the hearth feature was collected for radiocarbon dating.

Two C14 samples were taken and submitted from the 2006 excavations, one as a charcoal sample from a cultural layer in the HTU and one from hemlock bough sticks lining the excavated acorn leaching pit, Pit P. All dates compiled from 35MU4 are shown together in Figure 3.5, and the two recently derived dates will be discussed in more detail below. In general C14 dates from Sunken Village are evenly dispersed between approximately 130 to 660 years ago.

3.2.2 2007

Through a grant from the Japan Society for the Promotion of Science (No. 19200058) managed by Dr. Akira Matsui, Chief Archaeologist, Nara National Cultural Properties, National Institutes for Cultural Heritage, Nara, Japan, we were able to return to Sunken Village during low fall waters from September 16–22, 2007 to horizontally map and vertically core in the waterlogged intertidal areas of the site. The 2007 field methods were designed to greatly improve the accuracy of mapping the *in situ* features at the Sunken Village site: (a) acorn leaching pits, (b) wooden stakes, and (c) surface mapping and collecting of any exposed cultural materials, including lithics, animal bone, wood chips, basketry strips, and split wood. For special control, the ten transects established in 2006, each 25 meters wide, were re-established so the joint Japanese and U.S. crews could be divided into Transect areas to make sure each main 25 meter section of the beach was completely mapped, photographed and recorded (Figures 3.2–3.3) Professor Michael Martin, SPSCC Computer Aided Drafting (CAD) program, conducted the mapping with assistant Roy Griggs using a Sokkia Set5A (5 second gun) total station with tripod data systems software through an HP85 data collector.

To expand our vertical evaluation of the site depth, two cores were taken to a maximum depth of 6–7 meters (approximately 20 feet) in an area of the site that appeared to be well-preserved in 2006, with numerous vegetal mat layers exposed in Test Unit 4 (Figures 3.1–3.3c). Dr. Michele Punke, Archaeological Investigations Northwest, proposed a hypothesis in the 2006 final report that this area may reveal deep cultural

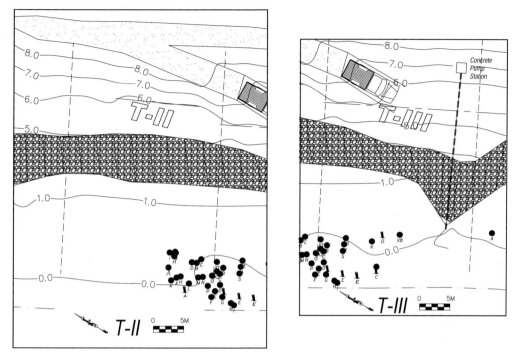

Figure 3.4a. Transects II and III with in situ acorn leaching pits and stakes with their transect designations (Maps by Michael Martin, CAD, SPSCC, 2008).

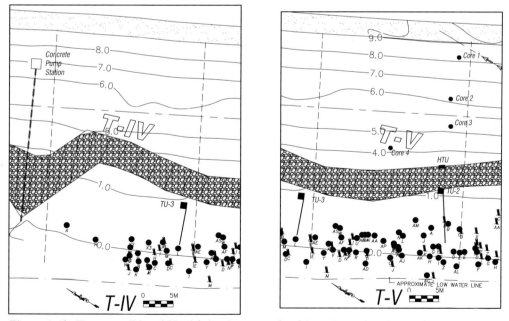

Figure 3.4b. Transects IV and V with in situ acorn leaching pits and stakes with their transect designations, Test Units and Cores (Maps by Michael Martin, CAD, SPSCC, 2008).

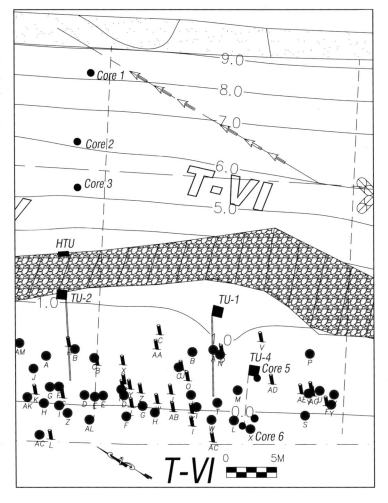

Figure 3.4c. Transect VI, where we found the deepest remaining vegetal mat layering preserved and where two deep cores were taken (see Punke, below; (Map by Michael Martin, CAD, SPSCC, 2008)).

deposits (Punke 2007, 28–58). A Geoprobe Model 7730 Track Rig, which is a direct push corer, was used; the cores are approximately 2 inches in diameter, providing enough sediment for litho-and bio-stratigraphic studies (Figures 3.2–3.4). We excavated two 2" cores from the current surface of TU 4 and another one a few meters down slope from TU 4 (Figure 3.4c). The second core, demonstrated a likely depth of vegetal mat deposits containing cultural layers to at least 4 meters below surface. The results of this analysis include two AMS dates that are from lower vegetal mat/cultural layers (see Punke, below).

The international mapping crew, consisting of 5 Japanese, 1 Canadian and 14 U.S. members, was divided into three teams, two covering a single transect area (25 M wide; Transects V and VI), and one team covering 3 transects (Transects II, III and IV, Figures 3.1–3.4) with assignments established on the basis of the 2006 distribution of mapped acorn leaching pits and wooden stakes—therefore each team had about equal numbers of known features to record in detail. The team's main tasks were to color flag and label, in the artifact recording sequence established in 2006, all (a) surface beach finds, (b) acorn leaching pits and (c) wooden stakes. These three categories of finds were mapped with the total station, and also photographed, drawn and measured. Measurements, observations, and collected items were recorded on standardized surface collection forms, specialize in situ pit forms, in situ wooden stake forms, feature forms and unit summary forms.

Additionally Dr. Curt Peterson, Portland State University, and students conducted north-south remote sensing tests, using a portable, digital pulseEKKO 100 Ground Penetrating Radar (GPR) system, and produced a preliminary report on their findings, summarized in Michele Punke's paper and conclusions below (Waibel *et al.* 2007; for full report see Appendix R, on website: http://www.library.spscc.ctc.edu/JWA9.pdf).

3.3 Geoarchaeological Investigations

By Michele Punke

3.3.1 Introduction

In 2005, Katherine Bernick, a Northwest Coast waterlogged sites expert, was commissioned by the U.S. National Park Service to prepare a report outlining possible archaeological investigations at 35MU4. A major component of Bernick's (2005) report focused on the need for geoarchaeological investigations at the site that would address site formation processes, regional landscape depositional histories, and cultural strata contexts.

Geoarchaeological studies were conducted at 35MU4 in 2006 and 2007. The 2006 first phase of work included the following activities: (1) geological sediment coring along an east-west transect through the levee deposit in order to define subsurface stratigraphy at the site and define the relationship between the different cultural components of the site; (2) stratigraphic profiling of test units and a pit feature to further elucidate the relationship between wet and dry portions of the site and to determine the nature of site occupation; and (3) limited diatom biostratigraphic study of sediments to further explore the depositional setting of 35MU4.

The 2007 second phase of work included the acquisition of two geological sediment cores from the area of the site closest to the shoreline. The work was designed to test the hypothesis put forth after the 2006 field work that at least 2.5 meters (8 feet) of cultural materials remained intact and *in situ* beneath the present-day land surface along the shorefront margin of the site. It was also hoped that the 2007 efforts might allow for a clearer picture of site formation processes to be painted – to elucidate what roles processes such as river meandering, channel bank slump, and tectonic activity may have had on the state of the site as it appears today.

The 2006 and 2007 geoarchaeological fieldwork and laboratory activities are outlined and their results discussed below.

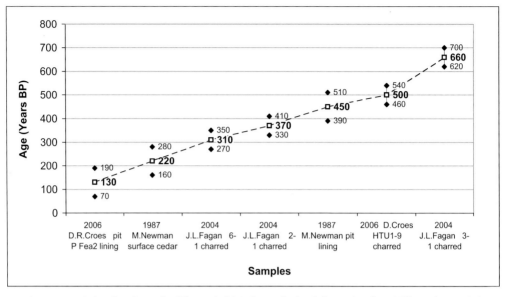

Figure 3.5. Distribution of calibrated C14 dates derived from Sunken Village (35MU4).

3.3.2 Natural and Cultural Impacts to the Site

The 35MU4 site, located near to the confluence of the Columbia and Willamette rivers, along the margins of Multnomah Channel, has been impacted by natural and human-induced erosional and depositional forces operating on various time scales. A discussion of some of these natural processes is presented by Diedrich (above), and will not be repeated here.

One geological variable not discussed in Diedrich's text that may have had an impact on the site is regional tectonics. As the name Sunken Village suggests, it has long been wondered if 35MU4 experienced, at some point in its history, a geological phenomenon that cause the site to fall in elevation relative to water level. In other words, did 'Sunken Village' really sink? Strong and Galbraith (1955, 2) write, "In some prehistoric time this camp had subsided until it was below normal water level. What caused this subsidence is unknown..." Jones (1972, 159) opens his discussion of the site with questions regarding its geomorphic history: "Has the land subsided in the Pacific Northwest? Did Sauvie Island drop down because of its silt foundation? Has the level of the sea risen?" Despite a long interest in the 'sunken' nature of the site, no formal work exploring this question has been conducted.

Sauvie Island lies at the northern end of the mapped extents of two faults within the Portland Basin: the East Bank fault and the Portland Hills fault. High resolution seismic profiling has shown evidence of late Pleistocene to Holocene deformation of sediments along the East Bank fault and possibly along the Portland Hills fault, although the timing and nature of movement has yet to be determined (Pratt *et al.* 2001).

The East Bank fault is a northwest-striking, high angle fault that runs along the southwestern corner of Sauvie Island (Figure 3.6). It is described as having a down-to-the-southwest displacement direction (Madin 1990; Beeson *et al.* 1991). However, seismic profiling work by Pratt *et al.* (2001) interprets movement along the fault as down-to-the-northeast. Data have yet to be acquired to resolve the question of the exact nature of this movement.

The Portland Hills fault is a northwest-striking fault mapped across Multnomah Channel from Sauvie Island (Figure 3.6), along the linear northeastern margin of the Tualatin Mountains (Portland Hills) (Personius *et al.* 2003). Sense of displacement along the fault is controversial, with original mapping indicating a down-to-the-northeast normal fault (Balsillie and Benson 1971). Other researchers have described the fault as a southwest-dipping reverse fault (Blakely *et al.* 1995) or a southwest-dipping reverse to vertical fault (Wong *et al.* 1999). Using multiple, high resolution geophysical techniques, Liberty *et al.* (2003) found that the fault had been active within the last 12–15 thousand years, although the nature of the faulting was not precisely determined.

If movement on either of these faults has occurred within the time period of occupation of 35MU4, the depositional setting of the site would have been affected. The exact effects of such movement will be discussed below.

Additionally, if movement along the faults had occurred when the site was being used by Native peoples it likely would have been notable, the type of event that might be incorporated into local oral traditions. There exist in the oral histories of the native peoples living in the Pacific Northwest stories relating to earthquakes, although much of the research regarding this topic has been discussed in terms of the coastal Cascadia Subduction Zone fault system (e.g. Carver and Carver 1996; Heaton and Snavely 1985; Losey 2001; Ludwin *et al.* 2005; McMillan and Hutchinson 2002). However, some stories referring to ground shaking have been recorded in association with interior and Columbia River tribes. Ground shaking associated with mythical figures engaging in battle is mentioned in the tale 'Speelyai fights Eenumtla' (Kuykendall 1889) and is thought to derive from the Yakama peoples (Ludwin 1999). The Clackamas Chinook refer to ground shaking events in their oral traditions (Jacobs 1959, 532–533), and the Chinook refer to dancing birds making the houses and the ground shake (Boas 1894, 148). Because the stories reference no specific locations, it is difficult to say whether they are associated with movement along faults in the Sauvie Island area, but the possibility remains.

Other factors have impacted the site's depositional setting and stratigraphy through time, including human modification of the landscape. In the early 1900's a county road was constructed along the western margin of Sauvie Island on top of and/or into the natural levee that runs parallel to the shoreline. Topographic maps from 1918 and 1920 display this road (see Newman 1991, Figures 6 and 7; and above). Newman (1991, 27) reports local informant descriptions that indicate the eastern portion of the site contained human burial mounds and that these burials were destroyed during the construction of a county road running south along the western edge of Sauvie Island. Subsequent work on both the road and the adjacent levee has not resulted in the discovery of any human remains or evidence of burials. It is likely that road construction affected the site on both sides of the levee, as cut and fill activities associated with leveling the ground surface for road building may have encroached upon the western portion of the site.

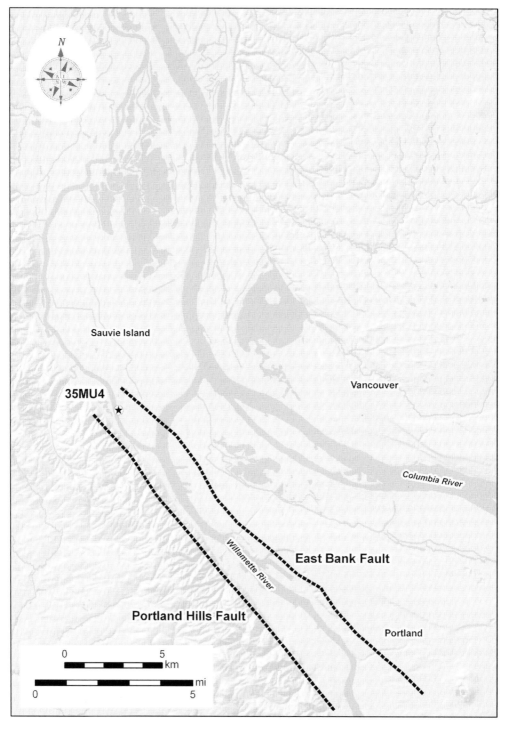

Figure 3.6. Tectonic setting of Sauvie Island and the 35MU4 archaeological site. (Modified from Pratt et al. 2001, Figure 1).

In 1938, the U.S. Army Corps of Engineers began construction of a dike that was designed to protect nearly 12,000 acres of land on Sauvie Island from flooding (Newman 1991, 27–29, and above). The dike was built to a height of approximately 32 ft and lined approximately eighteen miles of land along the southern portion of the island, including the land that contained 35MU4. Along the western margin of Sauvie Island, much of the material used in the construction of the dike was dredged from Multnomah Channel (McClure 1983). At the location of 35MU4, dredged material was deposited along the channel's bank and atop the natural streamside levee in order to build the dike to the required height. Construction of the dike and the associated dredging activity had a major impact on the site, as indicated in Strong and Galbraith (1955, 2): "It is now nearly all gone, what was not dredged up for fill is now under the dike, except for a narrow strip along the water's edge." Local residents have suggested that offshore portions of the site were included in the dredged material that was then re-deposited over other areas of the site, including the levee (Newman 1991, 28, 109).

Thickness of the fill material over the top of the natural levee was investigated as part of a study by Hibbs and Ellis (1988). They conducted auger testing across the dike, from east to west, and found that the fill depth was deepest at the dike apex, measuring approximately 1.8–2.4 m (6–8 ft) in thickness, thinning laterally to under 1.5 m (5 ft) (see Hibbs and Ellis 1988, Figures 10 and 11 for dike cross-sections).

An irrigation canal was constructed through the levee in the northern portion of 35MU4 in association with the dike construction and agricultural improvements of Sauvie Island lands (especially affecting 25 m collection transects III and IV, Figures 3.2–3.4a). Construction plans for the irrigation device show the natural levee in cross section, with the constructed levee, the irrigation intake pipe, and the control structure (concrete pump seen in Figures 3.2–3.4b) depicted. Fagan (2004, 6) noted "an extensive cut and fill feature centered on the intake pipe that cuts through the natural levee." The cut-and-fill feature sediments were noted to contain charcoal, shell, fire-cracked rock, and lithic flakes. Holes excavated within the cut-and-fill feature were the result of illicit looting activities. It has been suggested that sediments from the levee and beach surrounding the location of the intake pipe were used as fill during the construction process, and that much of the looting in the past has centered on this fill material due to ease of artifact recovery (Bernick 2005; Bernick, personal communication, 2007).

As mentioned above, dredging activities have been conducted at the site in the past in relation to the construction of the dike. Dredging has continued in the channel for both river navigation purposes and for the production of dredge spoils that can be used for dike reinforcement. Taber (1977, cited in Newman 1991, 112) indicates that as silt accumulates in the channel, dredging is performed and spoils from these channel deepening activities are dumped along the beach. Perishable artifacts have been found in these dredge spoils, indicating that the wet portion of the site is being impacted by the dredging. Jones (1972, 161) reports that a line of storage pits from the site that ran parallel to the shore was destroyed during dredging activities.

Looting is an ongoing problem at 35MU4. The site has been a collector hotspot for years, and methods of artifact acquisition have ranged from locals walking the beach in search of items to those collectors using more destructive methods such as loosening the soil with a rake (Steele 1978, 4) or digging holes into the beach or cutbank. Such invasive methods would have accelerated natural erosive processes that are active along the channel. Undercutting of bank sediments because of looting can lead to slump of the cutbank, causing upper cutbank sediments to slump down onto the beach, exposing them to erosion by fluvial forces.

3.3.3 Methods

The original call for proposals by the SIDIC for the 2006 work outlined the following tasks for the geoarchaeological portion of the study: the acquisition of 3–4 sediment cores into the levee, and the profiling of one cutbank exposure. As detailed in the scope, this portion of the study would define and characterize individual depositional units within site 35MU4. In particular, the origin of the cultural deposits would be defined both in the levee as well as in the intertidal zone. Natural levee formation processes and artificial impacts due to levee construction, dredging, erosion, and vandalism would be addressed.

In order to fully address the goals outlined in the scope for the 2006 work, the geoarchaeological portion of the study performed the tasks outlined above: acquiring four deep sediment cores from the levee and profiling the one meter exposure of cutbank revealed during excavation of the half test unit (HTU). Additionally, three test units (TUs) and one pit feature were profiled and limited diatom biostratigraphic analysis was performed.

The goal of the 2007 work was to test the hypothesis that intact, *in situ* nearshore cultural deposits reached depths of at least 2.5 m (8 ft) in the core area of the site, the area where the majority of the mapped acorn pits were clustered. The 2007 work included the acquisition and analysis of two additional geologic sediment cores.

3.3.4 Results – Sediment Stratigraphy

This section presents summary descriptions of the sedimentary properties of stratigraphic profiles of the (a) upper bank and in situ beach deposits of the Half Test Unit (HTU), (b) the organic rich and vegetal mat layering in Test Unit 4 (TU4), (c) the relatively complete acorn leaching pit (Pit P) and (d) six deep-core samples taken in 2006 and 2007. Summary descriptions of the sedimentary properties of stratigraphic profiles for Test Unit 1 and 2 were essentially culturally sterile and are described in the final report submitted to the Oregon State Historic Preservation Office, but, because of their lack of well-defined cultural deposits, are not described in detail here (see Croes *et al.* 2006; 2007a). Test Units 1–3 were excavated up next to the cutback, and were critical in evaluating the impact of placing rip-rap rock along the bank, and since they had very little cultural remains or deposits, these negative results provided the data used by the U.S. Army Corps of Engineers to issue a permit for the placement of rip-rap rock protection along this cutback in 2006 (Croes *et al.* 2006). Sediment stratigraphic descriptions for the HTU, TU4, and Pit P are presented below in tabular form, are referenced to Arabic numerals on the figure drawings, and are referred to in the text as Stratigraphic Unit number (SU #). All colors were recorded on dry sediments, unless noted. See Croes *et al.* 2006; 2007a for similar descriptions for TU1–2.

3.3.4.1 Half Test Unit (HTU)

HTU was excavated into the cutbank backing the beach, near to where AINW had described their stratigraphic Profile #7 (Figure 3.1; Fagan 2004). Two walls of the HTU were described, the south and east walls (Table 3.1, Figures 3.1–3.3, 3.4b–c, 3.7–3.9). The description below represents composite information from both walls. The bank appeared to have reached its current position as a result of erosion and slump of cutbank materials.

The HTU was excavated from the ground surface of the cutbank to a depth of 120 cm (47 in). The upper 50 cm (20 in) of the unit was a light yellowish brown loam that

HTU Stratigraphic Unit	HTU Description
1	Light yellowish brown (2.5Y6/4) loam; faint, diffuse yellowish brown (10YR5/6) staining and fine to medium mottles, located most commonly towards the base of the unit in pores and along root casts; medium to coarse, moderate granular; slightly sticky, slightly plastic, moderately hard; many fine roots and pores; clear and wavy lower boundary
2	Same as above, but increased clay content and strong, moderate granular structure; some faintly discernible masses of iron accumulation towards center of unit, at around 50cm below surface (cmbs); common pieces of charcoal (d < 2cm) and organic staining at ~50cmbs, especially in south wall
3	Light olive brown (2.5Y5/3) silt loam; coarse, strong subangular blocky; slightly sticky, slightly plastic, hard; few fine roots and pores; many mottles of reduced and oxidized iron throughout; common charcoal nodules and stains, some in apparently horizontal layers (charcoal content ~15–20%); clear, smooth lower boundary
4	Matrix same as above, but charcoal content much lower (<5%); distinct, wavy lower boundary
5	Cultural layer composed predominantly of charcoal, wood, burned bone and burned earth; Black (2.5Y2.5/1) silt loam; weak, fine to medium granular structure; slightly sticky, slightly plastic, hard; distinct, wavy lower boundary
6	Light olive brown (2.5Y5/3) silt loam; coarse, strong subangular blocky; slightly sticky, slightly plastic, hard; few fine roots and pores; common mottles of reduced and oxidized iron throughout; layer with charcoal and humified organic matter (~10%) at around 95cmbs, prominent in south wall; gradual, smooth lower boundary
7	Brown (10YR4/3) silt loam; weak to moderate, coarse columnar to coarse, strong subangular blocky; slightly sticky, slightly plastic, hard; few fine roots and pores; many mottles of reduced and oxidized iron throughout

Table 3.1 Description of Stratigraphic Units in HTU 1.

Figure 3.7. East and south wall stratigraphic profiles of the Half Test Unit (HTU) from 35MU4.

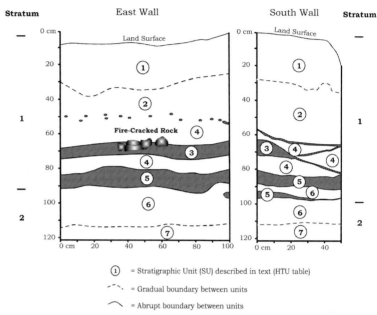

Half Test Unit (HTU)

Stratum   East Wall   South Wall   Stratum

① = Stratigraphic Unit (SU) described in text (HTU table)

⌇ = Gradual boundary between units

⌒ = Abrupt boundary between units

Figure 3.8. (left) Photograph of the east wall of the HTU showing two charcoal layers. (right) Photograph of the south wall of the HTU showing a beach-ward slope of the charcoal layering.

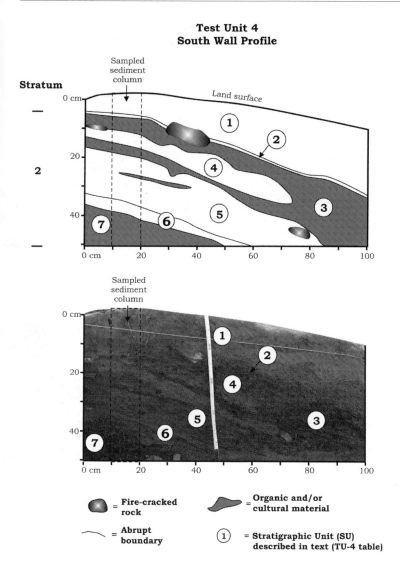

Test Unit 4
South Wall Profile

Figure 3.9. South wall stratigraphic profile and photograph of Test Unit 4.

showed signs of moderate soil development, including the development of soil structure and translocation of iron and clay into the lower portion of the unit (HTU SUs 1 and 2). A horizontal band of charcoal nodules and organic staining occurred at around 50 cm (20 in) and was especially prominent in the south wall of the HTU. This band separated HTU SU 1 and 2 from lower SUs.

Two prominent cultural layers occurred in the HTU, one from approximately 68 to 75 cm (27 to 30 in) and another from approximately 80 to 95 cm (31 to 37 in) (HTU SUs 3 and 5). The upper cultural layer contained a high concentration of charcoal, burned earth, and organic staining. An assemblage of fire-cracked rock (FCR) was also located in the profile wall at the elevation of the upper cultural layer. The lower layer contained a large concentration of charcoal, burned earth, and burned bone. The east-west dip of the culturally-rich strata in the south wall of the unit ranged from 0 to 20 degrees.

Sedimentary deposits of relatively charcoal-free sediment occurred above and between cultural layers (HTU SUs 4 and 6). These consisted of light olive brown silt loams that displayed moderate soil development, including increased soil structure relative to upper units and redoximorphic features (iron depletions and concentrations). However, redoximorphic features were related, in part, to water table fluctuations in the lower portions of the unit. The basal sediment unit in the HTU was a brown silt loam with increased soil structure and higher redoximorphic feature content.

3.3.4.2 TEST UNIT 4 (TU-4)

TU-4 was positioned along the beach nearer to the water's edge than TU-1 or TU-2 (Figures 3.2, 3.3, and 3.4c). Further stratigraphic information regarding TU4 sediments was gleaned by acquiring a column of sediment from the south wall of the unit (Figure 3.9) and performing litho- and diatom bio-stratigraphic analyses on the sampled sediment. The results of a simplified litho-stratigraphic analysis are listed in Table 3.2. The results

TU-4 Stratigraphic Unit	TU-4 Description
1	Black (10YR2/1) loamy fine sand; organic rich, many fragments of wood up to 7 cm in length; organic content of unit ~30%
2	Dark brown (10YR3/3) very fine sandy loam; organic content low (~10%)
3	Black (10YR2/1) highly organic loamy fine sand; organic content ~50%, with wood fragments up to 3.0 cm in length
4	Very dark grayish brown (10YR3/2) loamy fine to medium sand, some pockets of coarser sands; many fragments of wood up to ~3 cm in length; matrix contains approximately 15% organic matter and humified organics; thin layers (~1 cm) of iron oxide stained sands (dark yellowish brown 10YR4/4) and iron reduced sands (grayish brown 10YR5/2) throughout; many shell fragments
5	Dark brown (10YR3/3) loamy very fine sand; markedly less organic content than above, with few charcoal nodules, shell fragments, and organic stains noted; many thin (<1cm) laminae of lighter colored coarser sands and darker colored loams; artifacts noted in unit; abrupt, smooth lower boundary
6	Very dark grayish brown (2.5Y3/2) silt loam; very low organic content (<3%); appeared gleyed in field; abrupt, smooth lower boundary
7	Black (2.5Y2.5/1) fine to medium sandy loam; high proportion of humified organics and wood debris (~90%)

Table 3.2. Description of Stratigraphic Units in TU-4.

Figure 3.10. Location of TU-4 excavation (with backfill materials) within a small, remnant sediment outcrop along the beach portion of 35MU4.

of the diatom bio-stratigraphic analysis are discussed below and in Appendix C:164, on website: http://www.library.spscc.ctc.edu/crm/JWA9.pdf.

TU-4 was excavated to a depth of 50 cm (20 in) below the surface of a small, remnant sediment outcrop positioned just above the extant beach (Figures 3.10—3.11). The uppermost sediment within the unit was an organic-rich loamy fine sand that unconformably capped a series of sediment horizons containing variable amounts of organic materials. Most of the organic debris within SUs 3, 5 and 7 consisted of wood chips, twigs, and nut shells, while the organic constituents within SU 1 were more dissipated throughout the matrix. The matrix of SU 1 was poorly sorted and massive, displaying no features of soil formation regardless of its position at the surface. It is likely that this sediment was deposited relatively recently, a result of erosion and redeposition of sediments at a beach-front location. Thin beds of sandier materials separated organic units within TU-4, some displaying redox features. A thin (~3 cm [1 in]) layer of gleyed silt loam (SU 6) abruptly capped the rich cultural deposit of SU 7. This is more clearly seen in the unit's east wall stratigraphic profile, shown in Figure 3.11. The east-west dip of the strata averages 18%.

Figure 3.11 Photo of the east wall of TU-4, showing thin layer of gleyed silt loam (SU 6) capping a layer of cultural deposit (SU 7).

3.3.4.3 PIT P

Pit P was excavated into a low outcrop of remnant sediment towards the southern end of the site, near to the easting and elevation of TU-4. A stratigraphic drawing of the pit was drawn in the field, and sediment samples were taken at 5 cm intervals for analysis at AINW. Based on the drawings, photos, and sediment samples, a simplified stratigraphic description of Pit P is presented below in Table 3.3 and depicted in Figure 3.12.

Pit P was excavated as a half test unit to 50 cm (20 in) below surface. Sediments from within the pit consisted of discontinuous layers of silt loams, fine sands and sandy loams, and largely organic layers. More highly organic sediments line the base and lower sides of the pit. The discontinuous nature of the sediments is consistent with intermittent infilling. A second pit feature appears to have been dug into the primary pit and is represented by the portion of the unit labeled SU 7 in Table 3.3 and in Figure 3.12.

Pit P Stratigraphic Unit	Pit P Description
1	Dark gray (10YR4/1) and dark yellowish brown (10YR3/4) loam, mixed; low organic content (~5% charcoal nodules); slightly sticky, slightly plastic; abrupt, smooth lower boundary
2	Very dark grayish brown (10YR3/2) silt loam; slightly sticky, slightly plastic; clear, discontinuous boundary with Unit 3
3	Very dark grayish brown (10YR3/2) silt loam; with many dark gray (10YR4/1) mottles; slightly sticky, slightly plastic; clear, discontinuous boundary with Unit 4
4	Very dark grayish brown (10YR3/2) fine sand, with few mottles of dark yellowish brown (10YR4/6); high charcoal content (~40%); clear, discontinuous lower boundary
5	Dark grayish brown (10YR4/2) very fine sandy loam to loam; central portions of peds are dark grey (2.5Y4/1); abrupt, discontinuous lower boundary
6	Very dark grayish brown (10YR3/2) loam; charcoal nodules (~15%) and shell fragments (~5%); bottom of unit is lined with culturally imported twigs and wood fragments
7	Not sampled in field, but appears similar to Unit 2.

Table 3.3. Description of Stratigraphic Units in Pit P.

3.3.4.4 CORES 1–4

The four sediment cores extracted along an east-west transect through the levee displayed similar patterns of sedimentary stratigraphy through their lengths (Figure 3.13). The upper portions of each of the cores contained very poorly sorted materials, with sediment texture ranging from clay to gravels. These materials likely represent the dredged fill that was placed on top of the natural levee in the late 1930s to construct the dike. In cores 1 and 3, a buried soil was evident just below the fill material. This soil represents the former surface of the natural levee. Below this level, each of the cores contained a series of coarser and finer grained deposits. The cultural deposit that is visible in the cutbank was also found in the upper levels of cores 1, 3, and 4. Although no artifacts were noted during examination of these sections of the cores, charcoal and burned earth was found at levels stratigraphically in line with the cutbank's cultural materials. Fine- and coarse-grained laminae, or cross-beds, were present throughout much of the lower portions of the cores, some in fining-upward sequences. The central to lower portion of each of the cores displayed redox features, and the bases of cores 2–4 were largely gleyed.

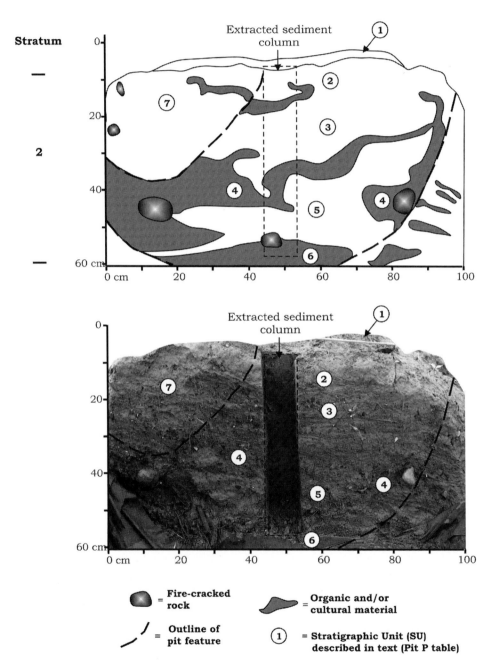

Figure 3.12. South wall stratigraphic profile and photograph of Pit P (FCR=Fire Cracked Rock).

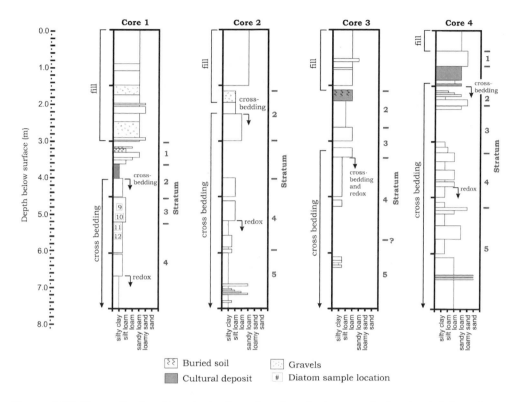

Figure 3.13 Generalized sediment stratigraphy of geologic cores 1–4 extracted from levee portion of 35MU4. Major features within core sections are noted, including depth of fill, buried soils, laminae, redoximorphic features, and gleying. Sedimentary Strata designations are also indicated (see text). Each core is depicted by boxes with differing widths representing the sediment textures encountered at depths below the land surface. The wider the box, the coarser the sediment texture encountered. Gaps between the boxes depicting core sediment textures indicate depths at which sediments were lost during coring activities.

3.3.4.5 Cores 5–6

Two cores were extracted during the 2007 coring endeavor. Core 5, which was extracted in three sections to a total depth of 2.7 m (9 ft), was extracted from a point directly west of the 1x1 meter (3.3 × 3.3 ft) test unit, TU-4, that was excavated during the 2006 fieldwork (Figures 3.2, 3.3, 3.4c). The second core, Core 6, was placed approximately 6 m (20 ft) to the west of Core 5, near the edge of the westernmost extent of mapped acorn pits. Core 6 was extracted in six sections to a total depth of 5.5 m (18 ft).

The upper portion of Core 5 contained relatively coarse-grained sediment, predominantly sandy loams to sands, to a depth of approximately 0.95 m (3.1 ft) below surface (Figure 3.14). A slight decrease in grain size was found below this, followed by another increase in grain size to a depth of 1.6 m (5.3 ft) below ground surface. Below this

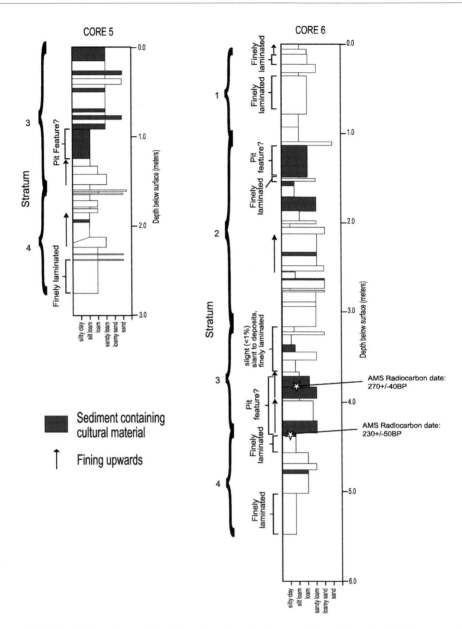

Figure 3.14 Detailed sediment stratigraphy of geologic cores 5 and 6 extracted from shoreline portion of 35MU4. Major features within core sections are noted, including sediment containing cultural material, laminae, fining-upwards sediment sequences, and possible pit features. Sedimentary Strata designations are also indicated (see text). Each core is depicted by boxes with differing widths representing the sediment textures encountered at depths below the land surface. The wider the box, the coarser the sediment texture encountered. Gaps between the boxes depicting core sediment textures indicate depths at which sediments were lost during coring activities.

point, the grain size decreased to a silt loam with a few, thin lenses of sandier materials intermixed. Fining upward sequences were noted in the mid- to lower section of the core, while finely laminated cross-beds were found at the core's base. Redoximorphic features were noted beginning at approximately 1.12 m (3.7 ft) in depth.

Core 6 contained relatively fine-grained materials 1.1 m (3.6 ft) in depth below ground surface (Figure 3.14). Below this grain size was coarser, generally loamy to sandy loam, to a depth of 3.3 m (10.8 ft). Grain size ranged from silty clay to sandy loam in the lowermost portion of Core 6, with finely laminated cross-beds found at the core's base.

Beginning at a depth of approximately 3.2 m (10.5 ft) in Core 6, the sediments appear to have a slight dip (<1%). Because the core was not extracted with directional orientation information recorded, it is not known exactly how this dip is oriented. In other words, it is not known if the sediments dip down towards the channel, down towards the levee, or up or downstream. What is notable is that the dip appears in this section of the core, since no other angled sedimentary layers are noted within cores 5 or 6.

Sediment samples from the two cores were fine-screened and examined under a microscope to identify non-mineral sediment inclusions or cultural materials. In total, 42 samples were extracted, 13 from Core 5 and 29 from Core 6. Most of the samples contained charcoal and woody debris. Many of the samples also contained shell, seeds, and burned bone. Of the 42 samples, 24 contained cultural materials. Nine samples from Core 5 contained cultural materials to a maximum depth of 1.93 m (6.3 ft). From Core 6, 15 samples contained cultural material to a maximum depth of 4.8 m (15.8 ft). Identified cultural materials included flakes of cryptocrystalline silica (CCS) and obsidian, a CCS core, and fire-cracked rock (FCR).

Distribution of cultural materials within cores 5 and 6 suggest that pit features may have been intercepted by the coring activity. In Core 5, a pit feature may have been represented by two samples containing cultural materials that were identified at 0.92 m (3.0 ft) and at 1.18 m (3.9 ft), with charcoal, wood and shell liberally distributed between the samples. A possible acorn shell was identified in the lower sample.

In Core 6, two potential pit features were identified. The first ranges in depth from 1.10 m (3.6 ft) to 1.31 m (4.3 ft) in below the land surface. Three samples containing cultural materials were extracted from these depths, with charcoal, burned bone, wood, bark, fish bone, and acorn shell found in and between the samples. A second possible pit feature was identified from 3.40 to 4.24 m (11.2 to 13.9 ft) in depth in Core 6. Five samples containing cultural material, charcoal, shell, wood, fish bones, burned bone, and acorn shell were extracted from these depths. A sixth sample was extracted from 3.96 m (13.0 ft) and was not found to contain cultural material; however, the matrix surrounding this sample appeared very similar to the artifact-bearing sediments above and below, and the same types of shell, wood, and charcoal were noted in this sample.

3.3.4.6 DIATOM BIOSTRATIGRAPHY

This section presents summary descriptions of the diatom biostratigraphy of sampled profiles and core samples. Specific observations are provided in Appendix C:208, website: http://www.library.spscc.ctc.edu/crm/JWA9.pdf.

A series of eight diatom samples was extracted from the sediment column that was taken from the south wall of TU-4 (Figure 3.15). All eight of the samples contained diatom assemblages consistent with a shallow water, plant-rich setting that incurs infrequent deeper inundation or flooding and deposition, such as a freshwater marsh with intertidal channels. Four samples were taken from the east wall of TU-4 which corroborate with these findings.

Four samples were extracted from Core 1, Section 3 (Figure 3.13). The lower two samples contained diatoms indicative of a shallow water setting with an increasing number of water plants through time. The upper two diatom samples from this core were from deeper-water deposits, perhaps associated with overbank flood deposition. This sequence of diatom assemblages may represent a slackwater marsh setting that abruptly changed to a deeper water, higher energy environment.

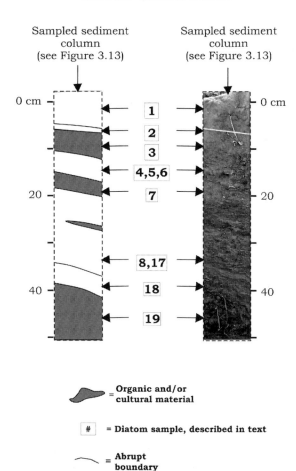

**Test Unit 4
South Wall Profile**

Figure 3.15 Diatom biostratigraphic sample locations from column sample extracted from the south wall of TU-4.

3.3.4.7 RADIOCARBON DATING

Two of the samples identified as containing cultural materials were chosen for charcoal extraction and dating. Both samples were from Core 6, the first from 3.80 m (12.5 ft) in depth and the second from 4.22 m (13.8 ft) in depth. The first sample returned a date of 270±40 BP (2–Sigma calibrated dates of 440 to 350, 340 to 280, 170 to 150, and 0 to 0 Cal BP) (Beta-239091). The second sample returned a date of 230±50 BP (2–Sigma calibrated dates of 430 to 370, 320 to 260, 220 to 140, and 30 to 0 Cal BP) (Beta-239092). Although the dates are reversed in terms of stratigraphic position of the samples and their dates (i.e. the younger sample was found stratigraphically below the older), there is significant overlap in their margins of error.

3.3.5 Discussion

3.3.5.1 SITE STRATIGRAPHY

A composite stratigraphic cross-section of the sediments composing the beach and levee was created using the stratigraphic drawings and descriptions from the cores, the HTU, Pit P and TUs 1, 2, and 4 (Figures 3.16 and 3.17). The cross section was constructed by plotting the units and cores along an east-west axis according to their easting and elevation relative to sea level. Although the cores and units were not at the same northing (Figures 3.2, 3.3, 3.4a–c), the similarity of sedimentary deposits along this portion of the beach allowed for a composite sketch to be drawn regardless of northing. A number of mapped pit locations and the location of Pettigrew and Lebow's (1987) Auger 8 are also shown on the cross section in order to provide reference locations for other known cultural features. The pits and auger northings are all within the same range as the HTU, Pit P, and TUs. None of the outlined sedimentary deposits is completely homogeneous in nature, nor do any represent a single depositional event. Rather, they are depositional units that are grouped based on common sedimentary and stratigraphic characteristics.

The upper unit shown in the beach and levee cross section (Figure 3.17) is a mixed loamy deposit that consists of fill material that was deposited at the location as part of dike construction. Below this is a relatively thin, discontinuous loamy deposit. This loam displays some signs of soil development and appears to have been a stable surface for an extended period of time. Below this is a loam deposit containing cultural materials and organic debris. The underlying silt loam appears to be sterile of cultural material in the levee portion of the cross section. However, this silt loam may be the same cultural material-bearing stratigraphic unit that is seen in TU-4 and the upper portion of Core 6 (Figures 3.16 and 3.17). A coarser-grained unit stretches though the profile just below the cultural and non-cultural silt loam and just above another silt loam deposit. Based on a small sample of material contained in the lower portions of five of the cores, it appears that a coarser-grained, sandy loam or loamy sand deposit is the lowermost sampled sedimentary unit at the site.

Based on composite stratigraphy outlined for the cores and test units, the upper sediment units from TU-1 and TU-2 appear to be unconformable with the lower sections of these units. Based on the amount of erosion that has occurred in the lower portions of the cutbank along the length of the site (due to both natural forces and looting activities), it is likely that the upper sediments in TU-1 and TU-2 were originally at an elevation similar to that of the upper portion of the cutbank HTU, were undercut by erosion, and have since slumped to their current position (Figures 3.16 and 3.17).

It has been suggested that the placement of the acorn leaching pits at this particular location on Sauvie Island is related to the presence of a freshwater aquifer that may run through the site (Croes et al. 2006, 140–141). This seems possible given the local hydrologic features and the sediment stratigraphy at the site. Early maps of Sauvie Island place a flooded basin or small lake behind the levee at the 35MU4 site. Some of the water that pooled at this location may have drained out beneath the levee and intercepted the cultural deposit (the acorn pits) at the sediment stratigraphic levels

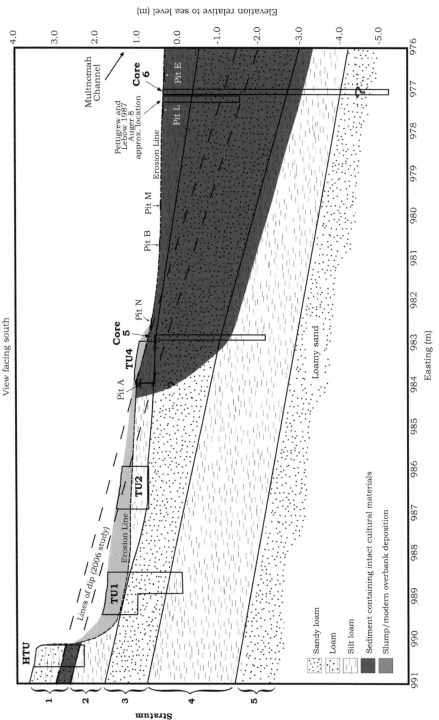

Figure 3.16 Composite stratigraphic cross section of the sediments composing the beach and cutbank portions of the site, including information from Cores 5 and 6, the HTU, Pit P, and TUs 1, 2, and 4. Locations of selected pit features and Pettigrew and Lebow's (1987) Auger # 8 are also shown for reference. Test units, pits, and the auger location are plotted according to their eastings and elevations. Sedimentary Strata designations are shown at left. Grey question mark at base of Core 6 indicates the potential maximum depth of cultural deposits identified in the core.

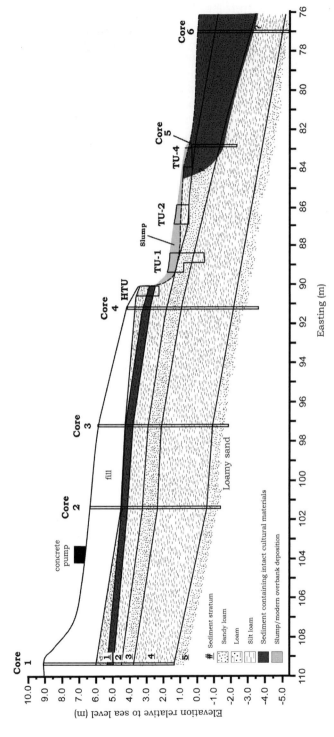

Figure 3.17. Composite stratigraphic cross section of the sediments composing the beach and levee portions of the site, including information from the cores, HTU, Pit P, and TUs 1, 2, and 4. All features are plotted according to their eastings and elevations. Sedimentary Strata designations are shown at left.

most conducive to water flow. Stratum 4, the silt loam to silty clay deposit, would have served as an aquatard, forcing water to perch above it as the water drained from the lake towards the Multnomah Channel, while Stratum 3, the overlying sandy loam deposit and the deposit into which the acorn pits were dug, would have allowed for water to flow through. Thus, the digging of acorn leaching pits by native peoples through the overlying silt loam and into the sandy loam would have allowed the acorns within the pits to be leached by the perched water flowing through the underlying sandier matrix. This contention is further supported by a recent study of the area using LIDAR data that suggests the basin behind the levee would have stored water seasonally, allowing for delayed seasonal discharge through the underlying aquifer for leaching purposes (Waibel *et al.* 2007; Appendix R, website: http://www.spscc.ctc.edu/crm/JWA9.pdf).

3.3.5.2 DEPOSITIONAL SETTING

Using information from the nature of the depositional units identified in the cross-section above, five sedimentary Strata were identified at the 35MU4 site (Figures 3.9, 3.13, 3.14, 3.16 and 3.17). The sedimentary strata of this sequence encompassing or surrounding the cultural deposit, Strata 1, 2, and 3, likely represent periods of deposition along the banks of a shifting river channel system (Ferring 1992; Miall 2006). Stratum 3 represents the relatively coarser point bar sediments that accrete laterally along the inside of a river bend. Point bar sediments typically display dipping beds of coarser and finer materials in their primary context, including laminae that represent ripple- and cross-bedding (Boggs 2001), features that were present and discernable in the core sediments (Figures 3.13 and 3.14). The presence of these coarser-grained sediments suggests that the main course of the channel has shifted through time, from east to west, leaving point bar deposits in its wake.

Once the channel had shifted position to the west, deposition of sediment continued. This deposition occurred as vertically accreting floodplain sedimentation. Floodplain sediments are represented in the sedimentary sequence as Stratum 2 (Figures 3.16 and 3.17), the silt loam that encompasses and directly underlies the cultural deposit within the site. Floodplain sediments are fine-grained materials that settle out of suspension from waters that overtop banks during flood events and inundate the lands surrounding a channel. Floodplain deposits often contain many organics and may be highly bioturbated. The silt loam found in the lower portion of TU-4 displays many vertical, reduced and oxidized iron features typical of infilled root casts, suggesting formerly vegetated conditions.

In addition to the evidence provided by the sedimentary and biological constituents, the diatom biostratigraphic record also suggests that Stratum 2 represents a floodplain deposit. The diatom assemblages from TU-4 are consistent with a shallow water, marshy setting that incurs infrequent deeper inundation or flooding and deposition, such as a low-relief floodplain or backwater swamp.

Overlying these deposits is Stratum 1, a coarsening upward silt loam to loam deposit that represents the formation of a levee. When streams overtop their banks during flood events, their power decreases and their ability to carry suspended sediment lowers resulting in the deposition of sediment. Over time the channel-side levee builds, requiring higher flood events (increased stream power) to overtop the banks. This situation results in increasingly coarser materials being deposited on the levee top. Stratum 1, seen in the HTU and cores 1 and 4, represents this latter stage of levee deposition.

The cores provide corroborative evidence for the migrating river channel and levee building depositional setting described above (Figure 3.17). In addition, the core sediments also provide information regarding the depositional setting of the site prior to human occupation (i.e. prior to the deposition of Strata 1–3). The Strata 4 and 5 couplet likely represents an earlier episode of channel meandering, with point bar facies represented by the basal component (Stratum 5) and overbank, floodplain sediment represented by the overlying unit (Stratum 4). These depositional groupings, Strata 5/4 and Strata 3/2/1, suggest that the 35MU4 site has undergone a long history of meandering river channel setting evolution, the latest episode during which human occupation of the location is recorded in the upper strata.

The diatom biostratigraphy from Core 1 supports this interpretation of landscape change. The lower two diatom samples were from sediments identified as Stratum 4. These assemblages indicated a shallow water setting, such as a floodplain or backwater swamp, with an increasing number of water plants through time. The upper two diatom samples from this core were from deeper-water deposits, perhaps associated with overbank flood deposition, and were from sediments identified as Stratum 3.

3.3.5.3 Cultural Deposits

The cultural deposits encountered during the archaeological investigations of 35MU4 were found both along the beach and in the channel levee (Figures 3.16 and 3.17). These deposits likely represent the same periods of occupation of the site, based on the overlap of radiocarbon ages between previously dated levee deposits and samples from pit features. In terms of their sedimentary contexts, the levee cultural deposits were found within Stratum 1 while pit features on the beach were found in Stratum 2. This difference in stratum location is logical considering the nature of the features. The levee bank deposit contained materials consistent with a hearth feature (FCR, burned earth, charcoal), the type of feature that would be placed atop the ground surface. In contrast, the pit features were dug at the ground surface into the underlying sediment. Many of the pits that were recorded during the 2006 and 2007 field seasons were thought to be truncated, their upper portions already eroded or destroyed. If this is the case, then the presence of pit bottoms in the sediment stratum underlying the levee cultural stratum should be expected, especially if pits were dug to depths of up to 2 m (6.6 ft) as a GPR study of the area suggests (Waibel *et al.* 2007; Appendices R, website: http://www.spscc.ctc.edu/crm/JWA9.pdf).

One of the most important outcomes of the stratigraphic profiling conducted in 2006 for the 35MU4 site was the illustration of the potential presence of deep, undisturbed cultural deposits at the site. When dotted lines were plotted extending from the top and bottom of the visible cultural deposits in TU-4 away from the channel, the cultural deposits located in the HTU were intercepted, suggesting that the dip of the original levee strata and the associated cultural deposits was similar to that seen in the TU-4 profile today (Figures 3.2, 3.4c and 3.9). When the dotted lines that bound the cultural strata were extended towards the channel, these lines of dip intercepted the easting of one of the mapped pits (Pit E) at approximately 2 m (6.6 ft) below the present-day land surface. A deep auger test excavated by Pettigrew and Lebow (1987) and mapped just east of Pit E (Figure 3.16) contained cultural materials throughout its length, to a depth of 2.5 m (8 ft) below the surface.

The 2007 work was designed to test the hypothesis that cultural deposits remained intact at that location to at least the depth hypothesized. The results if the 2007 coring support this hypothesis. Cultural deposits were encountered to a maximum depth of 1.93 m (6.3 ft) in Core 5. In Core 6, cultural materials were encountered to a maximum depth of 4.8 m (15.7 ft).

The radiocarbon dates acquired from Core 6 samples during this phase of coring at 35MU4 are problematic in terms of their depths below surface and age relative to other dated samples recovered from the site. Some samples from the site acquired during previous archaeological studies were much older, including from a pit feature at the ground surface that returned an age of 450±60 BP (see Figure 3.5). The radiocarbon samples submitted from the 2007 cores returned significantly younger ages, even though their vertical position was well below the ground surface (3.80 m [12.5 ft] and 4.22 m [13.8 ft] in depth) well below where previous samples had been extracted. There are many possible explanations for this apparent discrepancy, including sediment fall-in that may have occurred during core acquisition. We intend to use vibracoring techniques in future core testing, which should result in better, less mixed, samples.

Although the integrity of the lowest cultural deposits found in Core 6 is questionable, the next lowest intact cultural materials from Core 6 were found at a depth of approximately 3.3 m (10.8 ft) below the ground surface. Therefore, it can be stated with confidence that at the position at which Core 6 was extracted, cultural deposits are present to a minimum depth of 3.3 m (10.8 ft) and a maximum depth of 4.8 m (15.8 ft).

If deep cultural deposits are indeed present in the intertidal portion of the site at the westing of Core 6, the fact that other pit features are mapped at the land surface in the area between the location of Core 6 and TU-4 suggests that a wedge of deep cultural deposits remain intact below the surface at the 35MU4 site (Figures 3.16 and 3.17). The aerial extent of these deposits is not yet known. The western extent, into Multnomah channel, is dependent upon erosion due to natural fluvial processes, the distribution of past dredging activities within the channel, and the eastward extent of past human use of the site during low-water times. The north-south extent of the intact cultural deposit depends upon erosion or destruction due to dredging and irrigation pipe installation and past human use of the area. Although the exact north-south extent has yet to be determined, the presence of pits for over 100 m (330 ft) along the beach suggests a considerable amount of cultural material may still exist at the site.

A very rough estimate of the volume of cultural materials remaining at the site intact and *in situ* can be calculated using what information is known about the site today. An estimate of the north-south extent of the pits based on recent mapping of the site by Michael Martin indicates that the pit features extend roughly 100 m (328 ft) in length along the shoreline. Approximately 25 m (82 ft) of this length was disturbed by construction of the irrigation canal through the levee at the northern end of the site, leaving 75 m (246 ft) of length intact. The distance from the location of TU-4 west to the location of Core

6 is around 7 m (23 ft). The minimum depth of cultural deposits at the location of Core 6, based on the results of this study, is around 3 m (10 ft). Assuming the cultural deposits thin to the east, away from the channel, a triangular wedge of deposits can be constructed from these measurements and used to calculate volume (Figure 3.18). Using the formula (*length*width*depth)/2*, the estimated volume of this wedge of intact cultural materials is approximately 780 m³ (27,500 ft³).

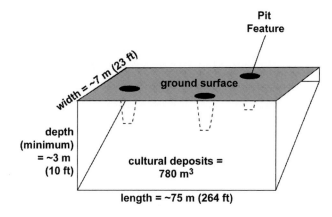

Figure 3.18. Volumetric estimation of intact cultural deposits remaining in the wet portion of archaeological site 35MU4 is approximately 780 m³.

3.3.5.4 Sunken Village?

The question remains as to whether 35MU4 has incurred a shift in elevation relative to water level some time in the past. While no geologic evidence of land subsidence due to tectonic movement has been recorded in the site vicinity, the presence of two major faults within the Portland Basin along the margin of Sauvie Island suggests the possibility of tectonic influence on the depositional history of the 35MU4 site (see Figure 3.6). If movement on the fault(s) dropped the site relative to the land around it, relative water level at the site would have risen and cultural deposits at the site inundated. Over time, sediment deposition and buildup at the site would have reformed the streamside beach and subsequent human occupation could have taken place. Such a scenario is depicted in Figure 3.19.

It is also possible that seismic shaking from regional quakes could have caused subsidence by liquefaction and spreading of the unconsolidated Columbia River deposits that underlie Sauvie Island, leading to a relative drop in land level relative to the water level of the river (Jim O'Connor, personal communication, 2007). Jim O'Connor, of the US Geological Service, indicates that there is good evidence of post-500 yr BP subsidence at the north end of the Sauvie Island where drowned young cottonwoods poke out of the water at lowest tides.

Other factors may have contributed to the deep cultural deposit recorded at 35MU4, but none offer a completely satisfactory explanation. One way in which river water level may have risen relative to land level is through a rise in sea level and concomitant rise in river base level. Global sea level rise over the last 3,000 years has averaged approximately 0.1 to 0.2 mm/yr (Church *et al.* 2001). If the cultural deposit at 35MU4 is assumed to date to no more than 1,000 years before present, then, at a maximum, 0.2 m of sea level rise has occurred since the beginning of site occupation. According to the distribution of cultural materials within Core 6, at least 3.3 m (10.8 ft) of cultural

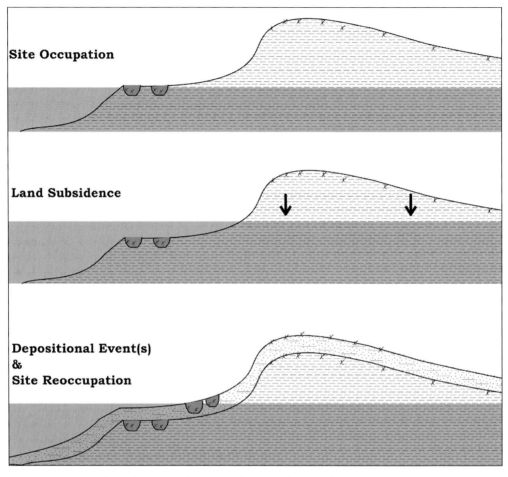

Figure 3.19 Hypothetical scenario for the production of deep cultural deposits at 35MU4 through the effects of human occupation, land subsidence, deposition, and reoccupation.

deposition has occurred at the site. Clearly sea level rise does not account fully for the depth of cultural materials at the 35MU4 site.

Another factor that may have affected the depth of cultural deposits at the site is slump. It is possible that early dredging activities within the channel may have encroached upon the edge of the site, leaving a steep scarp along its western edge. Over time, the edge of the site may have eroded and slumped down into the recently dredged channel, thus 'filling' it with cultural materials and causing an apparently deep cultural deposit to be left behind for later archaeologists to discover. A problem with this explanation lies in the fact that the deep cores extracted from the beach portion of the site were placed in the midst of surficial pit features, with some intact, *in situ* pits located adjacent to both cores. This suggests that dredging activities have not reached as far east as the cores' locations and thus the sediments that the cores sampled were indeed intact and undisturbed.

While the question, "Is Sunken Village really sunken?" has not been unequivocally answered, it is possible that movement along a local fault has occurred in the past, with land level dropping relative to water level. Other variables that may have affected the relative elevation of 35MU4 should be addressed with future research at the site. This research should include in-channel stratigraphic studies and acquisition of a series of radiocarbon dates from identified strata and cultural deposits.

3.3.6 Conclusion

Geoarchaeological investigations at the 35MU4, Sunken Village, archaeological site identified a series of depositional units consistent with a meandering river system, including point-bar construction, flood-plain deposition, and the formation of a stream-side levee. Stratigraphic investigations revealed that the cultural stratum identified at the site was associated with a former floodplain setting. The cultural deposits found in the wet, shoreline portion of the site, including the acorn pits, may have been placed at this locality to take advantage of a freshwater aquifer flowing through the subsurface. These cultural deposits trace into the dry portion of the site, as revealed in the levee cutbank and core sediments. Coring within the wet portion of the site revealed the presence of cultural deposits extending to a minimum depth of 3.3 m (10.8 ft) and a maximum depth of 4.8 m (15.8 ft). The volume of the remaining intact cultural materials within the wet portion of the site is roughly estimated to be 780 m³ (27,500 ft³). The possibility that the land surrounding the 35MU4 site has subsided in the past is a viable explanation for the deep cultural deposit seen at the site.

4 Ecofacts – Plant and Animal Analyses

4.1 Introduction

Wet sites, due to reduced oxygen, provide excellent preservation of both plant and animal remains. Due to the clear importance of Sunken Village as an acorn leaching and processing location – largely because of the aquifer streaming through this approximately 100–125 m of intertidal beach – the focus in Section 4 is on the leaching pits and acorn remains.

First we begin with a look at identifying the actual plant materials and fuels used at this site, requiring both visual observations of the plant remains and also cellular analysis of the wood, fibers and charcoal. Many of the perishable artifacts are introduced in this section while identifying their wood and fiber construction materials.

Second we report the abundant acorns and acorn leaching pit features, so numerous at Sunken Village.

Third, seed retrieval is explored, comparing the results of flotation techniques and fine wet screening.

And finally, the faunal analysis reflects the use of these animal resources in a secondary position, and probably to support the group while managing the acorn leaching pits from this site. The obvious contrast here to other Northwest Coast and Columbia River sites is the reduced focus on fisheries from this location.

4.2 Cellular Analysis of Artifact Plant Material and Charcoal

By Kathleen L. Hawes

4.2.1 Wood and Fiber Identification in Northwest Coast Wet Sites

The procedure of identifying wood and fiber materials by microscopic cellular analysis on the Northwest Coast of North America was pioneered in the 1970's by Dr. Janet Friedman, while conducting her research on the wealth of wooden artifacts from the Ozette Village wet site, Olympic Peninsula, Washington state, USA. Using information developed for the lumber industry, Dr. Friedman created a database of samples derived from the ethnobotany of the Ozette area, using this database for the basis of comparisons (Friedman 1978, 2005). The Ozette village had been partially covered by a landslide approximately 300 years ago, preserving normally perishable artifacts under anaerobic conditions, as well as plant materials such as sword fern, moss, berry seeds, and plant leaves (Gill 2005). The rich wood and fiber artifacts included basketry, wedges, fishing hooks, boxes, whale harpoons, ropes and cordage, arrow shafts as well as whole plank houses and furniture. The unique nature of Ozette and other wet sites on the Northwest Coast of North America has allowed plant material culture to be preserved and identified, adding a refreshing new understanding of the predominant ancient material culture and resources used by these ancient Peoples. The cellular identification of ancient plant material culture is complementary to information found in ethnobotanies, identifying traditional plant materials. Visual identification can be done on some plant materials, such as those made of western red-cedar (*Thuja plicata* Donn), which has a distinctive appearance; many times however features are obscured by silt and clay, long exposure to waterlogged conditions, and erosion.

4.2.2 Methods of Cellular Analysis

Cellular analysis of archaeological wood involves taking samples from three sections of a piece of wood (tangential, radial and cross-section), placing them on glass slides, and viewing these with a compound microscope. Differences between hardwoods and softwoods can be quickly identified by this method, and unique characteristics between softwoods can be observed in the rays, tracheids, and pit features (for more details about preparing the samples see Hawes in Croes *et al.* 2006, 2007a).

To identify plant material used in basketry and cordage, cellular analysis is used to determine if the material is woody tissue such as root or bough material; herbaceous dicot fibers; or monocot stem tissue.

4.2.3 Sunken Village Artifacts

Test excavations of the Sunken Village site in 2006 and 2007 yielded approximately 8600 artifacts (items that are the result of human activity, including abundant wood chips, split wood, charcoal, and basketry waste elements), of which approximately 80% were wood and fiber items. As examples, the wood and fiber artifacts recovered and examined by cellular analysis here include (a) an 'acorn' basket, (b) two wooden wedges, (c) branches lining an acorn leaching pit, (d) two *in situ* wooden stakes, (e) a carved wooden blade, (f) checker weave matting, and (g) a diamond-plaited soft bag.

4.2.3.1 THE ACORN BASKET

A beautiful basket, identified by master Warm Springs basket weaver Pat Gold as an acorn collecting basket, was recovered in 2006 in Transect V, Pit R (see Frontispiece and Ness *et al.*, below).This basket is well-preserved with intact base and sides, carefully cross-warp twined. Ethnography of basketry of the Lower Chinook area includes references to spruce root (Ray 1938, 132–133; Silverstein 1990), hazelnut boughs mentioned by Bud Lane (personal communication, July 2006), and cedar bark and root (Pat Gold, personal communications, 2006; Gunther 1973, 19).

Cellular analysis was performed on a fragment of basketry debris, which was

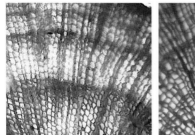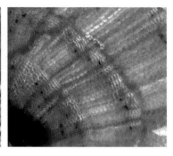

*Figure 4.1. (Left and center)Example of cross-section of acorn basket warp and a comparison of a modern example of a cross-section of Western red cedar (*Thuja plicata*) root. These both contrast to red cedar bough cross-sections (Right).*

identified as softwood, eliminating hazelnut (*Corylus spp*), a hardwood. Samples were taken of modern western red cedar roots and boughs, and Sitka spruce (*Picea sitchensis* [Bong.] Carr) roots. Microscopic examination positively identified the sample as conifer, with further comparison between the cedar and spruce roots showing characteristics that match cedar roots. Red cedar root samples, even taken from different areas show a similarity in the pith, with a star pattern seen in the cross section; whereas the Sitka spruce root cross section shows an elliptical pattern. A cross-section analysis between red cedar roots and boughs shows differences in the cellular structure, with that of red cedar roots having larger cells and extremely narrow (1–2 cells thick) or absent growth rings. A cross-section view of red cedar bough shows a denser cellular structure, with a wider transition between earlywood and latewood growth. Cellular analysis of a cross section of the artifact basket matches that of western red cedar root (Figure 4.1).

4.2.3.2 WOODEN WEDGES

Two wooden wedges were excavated from the Sunken Village site in 2006. A full wedge from Transect VI, Test Unit 1, Trench 7 is complete with collar (Figure 4.2), and shows much use through pounding of the proximal end (Figure 4.3), and the point broken off at the distal end. A smaller wedge, discovered in Transect IV, Pit D, was broken lengthwise and lacks a collar; but also reveals adzing. Wedges of this type have been used for millennia, with wedges of similar types found in wet sites around the Pacific Northwest and spanning from (a) 9,450 years BP with a wooden wedge excavated from the Kilgii Gwaay site on the Queen Charlotte Islands (Fedje and Mathewes 2005) to (b) 31 wedges from the Hoko River site on the Olympic Peninsula from approximately 3,000 BP (Croes 1995), and (c) over 1,100 wedges recovered from Ozette dating to approximately 300 years BP (Gleeson 2005). Wooden wedges of this type are also included in the ethnography of the Lower Chinook/Cowlitz area (Gunther 1973; Stewart 1984). Wedges were used for splitting cedar planks, splitting out canoes, and for splitting firewood. The ethnobotany of this area indicates the most common woods used for wedges were crabapple (*Pyrus diversifolia*) (Ray 1938, 136; Gunther

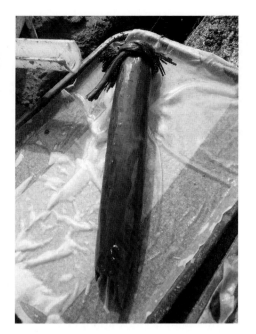 

Figure 4.2. Wooden wedge recovered – note fine adze faceting on body.

Figure 4.3 Wooden wedge, close up of rope collar to keep wedge from splitting while pounding – note the heavy wear from driving.

 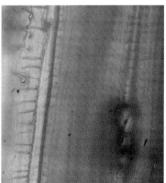 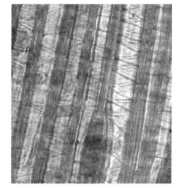

*Figure 4.4. Tangential section views of the wooden wedges from (left) Transect VI TU-1 Trench 7 and (center) Transect IV Pit D, showing the spiral thickening in the longitudal tracheids, a diagnostic feature of Pacific yew (*Taxus brevifolia*). (Right) identical example of modern Pacific yew.*

1973, 38; Silverstein 1990, 539), Pacific yew (*Taxus brevifolia* Nutt.) (Gunther 1973, 16), and western hemlock (*Tsuga heterophylla* [Raf.] Sarg.) (Silverstein 1990, 539).

Examination of samples taken from the artifact wedges indicates a conifer species, which eliminates crabapple, a diffuse-porous hardwood. The samples also showed spiral thickening in the tracheids in both tangential and radial views. Pacific yew and Douglas-fir have characteristic spiral thickening in the tracheids, shown in tangential view; however the spiral thickening in Douglas-fir is closer together and at a very short angle. The spiral thickening in Pacific yew has a steeper angle. Douglas-fir also commonly has longitudal and tangential resin canals, which is lacking in Pacific yew. Western hemlock was also analyzed but lacked the characteristic spiral thickening in the tracheids. The angle of spiral thickening in the tracheids, lack of resin canals and modern wood sample comparison identifies both wedges as Pacific yew (Figure 4.4). The collar of the full wedge also indicates a conifer species, with characteristics of red cedar root or bough. In this case, the diameter of the wood used for the collar would indicate the wood as red cedar bough; and a microscopic comparison between cedar root and bough show the cellular structure to most closely resemble red cedar bough (see Figure 4.1).

4.2.3.3 ACORN LEACHING PIT LINING MATERIAL

Plant lining material was removed from Transect IV Pit G including small twigs (less than 1cm diameter) lining the pit feature, found with needles still attached and identifiable as a conifer species. This feature also contained acorns, and was used for leaching and storage of acorns (Figure 4.5; Mathews 2006, below). The needles were short, generally between ½ and ¾ an inch in length, in double ranked rows along the branchlets, and detached very easily leaving small woody pegs. Several larger branches (1–1.5 cm diameter) were collected from Transect VI, Pit P for use in C-14 dating, and also were used for cellular analysis. Ethnographic information on the lining of these pit features is lacking, so comparisons were made among species of conifers which fit these observations, with the most likely being western hemlock, Grand fir (*Abies grandis* [Dougl.] Lindl.), and Pacific yew; all of which have needle attachments resulting in double ranked rows along the branchlets. Viewed with a dissecting microscope the attachment of the needles to the twigs, needle size and shape, and the alternating alignment of the branches identified the plant material as western hemlock. Examined with higher magnification, the cellular structure also was identifiable as western hemlock.

4.2.3.4 WOODEN STAKE FEATURES

34 stake features were identified in 2006 within Transects III–VII, most near or within the pit features (usually the south side of the pit as a re-location marker; see example Figure 4.5); two were excavated for analysis and identification in 2006. Stake A, Transect V (7.3 cm diameter) still has bark covering the area which had been beneath the surface of the beach. The bark is smooth with resin blisters visible, a characteristic of young noble fir (*Abies*) species (Pojar and MacKinnon 1994). Stake A from Transect VI is smaller (5.7 cm diameter) and has no bark remaining. Both have adzing on the distal ends.

Cellular analysis of Stake A T-V revealed the absence of resin canals in both cross-and tangential section views. Ray parenchyma cells contained dark reddish contents, with

Figure 4.5. Example of acorn leaching pit (Transect VI, Pit C) with branch lining and a wooden stake at the south end of the pit (arrow).

the end walls nodular, and cross-field pitting small and taxodioid. These characteristics, as well as the visual identification of the bark, identify this stake as noble fir (*Abies procera*).

A sample from Stake A, Transect VI revealed resin canals in both cross-and tangential section views. The latewood cells are thickwalled, with a gradual transition from earlywood. The longitudal tracheids contain 1 row of bordered pits, with no spiral thickening apparent in the tangential section view; a radial section view shows cross-field pitting small and piceoid, and non-dentate ray tracheids. These features identify the smaller stake as spruce, most likely Sitka spruce (*Picea sitchensis*). This tree is more commonly found in the coastal areas.

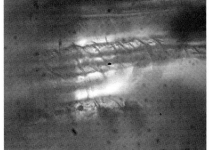

Figure 4.6. (Top) carved wooden blade fragment; (Bottom Left) close up view of incising on wooden blade; (Bottom Right) spiral thickening in tracheids identifying artifact as Pacific yew.

4.2.3.5 CARVED WOODEN BLADE SECTION

A section of a carved wooden blade was recovered from Transect III, Pit A; and originally identified as a possible rib bone (Figure 4.6). This section is 9.9 cm long, with a lenticular shape in cross section, and reveals fine incised lines on one side. The wood is very hard, which explains the original misidentification as bone. Cellular analysis revealed this artifact carved from Pacific yew.

4.2.3.6 WOVEN CHECKER MATTING

Several fragments of checker weave were recovered from Transects III, V, and VI. These were visually identified as Western red cedar bark, which has a characteristic appearance (Figure 4.7). Microscopic examination and comparison of modern cedar bark samples confirm the identification of cedar bark.

Figure 4.7. (left)Western red cedar bark checker-weave basketry (Transect VI, Pit D). (right) Sample of modern cedar bark.

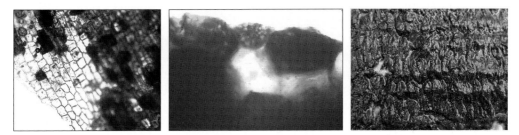

Figure 4.8. Tangential section view (left) and cross-section view (center) of soft weave fragment. (Right) Close-up of soft diamond plaiting weave.

4.2.3.7 Diamond-Plaited Soft Bag

The diamond-plaited soft weave fragment recovered from Transect VI, Pit G is a very unique specimen (Figure 4.8) (See Ness, below). Initial analysis indicated that the weave was not likely constructed from Western red cedar bark, and this was confirmed microscopically. The surface is very worn and impregnated with silt, which interferes with microscopic examination. A cross section view revealed characteristics of monocot fibers, with vascular bundles and epidermal cells visible. Cells with tannins were observed in the tangential view, which are characteristic of *Scirpus* species. Comparisons were made between modern samples of tule (*Scirpus acutus*) and sweetgrass (*Scirpus americanus*), with similarities between both species observed. Cell arrangement was also difficult due to crushing of the plant material, but size differences between vascular bundles and schlerenchyma cells appear to be similar to sweetgrass.

4.2.4 Charcoal

4.2.4.1 INTRODUCTION

Charcoal is one of the most common plant material recovered archaeologically, yet it often remains unanalyzed. Defined as the charred remains of a plant's woody structures, predominately from trees and shrubs, charcoal is frequently used for radiocarbon dating; but can also provide evidence of selection and use of wood at a site, and of ancient vegetation and environment (Smart and Hoffman 1988).

The use of particular wood types as fuel can depend on physical characteristics, such as heat content and quantity of smoke produced during burning. The form of wood is also considered in choosing firewood. Fuelwood collectors today generally prefer fallen trees and dead branchwood; this affects the taxa selected, as some trees are more likely to drop their branches than others (Smart and Hoffman 1988). Cultural values can affect the choice of wood for fuel. In a Straits Salish story of the Saanich People, arbutus (*Arbutus menziesii*) was the tree used by the survivors of the Great Flood (a tradition common to almost all Northwest Coast Peoples) to anchor their canoes to the top of Mount Newton. To this day, the Saanich People do not burn arbutus in their stoves, because of the important service this tree provided long ago (Pojar and McKinnon 2004).

Charcoal from Sunken Village had been used in radiocarbon dating of the site, and currently is being examined microscopically to identify the types of wood that have used for possible cultural fires. The results of this cellular analysis has been compared to the stratigraphic sampling and profiling of cultural layers in Test Unit 4, to correlate these charcoal samples to specific *in situ* vegetal mats that were laid down at different times on this river point bar beach deposit (see Punke, above, Figures 3.13, 3.15).

4.2.4.2 METHODS OF CELLULAR ANALYSIS

The same methods are used to identify charcoal larger than a thumbnail as for wood analysis, using the same planes of orientation (see above); however, due to its brittle nature charcoal is broken into the proper orientations rather than cut. Charcoal has reflective surfaces, which means a standard microscope using direct light sources generally creates too much contrast to view cells, so a metallurgical microscope is used to produce imaging of cellular structure (Figure 4.9). This has a light source that is transmitted directly down onto the sample through the objectives, and then retransmitted from the sample back through the objectives, eliminating reflection (Lepofsky 2007).

4.2.4.3 TEST UNIT 4 CHARCOAL CELLULAR ANALYSIS

Over 1700 pieces of charcoal were recovered from Test Unit 4, which was excavated to the 50 cm level in 2006. A 5% sample (n=85) was taken from each 10 cm arbitrary level and examined microscopically. This method was used for the sake of time, with further research planned to complete the appropriate sample size for taxa diversity. In this preliminary study, the majority of charcoal was identified as *Quercus* species, most likely Oregon white oak, also commonly know as Garry oak (*Quercus garryana*, the only native

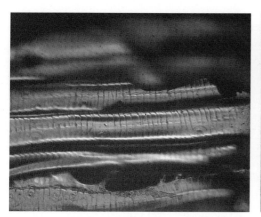
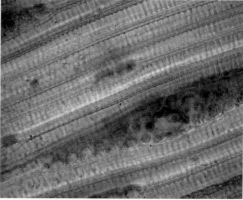

Figure 4.9. Example of cellular structure of Douglas-fir (Pseudotsuga menziesii) identified in archaeological charcoal from 35MU4 (Left) compared with the cellular structure of archaeological uncharred wood (Right),both revealing spiral thickening and resin canals.

Figure 4.10. Archaeological sample of Oregon white oak (Quercus garryana) charcoal (Left) and modern uncharred sample from Sauvie Island (Right).

oak in this region), which grows in abundance on Sauvie Island; with Douglas-fir the second most common species found (*Pseudotsuga menziesii*) (Figure 4.10, Table 4.1).

A litho-stratigraphic analysis of Test Unit (TU) 4 is defined by Dr. Punke with seven stratigraphic units (SU 1–7) analyzed (See Table 3.2, and Figure 3.9). A preliminary analysis of collected charcoal fragments (larger than a thumbnail) collected will be related to these SUs in order to explore areas of potential and concentrated cultural activity (Table 4.2).

The majority of charcoal fragments recovered were from the 20–30 cm level, which corresponds to Stratigraphic Unit 4 (SU-4) contained many fragments of wood up to ~3 cm in length (see Appendix F. Table 1. Website: http//www.library.spscc.ctc.edu/crm/JWA9.pdf); the matrix contains approximately 15% organic matter and humified organics; thin layers (~1 cm) of iron oxide stained sands (dark yellowish brown 10YR4/4) and iron reduced sands (grayish brown 10YR5/2) throughout; and shellfish fragments.

LEVELS (cm)	Quercus garryana	Alnus rubra	Pseudotsuga menziesii	Thuja plicata	Prunus spp	Acer spp	Salix spp
0–10	1		2				
10–20	12	4	2	1	1	1	
20–30	19	8	6		5	2	
30–40	4	3	5		1		1
40–50	3		3		1		
TOTALS	39	15	18	1	8	3	1

Table 4.1. Wood species identified in charcoal by TU-4 levels.

Stratigraphic Unit	Corresponding Level	Total charcoal fragments	5% samples analyzed
1	0–10 cm	56	3
2	10–20 cm	418	21
4	20–30 cm	808	40
3, 5	30–40 cm	287	14
6, 7	40–50 cm	142	7

Table 4.2. Number of charcoal fragments per stratigraphic Units in Test Unit (TU) 4.

The second highest number of charcoal fragments was found in SU-2 (10–20 cm), which had a very low organic content (see Punke, Table 3.2, above).

287 charcoal fragments were recovered from the 30–40 cm level, which included SU-3 and 5. SU-3 contained an organic content of~50%, with plentiful wood fragments up to 3.0 cm in length (see Appendix F, Table 1, Website: http://www.library.spscc.ctc. edu/crm/JWA9.pdf); whereas SU-5 had markedly less organic content. SU-6, 7 were from the 40–50 cm level, with 142 fragments of charcoal. SU-6 had a very low organic content; SU-7 however had a high proportion of humified organics and wood debris (~90%) (see Punke, Table 3.2, above).

4.2.5. Summary and Conclusions

The results of cellular analysis of artifacts and pit features made of wood, fiber and charcoal confirm many ethnobotanical and traditional uses of wood products of this area. Continuing research is also being done on the woodchips, split wood, and wooden wedge fragments recovered in 2006 and 2007 from the Sunken Village site to help identify materials used in woodworking (see below). With further excavation of the Sunken Village site and analysis of wood and fiber plant material, a greater knowledge and understanding of the technology of ancient Native People of Sauvie Island can be used to add to the history of this area. Continued archaeological research should be considered for this site, as more artifacts are likely to be found. In Test Unit 4, Transect VI, excavation was halted at the 50 cm level, and from 2007 coring clearly vegetal mat horizons continue for at least another 3 m.

The preliminary results of analysis of the charcoal in the TU-4 stratigraphic units reveals an abundance of Oregon white oak as fuel wood in the assemblage. Oaks form the genus *Quercus* of the beech family, Fagaceae. Oregon white oak (*Q. garryana*) is a member of the white oak subgenera, producing acorns that were processed in over 100 acorn leaching pits recorded at the site, carefully lined with western hemlock boughs and still containing acorns. This species of oak is seldom self-pruning; therefore it is possible that branches were being deliberately removed, either primarily as firewood, to access acorns, or to encourage acorn growth by pruning unnecessary limbs that compete for nutrients. Further research is planned to complete the appropriate sample size for taxa diversity.

4.3 Acorns and the Acorn-Leaching Pits

By Bethany Mathews

4.3.1 Introduction

During limited excavation in 2006 and mapping in 2007 approximately 100 pit features were recorded in a 125–meter section of the Multnomah Channel slough on Sauvie Island (see Figures 3.2–3.3). At the surface and after clearing a layer of silt, these remnant features contained wood, lithic, bone, and botanical artifacts, of which only acorns and hemlock branches and twigs (with needles) are found in every pit feature and are believed to be the liner and primary contents of these leaching pits. Charcoal is also found in all of these features, but because charcoal is found throughout the site it cannot be exclusively associated with the features, though ash would have served a practical purpose in acorn tannin leaching. Beyond examining the surface of the pits at 35MU4, one pit feature (Pit P, Transect VI) was excavated in 2006 so that a profile could be studied (see Punke, above). These acorns and pit features on Sauvie Island are evidence of a plant resource that has been previously underestimated in its importance to the ancient Northwest Coast of North America.

4.3.2 Defining the Sunken Village Site Acorn-Leaching Pits

The approximately one hundred pits recorded at 35MU4 were identified on the surface, sometimes because of the presence of acorns, but the more obvious marker of the leaching pits at the surface is a circle of branches protruding from the beach (Figures 4.11 and 4.12). Fire-cracked rock, found throughout the surface of the slough, tends to settle on pit depressions and was also used as an indicator, though circular formations of fire-cracked rock proved to be misleading at times. Associated with the pits were over forty wooden stakes, which may have served as markers for the pits on the beach surface. These stakes may have marked groups of pits, either for identification on the slough after silting, or for ownership purposes (see Figures 4.5 and 4.11).

Figure 4.11. (left) Branches protruding from edges of an acorn-leaching pit (right) A well-preserved wooden stake, possibly a marker stake for an acorn-leaching pit.

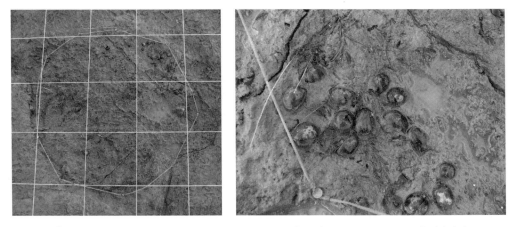

Figure 4.12. (left) Example of acorn leaching pit surface (Pit A, Transect IV); (right) acorns from upper right corner of the pit). Also notice hemlock needles showing as liner.

4.3.3 Acorns

Acorns are the most abundant botanical artifact associated with the pit features, and were identified as those of *Quercus garryana,* commonly called Oregon white oak (Young and Young 1992, 290; Figure 4.12). For comparison, some contemporary acorns were collected from trees growing on Sauvie Island, which were identified by leaf as the Oregon white, also known as Garry oak (*Quercus garryana*) (Pojar and MacKinnon 1994, 50). Girth measurements of a few large trees about a mile from the site estimate that the oak population has been there for at least 700 years (personal observation). The Oregon white oak is the dominant oak type in the Pacific Northwest oak woodlands north of San Francisco, California, USA along the coast of the northwestern United States and British Columbia, Canada (Agee 1993, 352). A small sample of acorn shells from the leaching pits on Sauvie Island was sent to Dr. Yang at Simon Fraser University for DNA testing. Researchers in the archaeology department at Simon Fraser will use these samples in a study on genetic similarities of *Quercus garryana*, which may have migrated north to the Fraser River in British Columbia through human transport (Dana Lepofsky, personal communication, 2008).

Acorns at Sunken Village were found complete, or in fragmented parts of the shell, nut, and occasionally cap. Though a large percent of the acorns were only found in fragments (73%), the fragments generally represent all parts of the acorn with the exception of the cap. Many acorns are whole (with the nut inside the shell) which means they were being left in these pits on the beach for later use instead of immediate consumption, unlike the numerous hazelnut fragments (see Mathews, below). Acorn caps, with three exceptions, were not found in the pits. Although they would have preserved as well or better than the thinner acorn shell in the archaeological record, acorns with caps attached probably would not have been collected, as these would be infested and are known to fall from the tree not because of ripeness but from insect movement.

A small portion of the acorn fragments are found completely charred, while most fragments and whole acorns show some mottled marks that appear to be the result of heat, but might also result in part from the leaching process. Heating could have killed any insects that might further infest the store. It might have aided in the removal of tannins and flavoring of the nuts. Experiments have shown that cracking or splitting the shells would speed up the leaching process considerably (personal observation), and this could have been accomplished through heating. Though removing tannins is not necessary when eating acorns in small servings, unleached acorns are unpleasantly bitter and consuming too much tannin can make a person ill. Heating would also prevent the acorns from germinating during the storage period as white oaks have a very quick germination period (Stein 1990, 657).

While being prepared for conservation in the South Puget Sound Community College laboratory, the acorns were measured for length, width and thickness so that a minimum number of individuals might later be determined (example in Appendix D:212, website: http://www.library.spscc.ctc.edu/crm/JWA9.pdf). These measurements were used to find the average acorn size, which was used to estimate how many acorns might have been stored in the pits at 35MU4.

4.3.4 Western Hemlock

Twigs protruding from the ground often mark a pit in a circular pattern on the surface, and the pits were lined from the sides to the base of the pit. Many of the twigs and branches, especially those at lower, less disturbed levels, still have their needles attached. Branches lining the bottom of Pit P (Transect VI) were radiocarbon dated at 1760 to 1880 CE (130 ± 60 BP) (Figure 4.13; and see Figure 3.4). The intact needles made it possible to identify the species, but wood cells identification confirmed the species was western

Figure 4.13. (left) In situ hemlock branches and needles near base of a pit, after silt cap has been washed away. Acorns and hazelnuts can be seen in this photo. (right) Base of north half of Pit P with hemlock bough lining exposed. The lining was C14 dated to 1760 to 1880 CE (130 ± 60 BP), indicating the last time this acorn leaching pit was used.

hemlock (*Tsuga heterophylla*) (Hawes 2007, above), which grows along the coastal areas of Oregon, Washington and British Columbia (Pojar and MacKinnon 1994, 30). Looking at modern western hemlock, it seems likely that this type of branch was selected over other conifers because of its thick coverage. Western hemlock boughs are flat and full, making very good cover while still allowing water to pass through easily, where other native branch types might require several layers to separate the acorns from the surrounding matrix. This would have been necessary for removal of the acorns from the pits, making the process less labor-intense for removal and cleaning after leaching. Hemlock was also considered an edible plant by many tribes of the Pacific Northwest, which might have led to it being chosen over other conifers (Moerman 2002, 571).

4.3.5 Charcoal

Charcoal is found throughout the site and at every level of excavation in pit features. Over 5000 thumbnail-sized or larger pieces were collected from 35MU4, with 2500 coming from the half-excavated Pit P. Though the charcoal could be remnants of cooking or wood burning done at or near the site, ash and charcoal are frequently used in leaching processes in California (Gifford 1936, 301). Ash is used to speed up the active leaching process, and adding ash and charcoal to the pits would ensure that the acorns were sweetened by the time they needed to be removed from the pits.

4.3.6 Pit Construction

Pits generally take on a circular shape at the surface, with diameters smaller than a meter. While only a few pits were tested, the depth of a well-preserved pit (Pit P, Transect VI) was 55 centimeters below the modern surface. Many pits were badly eroded with only a few centimeters of depth remaining. The acorn-leaching pits are concentrated in a 125–meter section of the slough (within Transects III–VI, Figures 3.2–3.4c), where aquifers under the natural levee would have moved water through the buried acorns (see Figure 6.7). The rising water of the Multnomah Channel would have covered the sealed pits after harvest in the fall until early spring (Diedrich 2007a, and Figures 2.4 and 2.5). This compares well with ethnographic reports of acorns leaching for several months after harvest.

4.3.7 Pacific Northwest Balanophagy

Oregon white oaks grow along the west coast from northeastern Vancouver Island in Canada, down to San Francisco, California, and extends at its eastern-most point to the Warm Springs area in Oregon (Peter and Harrington 2002, 189). Balanophagy, 'the eating of acorns', is rarely mentioned in ethnographic and historic accounts of the Northwest, and is even more rarely mentioned in archaeological site reports in the region. However, California is well-known for its acorn-dependent cultures. The typical process of preparing acorns in California, as followed by the Miwok/Pauite tradition in Yosemite, involves gathering, drying, shelling, winnowing, and pounding the acorns into flour, followed by actively leaching the acorn flour with water to remove tannins, sweetening the acorn flour (Ortiz 1991). Acorn flour was then frequently prepared as cakes, breads and porridges (Moerman 2002, 461). Though southern California leaching methods are always described as an active process, passive leaching has been recorded in northern California, where the white oak is the dominant oak type. For instance, the Wintu of northwest California leached acorns in swampy grounds through the winter, then removed them in the spring and prepared them by boiling or roasting. Paiute also buried acorns in mud in the fall to 'ripen' (Moerman 2002, 459). A passive leaching pit site north of San Francisco, dated to between 3370 and 4450 BP, suggests that passive leaching was a technique used in central California before active leaching techniques were widely adopted around 3000 years ago (Eric Wohlgemuth, personal communication 2008).

In the Pacific Northwest the methods of preparation range from eating the nut raw or roasted as the hazelnut is eaten, to various methods of leaching and preparing. Klallam ate acorns with no preparation (Gunther 1973, 28). The Snohomish and Suquamish (possibly Duwamish) set up camp on the Nisqually valley from August to October to gather acorns and berries, as did people from as far away as the Strait of Juan de Fuca (Norton 1979, 187). The Nisqually and Coastal Salish ate unleached preparations of acorn, while the Chehalis (Moerman 2002, 461) and Cowlitz are known to have used passive leaching methods to sweeten their acorns (Gunther 1973, 28). Erna Gunther recorded that Squaxin roasted acorns on hot rocks before consuming them (Gunther 1973, 28). Acorn shell fragments have been found at Qwu?wes (45TN240), a Squaxin archaeological site on Mud Bay near Olympia, in quantities that greatly outnumber hazelnuts, which are frequently mentioned in ethnographic information for the region (Bethany Mathews, personal observations 2007).

Further south, Lewis and Clark recorded people on the Columbia eating acorns raw and roasted. These people, who were probably the Wishram, said they acquired the acorns from people living near the falls (DeVoto 1997, 259). Acorns were used as a trade item by the mid-Chinook tribes, and the Wascopam of The Dalles are known to have baked acorns in the earth with hot rocks, and then leached them in pits dug near water through the winter. In the spring women were seen on a stream bank, removing acorns from the water. Their acorns were eaten with dried or pounded salmon (Aguilar 2005, 77–78).

In 1847 Paul Kane, an artist and explorer, recorded acorns being prepared as a delicacy by Chinook, in a way that was "a peculiarly characteristic trait of the Chinook Indian... confined solely to this tribe." According to Kane the preparation, called 'Chinook olives' by European explorers, was made by digging a hole in the ground close to the entrance of a home, filling it with a bushel of acorns, then covering the hole with grass and dirt, and depositing urine in the hole for four to five months. Kane writes that the Chinook considered these acorns "the greatest of all delicacies" (Harper 1971, 94). From discussions with California archaeologist Wendy Pierce, who is familiar with passive acorn leaching in California, it is believed that this would not have been a very effective way to leach tannins (personal communication 2006). If urine was used to process acorns, it is possible it was not the full method of preparation by the Chinook.

From the Wasco and Chinook also come the stories of Little Raccoon and his grandmother. This story about a greedy young raccoon describes five pits of acorns being stored by his grandmother for the winter. In the Chinook version of the story, grandmother stores her acorns in swampy ground, which suggests that passive leaching methods were used by the Chinook. Little Raccoon is tired of eating wapato, jerky and dried fish-eyes, so he sneaks acorns from the acorn pits, and in both versions of the story proceeds to get himself into one life-altering predicament after the next. (Hunn 1990, 186–187, Ray 1938, 148–151). This story of Little Raccoon and the acorns not only adds strength to ethnographic reports on acorn use by the Chinook and surrounding tribes, but implies that acorns were an important and desirable winter food.

The memory of passive leaching is alive in northwest tribes today. The Siletz of western Oregon call acorns that are leached in stream banks for several months to a year 'tus-xa', and acorns are still gathered, stored and eaten by people living there (Bud Lane, personal communications 2007). Observations of passive leaching methods in the Northwest at contact and ethnographic descriptions are fairly wide-spread, though rare. Future understanding of the extent and antiquity of these passive leaching features might explain whether there was a migration of the idea through the northwest to California or vice versa, where the same species of oak is found.

4.3.8 Population Estimate

An estimate of the possible human population supported by the acorn-leaching pits on Sauvie Island was made by determining the size of the individual pits, how many

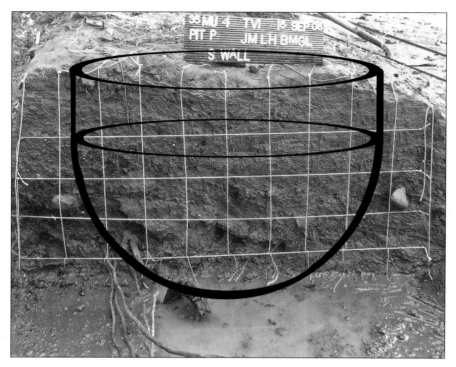

Figure 4.14. The volume of the leaching pits was calculated using Pit P in Transect VI as a model (grid 10 cm sq). Note the hemlock bough lining near base and rocks to either side of outer edges, which help to define the pit boundaries.

acorns they might store, and how many people could be fed by the estimated total of acorns present. Estimates were then compared to historical statistics on populations living near the site of the leaching pits, and to California ethnographic information on populations that relied on acorns as a staple food.

4.3.9 Acorn-Leaching Pit Volume

The volume of the leaching pits was calculated using Pit P in Transect VI as a model (see Figure 3.4c for location). Pit P was a well-preserved pit and is probably representative of the size of the ancient leaching pits (Figures 4.13 and 4.14). This feature was first measured at the surface, and then a one meter by one-half meter unit was excavated so that a profile of the pit could be seen. The general shape of the pit can be described as a half-sphere at the bottom, with a cylinder extending the pit to the surface (Figure 4.14). A formula for the volume of this shape was created by adding these shapes together. The formula for the volume of a cylinder and half sphere is $V= r^2h + \frac{2}{3} r^3$ (based on volume formulas in Percy and Waites 1997, 107, 409).

The surface of Pit P was 84 cm at the widest, and 71 cm at the narrowest area of the pit, which is closely comparable to the average recorded pit surface of an oval that measures 82 cm by 72 cm. For the purpose of making a conservative estimate, the narrowest diameter of 71 cm was used to calculate the volume of Pit P. Though the cap of the pit has probably eroded to some degree, the bottom of the feature is marked by hemlock boughs lining the pit at 55 cm below surface. This means that the pit originally extended at least 19.5 cm above the half sphere shape. Plugging these numbers into the volume formulas for the pit shape, the total volume of Pit P is found to be about 170,900 cm^3.

4.3.10 Ancient Quercus garryana Acorn Volume

Similarly, the general shape of the average acorn found at 35MU4 is that of a divided sphere joined by a cylinder of the same diameter (see acorn examples, Figure 4.12). The formula for this volume is V= r^{2}h + 4/3 r^3 based on volume formulas in Percy and Waites (1997, 107, 409). The average size of acorns leaching at Sauvie Island was found by measuring the length and width of excavated whole acorns. Sixty examples were used to find the average size, which at present is believed to be 2.218 cm long, and 1.610 cm wide. Like the pit volume calculations, these numbers were used in the volume formula and the volume of the average acorn is believed to be about 3.423 cm^3.

4.3.11 Acorns per Acorn-Leaching Pit

To estimate how many acorns each pit is capable of holding, the pit volume is divided by the volume of the average acorn. An estimate of volume displacement had to be made to account for the space being displaced by the rounded acorns. Using one liter of Oregon white oak acorns, displacement was found to be about forty percent. The volume occupied by the acorns when pits were full would be about 102,540 cm^3, meaning that nearly 30,000 average acorns could fit into each pit. The displacement calculation also showed that 120 acorns fit into a one liter container, meaning that about 20,500 might fit into a pit. The rest of the calculations will use 25,000 as an average of the two.

4.3.12 Acorn Totals at 35MU4

Using the estimate of 25,000 acorns per pit, and a minimum of 100 pits, there may have been approximately 2,500,000 acorns being processed at the site every winter, if these pits were filled annually. Aside from the uncertainty of consistency of original pit sizes and the possibility of ash or other fill, the biggest potential problem with this figure may be that pits seem to overlap in places and may not have all been used contemporaneously. However, as far as possible at present, these estimates are conservative. Further research may result in identifying more leaching pits, so it is reasonable to assume that these one hundred or more pits might have been used at the same time.

    Large crops are produced once every three years on the Oregon white oak, followed by a year of moderate production, and a year of crop failure before the bumper crop year returns (Peter and Harrington 2002, 198). One study showed that Oregon white oaks in the Willamette Valley can produce up to 1737 kilograms of acorns per hectare (Stein 1990, 657). The average mature acorn from *Q. garryana* weighs 5.35 grams (Young 1992, 292) meaning that about 325,000 acorns can be collected from a hectare of Oregon white oak grove in the Willamette Valley south of Sauvie Island, which means that less than eight hectares of oak would have to be collected from to fill these pits during bumper years.

If the acorns were collected during a moderate production year, it seems likely that the trees needed to fill the leaching pits would be available, given the proximity of oaks today. During a crop failure year though, it could be that few pits were utilized on the Multnomah slough.

4.3.13 Acorn Nutrition

To calculate the amount of calories these acorn-filled pits could provide a population, the calories per acorn were multiplied by the possible total amount of acorns. Though data has not been located for the calories per acorn, other important nutritional values are comparable to the acorns from *Q. lobata*, another white oak, which grow in regions of California with *Q. garryana*. *Quercus lobata* contains 4.44 calories per gram. (Bainbridge 1986, 2; Basgall 1987, 25). Based on data in Young 1992, the average mature acorn from *Q. garryana* weighs 5.35 grams. Though I have not located data for the calories per acorn, other important nutritional values are comparable to the acorns from *Q. lobata*, another white oak, which grow in regions of California with *Q. garryana*. *Quercus lobata* contains 4.44 calories per gram. (Bainbridge 1986, 2; Basgall 1987, 25). Using the estimate of 4.44 calories per gram, each *Q. garryana* acorn contains about 23.75 calories when consumed raw. If the site has 2.5 million acorns leaching for use every year, these leaching pits on Sauvie Island could provide over 59 million calories to the group or groups who owned them. About seventy percent of the Oregon white oak acorn's nutrition is in the form of carbohydrates (Bainbridge 1986, 2), which people in the area might have had a great need for it in the winter months when the acorns might have been retrieved from pits after leaching for as much as a year. I suspect that the use of acorns was overshadowed by the importance of wapato in the area for general subsistence, and acorns may have been more important as a delicacy trade commodity produced by the owners of this acorn leaching station (Darby 2005; see also Section 6.3 below).

4.3.14 Possible Population

To understand how many people this calorie figure is capable of supporting, the Mono of California can be looked to as a model for a minimum population. The Mono provide an example of a group that depended on acorns as a staple throughout the year, which would represent the use of the food at its maximum. According to information in McCarthy 1993, the Mono consumed a preparation of acorns that required as many as 207 grams of whole raw acorns a day per person, the equivalent of about thirty-nine *Q. garryana* acorns a day. Consuming thirty-nine acorns a day for 365.25 days would mean that every individual would consume nearly 14,250 acorns annually. A society that had 2,500,000 acorns available, and depended on acorns as a staple food, would at minimum support 175 individuals. Though the people on and around Sauvie Island probably did not use acorns to the same extent as the California groups (and, again, it might have been a delicacy trade item as much as a staple at Sauvie Island), we can gain an understanding of how far this quantity of acorns might go. A group that had 2.5 million acorns available could support 175 individuals who consumed thirty-nine acorns a day for 365.25 days, the equivalent of the Mono staple preparation.

Since we can assume that acorns on Sauvie Island were not relied on for as great a portion of diet as they were in California, given their near absence in historical and ethnographic reports, the millions of acorns leaching on Sauvie Island could potentially support a larger population throughout the year. If acorns supplied only 500 calories to a person per day, the population supported might number over 300 individuals. If the acorns represent a smaller portion of the diet, as is suggested with the 'Chinook olives' idea of delicacy, the population estimate grows to such a large number that trade to other communities would have been likely, to make use of the acorns throughout the year.

It is interesting to compare these population estimates to the 1805/6 Lewis and Clark statistics for the area. Populations varied seasonally, increasing in the spring when more resources were available on the rivers than in the outlying areas. For the Multnomah Channel this meant that populations increased from 420 individuals in the fall of 1805, to 970 in the spring of 1806. Along the Lower Columbia River, Lewis and Clark statistics nearly doubled from 9800 in the fall, to 17840 in the spring (Boyd and Hajda 1987, 313). This seasonal population increase could coincide with the time when waters on the slough would have receded, and acorns might have been retrieved to support a population that was coming to the area for foods before spring produced abundant resources in their area.

4.3.15 Summary and Conclusions

Historic, ethnographic and archaeological information support the idea that acorns were commonly used as a source of food by people throughout what is now Oregon and Washington. If acorns were not a significant source of nutrition throughout the year, they were at least marginally important seasonally for many groups. Tribes traveling long distances, camping and trading for acorns demonstrate that this food source was worth the energy it required to obtain and prepare it. Further ethnographic and archaeological research, as well as future study of the acorn pits of 35MU4, may show that this valuable resource was used by many groups of the central and southern Northwest Coast.

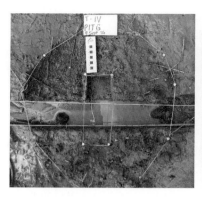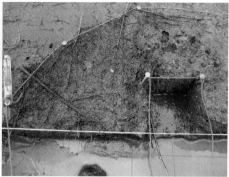

Figure 4.15. (left) Plan view of Acorn Pit G lined with western hemlock boughs, that has been sectioned by the 10 cm wide drainage trench from TU-3 . Acorns are visible lower right. (right) Close-up of same pit, showing location of 10 × 10 cm 100% sample removed for analysis. Acorns are visible upper right.

4.4 Seed Retrieval

4.4.1 Flotation vs Wet-sieving as Methods of Seed Retrieval

By Melanie Diedrich, James W. Goebel Jr., and Tressa Pagel

4.4.1.1 INTRODUCTION

As is found in most wet/waterlogged archaeology sites, the macro flora is well-preserved though often delicate. The usual processing involves careful wet-screening, cleaning and preservation in polyethylene glycol. Accepted flotation methods employed to isolate small seeds necessarily require drying the matrix more than once as well as agitation to disassociate the light-fraction material from the soil. Kidder has argued that rewetting dried carbonized plant remains can result in considerable damage or even the total destruction of delicate seeds (1997). Also, because the organic material has been waterlogged, some of it may not readily float. Therefore a comparison of flotation vs. fine wet-screening was determined to be necessary before full-scale lab work and analysis could proceed.

4.4.1.2 METHODS AND MATERIALS

One hundred percent 10x10 cm soil column samples were taken from surface to bottom of five acorn-leaching pits (see example Figure 4.15), as well as one highly concentrated seed sample, possibly a corprolite, called a special soil sample (SSS) from 30–40 cm in TU4, Transect VI. AINW processed and screened material from the second (southern) ½ of Pit P, Transect VI. Lab procedures were written, combining methods from Nancy Stenholm (1994) and Sarah Walshaw (2004), adapting them to the size of the samples from this site. Experimental flotation and fine wet-screening began using 10 randomly chosen samples taken from four of the five acorn leaching pits and the special soil sample from TU4. From each of these ten, a 10% (by weight) sample was removed for flotation, and a 10% sample was removed for wet-screening.

The 10% flotation samples were dried on trays for two or three days. Screens for both procedures were made using fine tulle and even finer sheer fabric stretched over plastic embroidery hoops. These were stacked, coarser on top, for the light fraction A and B. The samples were placed in small buckets with milliliter markings, ⅔ full with water, and agitated. This procedure was repeated two or three times till flotation had ceased. Screens with finer sheer fabric were used individually for heavy fraction C and D. Heavy fraction C was agitated using one teaspoon of Calgon bath powder, which contains a defloculant, sodium hexametaphosphate, for a chemical separation of sediments. For heavy fraction D, the remanding sample was screened with a soft mist to remove clay and fine sand. The flotation fractions were again dried for one to two days then placed into containers.

The 10% wet-screening samples were poured over the stacked coarse and fine screens. A soft spray was used to carefully wash away clay and sand. The remaining material was then labeled, screens A and B. The wet-screened samples were slowly dried in closed containers.

Once the flotation and wet-screening process was finished, isolation of needles, seeds and small bones was accomplished using a dissecting microscope and tweezers. Counts were made of seeds for each 10%, totaled, and compared with the corresponding samples (Table 4.3, Figure 4.16). Identified seeds were separated and counted. The types and counts were then put into a spreadsheet for tabulation.

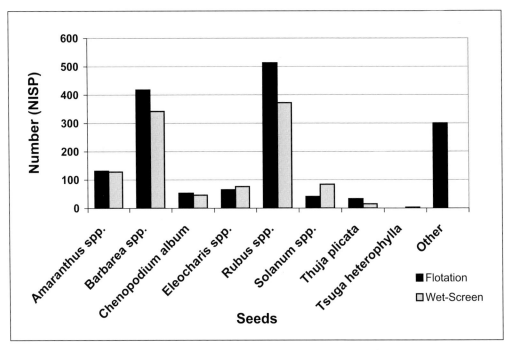

Figure 4.16. Comparing number of seeds (complete and fragments) found in flotation versus wet-screening.

Flotation Totals	Pit A 20–24cm	Pit A 24–28cm	Pit B 4–6cm	Pit G 2–4cm	Pit G 6–8cm	Pit N 4–8cm	Pit N 16–20cm	Pit N 24–28cm	Pit N 28–32cm	SSS 30–40cm	totals Flot
Amaranthus spp.	29	17	0	33	38	17	16	18	51	0	219
Barbarea spp.	77	34	1	3	16	34	57	25	91	133	471
Chenopodium album	15	12	0	0	5	6	12	4	10	0	64
Eleocharis spp.	25	14	6	0	3	5	1	7	11	1	73
Rubus spp.	18	20	0	2	5	4	5	13	23	434	524
Solanum spp.	4	2	0	0	2	6	9	11	14	1	49
Thuja plicata	0	0	0	0	0	0	0	29	4	0	33
Tsuga heterophylla	0	0	0	1	5	2	0	0	0	0	8
Other	1	6	0	0	2	0	4	1	9	279	302
SubTotals	169	105	7	39	76	74	104	108	213	848	1743

Wet-Screening Totals	Pit A 20–24cm	Pit A 24–28cm	Pit B 4–6cm	Pit G 2–4cm	Pit G 6–8cm	Pit N 4–8cm	Pit N 16–20cm	Pit N 24–28cm	Pit N 28–32cm	SSS 30–40cm	totals SSS
Amaranthus spp.	15	15	0	20	30	6	19	33	46	0	184
Barbarea spp.	76	12	1	2	1	24	52	44	89	68	369
Chenopodium album	4	6	0	0	0	7	9	15	12	0	53
Eleocharis spp.	36	12	2	1	3	4	9	6	11	0	84
Rubus spp.	30	26	2	2	3	12	19	14	23	258	389
Solanum spp.	13	5	0	0	0	9	11	22	33	0	94
Thuja plicata	6	0	0	0	2	0	6	3	0	0	17
Tsuga heterophylla	1	0	0	6	5	0	2	0	0	0	14
Other	3		0	0	4	0	7	4	6	121	145
Sub Totals	184	76	5	32	48	62	134	141	220	447	1349

Table 4.3. Comparison of seed counts (complete and fragments) from flotation (top table) and wet-screening (lower table). Higher flotation count may be deceiving, see Results section below (4.4.1.3). SSS=special soil sample of concentrated seeds from TU4.

4.4.1.3 Results

Samples of the various seeds found were sent to the Washington State Department of Agriculture Seed Inspection Program Office in Yakima, Washington, for identification by Victor Shaul and Nancy Ashby. They identified *Amaranthus spp.* (pigweed), *Barbarea spp.* (American winter cress), *Chenopodium album* (lamb's quarters), *Eleocharis spp.* (spikerush), *Rubus spp.* (berries), and *Solanum spp.* (nightshade) (Table 4.3). Needles of *Tsuga heterophylla* (Western hemlock) and the leaf scales of *Thuja plicata* (Western red cedar) have also been isolated. The few small fish bones that have been isolated will be sent to Dr. Virginia Butler of Portland State University for identification when all of the seed and bone isolation is completed (see Butler, below, for current fine screened faunal remains identification).

The Flotation and wet-screening samples were then counted to do a comparison of the quantity and quality of the samples. Each of the flotation fractions were individually counted to compare and consider the effectiveness of the flotation process before they were subtotaled for each level, giving us an overall total of seeds collected during flotation. The flotation samples collected were 56% and wet-screened samples were 44% of the total seed count. The most prevalent types of seeds were the *Rubus spp.* seeds and the *Barbarea spp.* seeds. The flotation method yielded 524 and 471 respectively, and wet-screening yielded 389 *Rubus spp.* and 369 *Barbarea spp.* The highest concentration of seeds came from the Special Soil Sample, TU4, Transect VI, 30–40cm, from both flotation and wet-screening (Figure 4.16, Table 4.3).

Although it appears flotation resulted in a higher number of seeds recovered, the totals may be misleading. In fact, this process resulted in considerable damage to the seeds. While working under the dissecting microscope the fragile condition of the seeds could readily be seen. At times, the seeds were hard to find because each fraction had a coating of tiny mineral crystals left after the procedures. The plastic containers used to store the samples created static, which would cause the seeds and other light material to stick to the side of the dish. This made isolation difficult. Another problem that was observed during isolation was that the flotation sample seeds were dry and brittle. These seeds tended to fall apart when touched with the tweezers.

The wet-screened samples, on the other hand, were much easier to work with. Although there was more coarse sand to pick through, the seeds were cleaner, were firm, and held up better under the pressure applied by the tweezers when isolating the seeds. The wet-screened seeds continued to hold up better in storage, and the majority remained intact.

When the sample counts were totaled it became relevant to note that the seeds in the flotation samples were broken into many pieces. This could have ultimately skewed the final total in flotation's favor, and because these seeds are now broken, a recount is not possible. It is also relevant to note that for some species the difference between the flotation and wet-screening totals is minor, and in three cases the wet-sieving total is the greater.

After the totals were charted for both wet-screening and flotation a significant observation was made regarding the special soil sample (SSS) from TU4, Transect VI, 30–40 cm level. With the 20% sample used totaling only 13.6 grams it accounted for 1295 seeds, 42% of the experiments seed total. This compared with the 20% of all other matrix at 865.96 grams for a total of 1797, 58%. The high concentration of seeds found in this small sample may indicate a coprolite location (though source of the coprolite is indeterminate – could be human, but also dog, bear, raccoon, large bird, or from many other animals). Seeds found in the SSS for both flotation and wet-screening also support the conclusion of a coprolite. Within this matrix a total of 400 unidentified seeds have been found which appear to be burnt or partially digested; the *Rubus spp.* seeds also showed signs of having been burnt.

Four of the six seeds identified come from possible non-native origins. These four are *Barbarea spp.*, *Chenopodium album*, *Eleocharis spp*, and *Rubus spp.* During the recent excavations at 35MU4 *Tsuga heterophylla* (western hemlock) boughs were taken from Pit P for carbon 14 dating (see Figures 3.4c and 4.13). The results placed the age of the hemlock at 130 ± 60 years, indicating the last time this acorn-leaching pit had probably been used was between 1760 and 1880 AD. We determined it would be reasonable for seeds found within the pits, most likely deposited with natural river sedimentation, to be post-contact seeds. Non-native seeds are therefore not unexpected.

While working with the dissecting microscopes during seed isolation a number of small black seeds were turning up that had the appearance of being tiny mollusks. The shells were thin and looked like they were attached by a hinge, with a shiny black periosticum-like exterior. Before we sent a sample of these seeds to Victor Shaul for identification, it was determined that a hydrochloric acid test should be preformed. If these were mollusks, the calcium carbonate would immediately dissolve in hydrochloric acid. A sample of 1M HCL was obtained from the South Puget Sound Community College biology laboratory, and three of the small seed/mollusks were isolated from the Pit N, 24–28cm. Under the dissecting scope a drop of hydrochloric acid was added; a probe was used to override surface tension on the seed. No fizzing or dissolving occurred. The only reaction was that after two minutes the black seeds shell began to turn a light brown, allowing us to conclude this was indeed a seed, not a mollusk. After a sample was sent to Victor Shaul the seeds were identified as *Amaranthus spp.* (pigweed).

4.4.1.4 Discussion and Conclusion

Due to the unknown sediment change from the dams and deforestation, the age of the macro-flora and fauna could not be determined. Further research will involve more soil samples taken from deeper levels. However, we were able to determine through a carbon 14 date of 130±60 calibrated years BP, taken from hemlock boughs lining acorn leaching Pit P (see Figure 3.4c) that it is chronologically possible for non-native species to be present within the fill of the pits.

The purpose of this experiment was to determine by comparison if flotation or wet-screening would be a better choice for wet-site material. Using the 10% samples from the 100% soil column samples, flotation and wet-screening procedures were carried out. Once the seeds were identified and counted we found that the flotation procedure offered a higher quantity of seeds, but this may not be an accurate reflection of recovery success because the seeds from flotation were in poor condition, and fragments were counted as well as whole seeds. The quality of the wet-screened samples was much better, with more whole seeds. Moreover, the seeds were easier to work with, and they continue to hold their condition in storage.

It appears from the research that has thus far been completed that a quantitative evaluation is problematic due to seed breakage. The qualitative evidence, however, indicates that fine wet-screening yields a good number of seeds in good condition, and this will be the preferred method of seed extraction in the future.

4.4.2 Flotation and Screening Samples from 2007 Cores 5 and 6: Seed Analysis

By Melanie Diedrich

On September 21, 2007, the two deep soil cores (5 and 6) were taken from the beach level near Test Unit 4 (TU4; see description in Punke, above). Core 5 was taken from directly west, in front of TU4 and achieved a depth of nine feet, three sections in three foot lengths. This core sample would have gone to deeper levels, but the coring crew lost the drilling head, due to suction. Work on Core 6 was more successful and went much deeper. This core had six 3 foot sections, achieving a depth of 18 feet, or slightly less than six meters. The sections were quickly capped, taped and labeled as they were brought up, transported to AINW and then split lengthwise at a later date.

During the lengthwise splitting, in core 6, section 5 a mammal bone was found at 15cm from the top of the section, which relates to approximately 4.15 m below the surface of the beach. A lithic core was also found in section 5 at 55 cm from the top of the section, or ~4.55 m below the beach surface. The charcoal for AMS dating was taken from close to these two locations in section 5 of core 6.

Dr. Punke created detailed drawings and notes for each of the core sections; samples for flotation and screening were taken from 13 of the 42 possible locations of interest along the length of the cores. In addition to these locations of interest it was decided to take samples from 5 cm above and 5 cm below each point as well (Table 4.4). Each sample resulted in three flotation screens: light fraction fine screen, light fraction coarse screen, and heavy fraction.

All of the screened samples were examined, described and digitally photographed under the dissecting microscope. Dr. Punke's samples were also examined for seeds, adding additional data. Seeds found were identified at least to genus when possible (Table 4.5), some were mere fragments, heavily coated in silt, and/or in such fragile condition it was difficult to make identification. The six taxa found in the pits in 2006 were evident within both of the 2007 cores. These were *Amaranthus sp., Chenopodium album, Eleocharis sp., Gaultheria shallon, Rubus sp.* and *Solanum sp.* A few unidentified seeds were noted. Though the NISP were far fewer in the cores than the pit samples due to sample size, the percent of *Gaultheria shallon* and *Rubus sp.* is comparable.

The *Amaranthus sp.* seeds were found in both cores; the *Chenopodium* were found primarily in core 6. This may be the result of disturbance along the shores of the channel adjacent to the site, possibly seasonal human traffic. Since *Amaranthus sp.* generally prefer the drier weather east of the coastal mountains along the Columbia River gorge and south into the Willamette valley, there is also a remote possibility these seeds washed downstream or blown in from other areas. A sprinkling of *Eleocharis sp.* seeds were found within both cores.

In total, five (5) *Solanum spp.* seeds were found in both cores at 0.15 m, 1.21 m, 2.81 m, 4.70 m, and 4.76 m. Although a species of this taxon, *Solanum americanum* P. Mill, is noted by the United States Department of Agriculture Natural Resources Conservation Service (USDA 2008) to be native, other sources, including the Burke Museum Herbarium Collection (2006), list this as introduced. Although they grow in abundance in the area now, *Amaranthus, Chenopodium, Eleocharis,* and *Solanum* are non-native plants that would not have been found at this location prior to Euro-American

Core 5		Salal	Rubus	Core 6		Salal	Rubus
Section 1	Meter level			Section 1	Meter level		
5cm	0.05	1					
10cm	0.1						
15cm	0.15			15cm	0.15		
20cm	0.2			20cm	0.2		
25cm	0.25			25cm.	0.25		
30cm	0.3						
				35cm	0.35		
				40cm	0.4	3	
45cm	0.45			45cm	0.45	3	
50cm	0.5	1					
54cm	0.54		1				
Section 2				Section 2			
20cm	1.11						
25cm	1.16			25cm	1.16	1	
	1.21			30cm	1.21		1
				35cm	1.26		
				Section 3			
				55cm	2.37		1
				60cm	2.42		
				65cm	2.47		1
				Section 4	M. level		
				7cm	2.81	2	1
				12cm	2.86		1
				17cm	2.91	1	
				Section 5			
				10cm	3.75	3	
				15cm	3.8		
				20cm	3.85	1	
				50cm	4.15	1	
				55cm	4.2		1
				60cm	4.25		
				Section 6			
				15cm	4.71		1
				20cm	4.76		2

Table 4.4. Cores 5 and 6 sampling plan and occurrences of whole salal (Gaultheria shallon) and Rubus seeds in the 1 cm^3 samples.

	Pits A–N		Cores 5 and 6	
	Total NISP	Percent	Total NISP	Percent
Amaranthus	173	16.31%	92	28.66%
Chenopodium	68	6.41%	49	15.26%
Gaultheria	359	33.84%	94	29.28%
Rubus	146	13.76%	44	13.71%
Eleocharis	119	11.22%	13	4.05%
Unidentified	106	9.99%	25	7.79%
Solanum	90	8.48%	4	1.25%
Totals	1061		321	

Table 4.5. Seed type total counts (complete and fragments) and percentages in pit samples and 2007 core samples.

settlement; the occurrence of these seeds may reflect fall-in contamination that occurred during the coring process.

The culturally important *Gaultheria shallon* (salal) and *Rubus sp.* (most likely *R. spectabilis* or salmonberry, *R. parviflorus* or thimbleberry, and *R. ursinus* or trailing blackberry) were found in nearly all samples below 35 cm. As the samples were primarily taken, and very few seeds were found outside the charcoal layers, these layers appear to indicate both riverbed exposure and site use (Table 4.4 and see Punke's core diagrams, Figure 3.14, above). The presence of salal and all of the native *Rubus sp.*, which ripen from May to late August, when the acorns placed in leaching pits should be exposed and ready to retrieve (see Diedrich, above, Figure 2.5).

While analyzing these core samples it is important to keep in mind the small quantity of samples taken, their small size (approximately 1 cm³), and the fact that the cores are only little more than 5 cm (2 in) in diameter. Additionally, possible contamination of the samples by fall-in during the coring process makes analysis difficult. Further sampling of these existing cores is warranted, and additional excavation or better controlled cores (such as vibracoring technologies) may help further explain the layers and seeds found to date.

4.5 Hazelnuts

By Bethany Mathews

The hazelnut fragments found at 35MU4 were identified as coming from *Corylus cornuta* Marsh var. *californica*. The California hazelnut is the only native variety of hazelnut currently growing in Oregon (USDA 2008). Though hazelnuts are found in larger quantity than the acorns at 35MU4 (60% of acorn and hazelnut total), they are not found in the same condition. Of the nearly 500 hazelnut fragments that were excavated, only one was found unbroken (from TVI, Pit M, surface). This single hazelnut represents about 0.2% of the excavated hazelnuts, while over 25% of the acorns were found whole, with the nut still encased. Many acorns were found fragmented, but because all parts of the nut and shell were found the acorns were likely placed in the features whole, where the hazelnuts appear to have been broken and probably eaten on the spot instead of stored.

The single hazelnut that was found complete was damaged at the radicle (pointed) and base (flat) ends of the shell. The marks look as if they are the result of the nut being set on its base on a stone, and struck with another stone at the radicle end. An experiment using store-bought large hazelnuts, a somewhat flat anvil stone, and a small hammerstone held parallel to the anvil demonstrated that this was the easiest way to crack open hazelnut shells without damaging your fingers. While the hazelnuts were from a different species, and were much larger than those at 35MU4, the breaking patterns seem to be comparable.

Hazelnuts are ripe in the late summer and early fall, as are acorns, so it is possible that they were eaten while acorns were being processed, stored, and safeguarded at the site. Like the acorns, many of the hazelnuts have scorch marks on the outside of the shell that suggests they were roasted before they were eaten.

4.6 Faunal analyses

Fauna elements recovered in the limited two excavations at 35MU4 were rare compared to the abundance of floral remains (above). For example, 32 salmon vertebrae were identified from the entire site in 2006, and since salmon generally have 64 vertebrae, this would be the equivalent of half a salmon. The brief 2006 faunal analyses are presented followed by a synthesized 2006–2007 overview report (data spreadsheets can be found in Appendix E, Tables 1–3:219 in website: http://www.library.spscc.ctc.edu/crm/JWA9. pdf).

4.6.1 Mammal, Bird, Fish and Shellfish Fauna from 35MU4 2006

By R. Todd Baker

The faunal collection from 35MU4 contains mammals, birds, fish, and shellfish. Most of the recovered faunal specimens represent animals that would have been commonly found within the area and some represent species that live close to water or in water. The animals represented in the faunal collection include Black-tailed Deer (*Odocoileus columbianus*), Elk (*Cervus elaphus*), Beaver (*Castor canadensis*), Bobcat (*Lynx rufus*), Mink (*Mustela vison*), Muskrat (*Ondatra zibethicus*), Jackrabbit (*Lepus sp.*), Harbor seal (*Phoca vitulina*), Canada Goose (*Branta canadensis*), and Western pearlshell Mussel (*Margaritifera falcata*). The fish bone from the site has been identified to genus and species by Dr. Virginia Butler, Portland State University, who has volunteered to do this for us, since so little fish fauna was recovered from the screening (though the fine screening of Pit P, Transect VI, reveals a number of smaller fish bones, that Dr. Butler has reviewed for us (below)). The majority of the faunal remains are burned and many have cut marks, which indicate animal processing was taking place at the site. Several of the unidentified bone fragments are pieces of bone shafts. An abundance of shaft fragments is usually a good indication of marrow processing taking place (see Table 1, Appendix E:219 in website: http://www.library.spscc.ctc.edu/crm/JWA9.pdf).

4.6.2 Fish at Site and in 100% Samples 2006

By Virginia Butler

From the 100% sample collected from Pit P in 2006, the fish remains were recovered through wet screening to see any small fraction. Other examples of fish remains were recovered through surface collecting, either while hydraulically cleaning the surface of pits for mapping, or flagged on the surface survey.

In total, 53 specimens were identified (Table 4.6). Remains of *Onchorhynchus* sp. (salmon and trout) are most abundant, followed by *Acipenser* (sturgeon), then the Cyprinidae-Catostomidae (minnow and sucker) and *Catostomus* (sucker).

The Appendix E:224 – Table 2: 2006 in website: http://www.library.spscc.ctc.edu/ crm/JWA9.pdf) lists the taxon and element that were identified from each of the provenience units.

4.6.3 Synthesis and Summary of Sunken Village Fauna, 2006–2007 excavations

By Rebecca Wigen

The Sunken Village explorations in 2007 more than doubled the number of elements in the site assemblage. In 2007 a total of 292 elements were recovered from the beach surface collection and pit/unit sample with a further 1216 elements recorded from the fine screen samples of HTU and Pit P. The bulk of the elements from the surface collection and pit/unit samples are mammal (90%), with a few fish (5%) and birds (4.5%). In the fine screen samples this basic pattern is quite different, with the bulk of the sample being fish (97%), with only 2% mammal and 1% bird. The density of bone was so high in the fine screen samples that unidentified bone was not counted, so figures reported are NISP. New taxa identified from the 2007 material include peamouth chub, eulachon, three-spine stickleback, sculpin, trumpeter swan, small, medium, medium-large and large ducks, northern pygmy owl, a canid, raccoon and black bear (Table 4.7, and Appendix E, Table 3:225 in website: http://www.library.spscc.ctc.edu/crm/JWA9. pdf). Considering the different collection techniques and resulting assemblages it is best to discuss the two data sets separately.

Taxon	Frequency (NISP)
Oncorhynchus sp.	32
Acipenser sp.	11
Cyprinidae-Catostomidae	5
Catostomus sp.	5
Total	53

Table 4.6. List of fish taxa from 2006 100% Samples.

4.6.3.1 Surface Collection and Pit/Unit Sample Bones

The bones in the 2007 assemblage found on the surface or in surface cleaned acorn leaching pits in the river sediments all appear to be in disturbed archaeological deposits. It could reasonably be asked whether these bones are actually associated with an archaeological deposit or whether they are from natural deaths. Several lines of evidence suggest they are indeed archaeological. Many of the elements show cultural modifications such as cutting, chopping or burning. In addition some of the species are no longer found in the area, such as elk and black bear, so could not be recent deposits on the river bank. Finally, these surface bones (as well as lithics) are only found concentrated on the intertidal beach in Transect II through Transect VI, and not north or south of these transects, and this is the only area containing the ancient *in situ* acorn leaching pits and stakes. As result, it is reasonable to assume the bulk of the assemblage is eroded from the archaeological deposit.

The mammal assemblage (combining both 2006 and 2007 material) is quite varied considering the small numbers present (Table 4.8, below), although most of the species are represented by less than 5 elements. Many of the species of small mammals, including muskrat, beaver, river otter, mink and raccoon, are typically found associated with riverine, lacustrine, shoreline or marshy habitats. These animals may not be found in the main river stream, but they would certainly find prime habitat along side-channels such as Multnomah Slough, and along the river edges.

Several elements have been identified as *Lynx* sp., either bobcat (*L. rufus*) or lynx (*L. canadensis*). These two small cats are quite difficult to separate skeletally. The bobcat would certainly be present in the general site area and is the most likely candidate. However, potentially lynx are present in the Washington or Oregon interior or Cascade Mountains and so might have been traded to this area or captured during a hunting trip. These cats are probably hunted mainly for their high quality pelt. A single canid element was recovered. Size suggests identification as either domestic dog (*Canis familiaris*) or coyote (*C. latrans*), and either of these is possible at this site. A single rabbit element was identified from the 2006 excavation, tentatively identified as one of the *Lepus* species. The most probable candidate is the snowshoe hare (*L. americanus*), which is recorded in the area and lives in a wide variety of habitats.

Few of these small mammal bones are modified. However in the 2007 sample, one of the muskrat elements is burned and a raccoon tibia shows faint grinding and scraping marks as well as having been chewed by a carnivore such as a dog.

In addition to these small mammals, black bear and harbor seal are identified from a single element each. Black bears are found throughout the region and could certainly have been hunted in the local vicinity. Harbor seals are typically a marine species, however they are known to enter the lower reaches of the Columbia River and reported to travel upstream to at least Willamette Falls.

The most abundant identified taxa in the 2006–2007 assemblages are deer and elk (elk are called red deer in British English) (Table 4.8). In the 2007 assemblage, deer contribute 33% of the mammal elements, while elk contribute 5%. The deer elements could come from either mule/black-tailed deer (*Odocoileus hemionus*) or white-tailed deer (*O. virginianus*). Both species are found along the Columbia River. Unfortunately, they

Table 4.7. List of Taxa Identified from 35MU4 including all 2006–2007 samples.
*Note: * indicates species found only in HTU and Pit P samples.*

Bird	
Trumpeter swan	*Cygnus buccinator*
Canada goose	*Branta canadensis*
*Duck, small	Anatidae
Duck, medium	Anatidae
*Duck, medium-large	Anatidae
Duck (large)	Anatidae
Northern pygmy owl	*Glaucidium gnoma*
Fish	
Sturgeon	*Acipenser* sp.
*Eulachon	*Thaleichthys pacificus*
Salmon	*Oncorhynchus* sp.
Chub sp.	Cyprinid sp.
Peamouth chub	*Mylocheilus caurinus*
Sucker sp.	*Catostomus* sp.
Chub/Sucker	Cyprinidae/Catostomidae
*Three-spine stickleback	*Gasterosteus aculeatus*
*Sculpin sp.	Cottidae
Mammal	
Jackrabbit	*Lepus* sp.
Muskrat	*Ondatra zibethica*
Beaver	*Castor canadensis*
Canid	*Canis* sp.
Bobcat	*Lynx rufus*
Lynx/bobcat	*Lynx* sp.
River otter	*Lutra canadensis*
Mink	*Mustela vison*
Raccoon	*Procyon lotor*
Black bear	*Ursus americanus*
Elk (red deer)	*Cervus elaphus*
Mule deer	*Odocoileus hemionus*
Deer (mule or white-tail)	*Odocoileus hemionus/virginianus*
Ungulate sp.	Artiodactyla
Harbor seal	*Phoca vitulina*

are difficult to distinguish skeletally (although not impossible) and the comparative collection used in 2007 from the University of Victoria Department of Anthropology lacks a white-tailed deer specimen. As a result it was decided to leave the identification at the genus level. Black-tailed deer was definitely identified in the 2006 assemblage. It is probable that both are present in the assemblage.

The deer bones from 2007 are all from adult (epiphyses fused or adult size) or sub-adult (epiphyses unfused but adult size) individuals. A single cranial fragment with

	II	III	IV	V	VI	Total
Sturgeon			1	1		2
Salmon		2	1	4	1	8
Peamouth chub	1					1
Chub sp.	1					1
Sucker sp.				1		1
Unidentified fish		1		1		2
Total fish	2	3	2	7	1	15
Trumpeter swan				1		1
Duck (large)	1					1
Unidentified large bird	2					2
Unidentified bird			1	2	3	3	9
Total bird	3	1	2	4	3	13
Small mammal\bird			1			1
Beaver				3		3
Muskrat				1		1
Raccoon	1		2			3
Canid				1		1
Lynx/bobcat	1				1	2
Black bear	1					1
Deer	11	17	21	27	12	88
Elk	3	4	2	4		13
Ungulate (antler fragments)			1	2		3
Very large land mammal				2		2
Large land mammal	14	13	25	31	24	107
Large mammal			1			1
Unidentified mammal	4	8	1	21	4	38
Total mammal	35	42	53	92	41	263

Table 4.8. NISP by Transect, 2007 data.

the antler chopped off was present, indicating the capture of a male sometime in the fall/winter season. At least four individuals were present based on the presence of four left astragali. All parts of the body were present with front and hind limb elements most common, suggesting complete, or substantially complete, deer were being processed at the site. Metacarpals and metatarsals were particularly common, 21 in total, and of these 8 were cut or worked in some fashion. The cut marks on these bones, which have little flesh on them, probably indicate debris from bone tool manufacturing and their abundance suggests they were being preferentially chosen. In contrast, cuts on a humerus, rib and scapula probably result from food preparation.

Elk are the second ranked mammal (Table 4.8), but with many fewer bones than the deer. At least two elk are present based on the presence of 2 left femurs from an adult and juvenile individual. Although there are not very many elements, there are still representatives from most parts of the body, including the hind limb, skull (teeth), ribs, and fore limb (a carpal) indicating complete or substantially complete animals were present. Two of the podials (a calcaneous and radial carpal) have deep cut marks and one of the rib shaft fragments has shallow cuts. The cuts on the podials probably occurred during removal of the metapodials and the cuts on the rib shaft may indicate flesh removal for consumption.

The single most abundant faunal category is the large land mammal group. This accounts for 41% of the mammal assemblage. This size category could include bones from such mammals as deer, black bear and wolf. These bones are usually shaft fragments that are thick enough to indicate they came from a large mammal. Considering the abundance of deer in the assemblage, it is probable most of these are deer as well. Many are spirally fractured suggesting humans as the agent of breakage.

Very few bird bones were recovered either in 2006 or 2007 and the majority is unidentifiable. A single swan element is identified as trumpeter swan rather than whistling swan (*Cygnus columbianus*), based on its large size. Both swans winter on the Columbia River, and in the past, in very large flocks (Jewett *et al* 1953, 101–102). A single goose element, identified as Canada goose, was identified in the 2006 assemblage. Canada geese are also most common during spring and fall migration, but some might be found in the area all year. The only other bird identification is large duck, which is too generic to provide any seasonal or habitat information.

The sample of fish bones is also quite small (Table 4.8). In the 2007 sample only 15 fish bones were present. More than half of these are salmon. The salmon bones are all vertebra from medium sized individuals (estimated to be between 45–60 cm in length). The dominance of salmon is not a surprise as the Columbia River has enormous salmon runs. A few sturgeon elements were identified. It was not possible to identify the sturgeon to species, so the elements could either be white (*Acipenser transmontanus*) or green (*A. medirostris*) sturgeon. The other elements belong to freshwater taxa, including the peamouth chub and unidentified chub and sucker bones. The peamouth chub is a permanent resident in the area, preferring slower flowing areas of the river (Page and Burr 1991, 70). Suckers (Catostomidae) are difficult to identify to species. In this case the bones were from one of the larger species such as the largescale sucker (*Catostomus macrocheilus*), bridgelip sucker (*C. columbianus*) and mountain sucker (*C. platyrhynchus*).

A larger number of fish elements (53) were recovered in the 2006 surface collection and pit/unit excavations, although this is still not a large number. Again, salmon is most common, followed by about equal quantities of sturgeon and chub/sucker. So, despite the small samples, the 2006 and 2007 assemblages produced quite similar results.

Despite the relatively small samples, some patterns seem clear in this assemblage. Certainly the abundance and variety of mammals indicates that hunting was a significant activity at this site. Deer and elk were the primary mammal resources, but the wide variety of other species indicates they were not the sole focus. The presence of many deer metapodials, some with cut marks, shows that bone tool manufacturing was a significant activity. The smaller mammals include several species, such as bobcat, river otter and mink, which may have been hunted for their pelts. The raccoon may have been an invader, interested in the hundred plus acorn leaching pits containing millions of acorns (Mathews, above) and/or been hunted for its pelt as well. Others, such as muskrat and beaver, would have supplied both high quality pelts and substantial food.

Apparently few birds were hunted. Water birds were the only group represented suggesting a focus on riverine habitats, although the sample is very small. The presence of the swan and Canada goose suggests some bird hunting took place in the fall through spring.

The small fish assemblage also shows some clear patterns. Salmon is the most abundant fish taxa identified by far, followed by sturgeon and then the suckers and chubs. However, the most striking aspect of the fish assemblage is its small size, as the setting of the site, on the Multnomah Channel, would appear to lend itself to a focus on fishing.

At this point in the analysis, it appears fishing was not a particularly important activity at this site, despite the ethnographically recorded preference for fish as a resource (Boyd and Hajda 1987). Considering the abundance of plant resources recovered, particularly acorns, it is possible that the focus here was on those resources rather than fish. Acorn harvesting would take place in the fall and then would be collected from the leaching pits in the late winter/spring. In the fall, chum salmon (*O. keta*) and possibly the last of the summer run sockeye (*O. nerka*) and chinook (*O. tschawytsha*) would be available in the channels around Sauvie Island. In the late winter/spring eulachon (*Thaleichthys pacificus*), white sturgeon (*Acipenser transmontanus*), which feed upon the eulachon and spring chinook salmon are available. So it would theoretically be possible to collect acorns and catch a variety of fish in the same season. Hunting was obviously important, so why not fishing as well? And the evidence for bone tool manufacturing adds to the picture of a variety of activities taking place at this site.

Alternatively, if fall acorn harvesting and processing and late winter/spring collection was the focus of activities by a large group of people at Sunken Village and it was occupied by only a few people through the winter to guard the acorn leaching pits then large scale harvest of salmon and/or eulachon may not have occurred. In that case, the few fish bones may accurately reflect occasional fishing by the small number of longer-term residents.

Another possibility is that site deposition is affecting the recovery of fish bones. All but one of the 2007 fish bones were recovered from the pit deposits. The acorn pits were presumably left open when not in use and when abandoned and subsequently were filled in with river sediments. When open they could have created an eddy, slowing the slough current and trapping smaller, lighter weight bones. Larger, heavier mammal bones would also be caught in the eddy created by the pits, but would also be deposited in the bank sediments, while many (most?) of the lighter weight fish bones could have been carried away by the currents. So, if there were more fish remains in the eroding midden, they may have been carried away by the slough, rather than being deposited on the adjacent river bank.

This is where the analysis stood when I was given the opportunity to examine fine-screened samples that were collected from the Half Test Unit and Pit P. As a result of this analysis, the interpretation of the fish bone in particular changed dramatically.

4.6.3.2 Half Test Unit (HTU) and Pit P Fine Screened Samples

HTU Assemblage. The Half Test Unit was excavated into the cutbank above the beach (see Punke, above). The faunal samples came from Stratigraphic Unit 5, an area with fire-cracked rocks, charcoal and burnt bone (Figure 3.7). This appears to be an in-situ cultural layer. This unit is above the water level and so there are no waterlogged wood and fiber materials present.

Two level samples were water-screened through a 1.00 mm mesh and produced more bone than had been recovered in both the 2006 and 2007 excavations. Almost all of this bone was burnt and/or calcined, probably the only reason it survived. No attempt was made to count the unidentifiable bone due to the high density of bone and time constraints, so the figures in Table 4.9 are NISP only.

Most of the bone identified is fish, 594 of 601 elements (Table 4.9). The only identifiable mammal element is from a medium sized rodent, possibly mountain beaver. There are 6 other fragments that appear to be antler. There is more mammal bone present in the sample, but it was all unidentifiable and so was not counted in this case. There is a small amount of bone from salmon, sturgeon and the sucker/chub group (more than was recovered in the rest of the site!), but there is an astonishing amount of three-spine stickleback, 542 elements, contributing 91% of the sample. Most of the stickleback bones are dorsal and pelvic spines. The MNI for stickleback is at least 60 based on the pelvic spines (see Appendix E, Table 3e in website: http://www.library. spscc.ctc.edu/crm/JWA9.pdf).

The association with fire-cracked rock and charcoal and the calcined nature of the bone, suggests this deposit might be from a hearth. If so, this deposit might represent a short-term event. Although the great abundance of 3-spine stickleback might seem unusual, it has been recovered in large quantities at Cathlapotle (a similar site on the Columbia River) when fine screens were used (Virginia Butler, personal communication). Whether people are collecting three-spine stickleback as bait, inadvertently while netting other fish, in the stomach of other animals or deliberately for food is unknown at this point. The burning of the bones indicates they were deliberately discarded into the fire, which might suggest these small fish were discarded whole.

Pit P Assemblage. The second group of samples taken from each level of Pit P were also water-screened through 1.00 mm mesh and produced an abundance of bone; a total NISP of 615 (Table 4.9; also see Pit P description in Punke, above, Table 3.3, Figure 3.12). This bone is about 38% calcined or burnt, a lower proportion than in the HTU. In addition to the bone, the samples contained some stone flakes, small bits of shell, some wood chips, fragments of worked bone and abundant charcoal. Although excavated in 10 cm levels, I could see no particular vertical pattern beyond an overall increase in the density of bone in the lowest levels. As a result all bone from Pit P was combined into a single assemblage for analysis.

There is a modest amount of bird and mammal bone. In fact, there is more identifiable bird bone in these samples than in the rest of the site (Tables 4.8 and 4.9). Ducks of varying sizes are most common, contributing 64% of the bird NISP. Variation in size of the elements indicates an MNI of at least four ducks in this pit. The only other bird present is northern pygmy owl, represented by three vertebrae and a foot phalanx

Taxon	HTU	Pit P	Total NISP
Sturgeon	11	43	54
Salmon	13	169	182
Chub sp.	1	64	65
Sucker sp.	3	28	31
Chub/Sucker	23	108	131
Eulachon	1	148	149
3–spine stickleback	542	17	559
Sculpin sp.		3	3
Total fish NISP	594	580	1174
Small duck		1	1
Medium duck		4	4
Medium-large duck		1	1
Large duck		1	1
Northern pygmy owl		4	4
Total bird NISP		11	11
Small rodent		2	2
Mountain beaver?	1		1
Muskrat		3	3
Canid		1	1
Deer		2	2
Ungulate (antler?)	6	19	25
Total mammal NISP	7	27	34

Table 4.9. NISP for Half Test Unit (HTU) and Pit P Bulk Samples.

probably from the same individual. This sparrow-sized owl is an unusual find in an archaeological site, but they are permanent, and probably common, residents in this area (Jewett *et al.* 1953, 361).

More mammal bones were identified than bird (Table 4.9), although 67% of the NISP is antler fragments. Several of these fragments appear to be detritus from chopping or adzing the antler. Muskrat is the next most common mammal taxon with 12.5% of the NISP, followed by deer (8%) and a small rodent (8%). A single canid tooth was recovered. Size suggests this is either domestic dog or coyote.

By far, the largest portion of bone was fish (NISP = 580), a bit lower than in the HTU samples. The breadth of species is almost the same, only adding sculpin to the list. However, the proportions are fundamentally different.

In Pit P, salmon is most abundant, 29% of the NISP. The elements consist mainly of vertebra and vertebra fragments, with a few teeth present, indicating at least some whole salmon were being processed. About half of the salmon bone is calcined. The bones appear to be from medium-sized individuals, although size is a bit difficult to determine with fragmentary vertebra.

Following closely behind the salmon is eulachon with 25.5% of the NISP. All of the eulachon bones are vertebra and they are the only abundant taxon where none of the bones are burned or calcined. These are very fragile vertebra (essentially a thin ring) and it is possible burning, which tends to make bone more brittle, caused them to disintegrate. Of course, it is also possible none of them were burned. Eulachon are the best seasonal indicator of the faunal remains, entering the area in February and March to spawn (see Diedrich, 2.2.8 above).

The next ranked group is the sucker/chub group, which consists mostly of vertebra. Chub and sucker vertebra are difficult to identify, so have been combined. Cranial bones of chubs and suckers are more distinctive and indicate both are present, although it wasn't possible to identify any to species. For comparison purposes it is easiest to combine all three groups together. If you do that, this group becomes the most abundant in the sample, with a combined NISP of 200 or 34%. Both vertebra and cranial elements are present for these fish and in a variety of sizes, from large to small.

Sturgeon is fourth ranked. Unfortunately, these were mostly small fragments of large elements identified mainly by the texture. As a result it was usually not possible to identify either element or to estimate the size of the sturgeon. Some scutes were present and some fin rays, but that was the most that can be determined.

And in complete contrast to the sample from the Half Test Unit, only a few 3-spine stickleback elements were present (Table 4.9). Again, these were mostly spines, but in this case not all were calcined.

The derivation of this sample is a complex question. It is likely that Pit P was left open the last time it was emptied of acorns leaving behind its hemlock branch lining (dated to 130±60 calibrated C14 years ago, Table 3.5, above). Presumably it was filled by sediments settling into the eddy it would create. So these bones, artifact fragments, flakes, etc, may have been washed into the pit after eroding from the bank. The eddy created by the open pit would certainly tend to catch this type of material as well as the silt in the water. However, none of the bone appears to be water worn. Potentially it didn't move far enough to be worn, but this is at least suggestive of the notion that the material might not have been washed into the pit.

The large amount of charcoal and calcined/burnt bone suggests an alternative possibility. As has been noted by Beth Mathews above, charcoal and/or ash were sometimes included in the acorn processing. Perhaps in addition to the pit being lined with hemlock branches, it was also lined with ash or ash was layered in with the acorns. The most obvious source of ash and charcoal would be fire hearths, and hearths might contain all of the material listed above. The unburnt bone might have been included if some floor material was collected along with the hearth material. I believe this is the most likely source of this sample.

4.6.3.4 Summary. With the addition of the bulk samples, fish become the most abundant fauna recovered from this site; a very different conclusion than was reached before the bulk samples were analyzed. The most common fish are stickleback, the chub/sucker group, salmon, eulachon and sturgeon, although not necessarily in that order. The abundance of stickleback and eulachon is quite variable, with a very high number in the HTU and few in Pit P. The sheer quantity of fish in the two samples from the Half

Test Unit and Pit P suggests that fishing *was* important at this site, in direct contrast to the conclusion drawn when only the surface and test unit materials were present. However, these are only two small samples from what may be unusual settings. More work would be necessary to determine if they are typical of the site. Certainly the proportions and species present are quite similar to those from Cathlapotle, suggesting this sample may be typical for the area.

It is also clear that mammal hunting was important as well, perhaps just as much as fishing. The breadth of the species recovered from what is a still a small sample of the site seems a good indication of this importance. Deer and elk are the most common mammals hunted, but a wide variety of smaller fur-bearers were also hunted. The presence of a deer cranial fragment with antler attached indicates at least late summer to early winter hunting.

Surprisingly, birds don't seem to have been particularly important, even though this area is known for large wintering populations of ducks, geese and swans.

The cut deer metapodials and fragments of antler detritus also indicate bone and antler tool manufacturing was taking place on site.

In the end, the faunal remains suggest a broad range of resource collection was taking place at this site and lends support to the suggestion that it was occupied by at least some people for most of the year.

5 Artifact Analyses

5.1 Introduction

Over 50 years of collecting and intentional vandalism at the Sunken Village wet site has demonstrated the potential material culture data preservation at this waterlogged site, and finally we can report a systematic characterization of the overall material culture – both debitage and examples of discrete artifacts. The previously and unprofessionally collected basketry, cordage and wooden artifacts reflected the wealth of wood and fiber artifacts thanks to the waterlogged preservation of the site, however collecting is very selective. The analytical power of the basketry was noted over twenty years ago, reflecting a distinct Chinookan style (Croes 1987). As reported next, this artifact analysis may even have a much broader implications for a North Pacific cultural sharing, both in the use of acorn pit processing and distinct basketry styles, factors never perceived before these initial professional explorations.

In two limited field investigations we have stabilized and reported approximately 8,499 artifacts recovered (items that are the result of human activity) from the Sunken Village wet site – itself a reflection of the wealth of data from this wet site. All these materials are concentrated only within Transects II–VI along the intertidal beach and bank (see map, Figure 3.2). In total the 2006–2007 field efforts recorded 2,022 wood chips, 1,669 pieces of lithic debitage, 1,244 split wood pieces, 89 basketry waste elements (both bark and bough/root splints), 890 acorns, 502 hazelnuts, 29 cherry bark curls, 8 bone artifacts, 45 stone artifacts, 48 wood or fiber artifacts, 1,018 faunal elements (both shell and animal bones) and 935 thermally altered rock (TAR, often called fire-cracked rock; Appendix F, Table 1:237 in website: http://www.library.spscc.ctc.edu/crm/JWA9.pdf). If we include the 5,939 pieces of charcoal (larger than a thumbnail pieces) collected, then approximately 14,438 items that are likely the result of human activity are being processed from the limited total of four weeks evaluation of National Historic Landmark site. The exact counts of the artifact types have changed following further cleaning and analysis; For example, the split wood sticks (often with burnt ends) are far more common than recorded, having been originally identified as wood chips. Probably acorns, hazelnuts and cherry bark curls are more numerous than the original calculations following cleaning and some analysis. Some of these changes will be reflected below in the specific artifact analyses. A general discussion of the artifact distributions here will be followed by specific studies.

If we review the 14,438 items cataloged from the site, 18% of the collection are stone, bone and shell elements, with 82% consisting of wood and fibers items. In Northwest Coast wet sites further north, the wood and fibers items often account for 90–95% of the material culture (Croes 1995), therefore Sunken Village reflects a stronger emphasis on stone artifacts, a trend that probably separates ancient cultural trends in the Portland Basin and Puget Sound northward (see Lithic artifact and Projectile Point studies below).

5.2. Artifact Debitage and Debris – Overall Characterization, Distribution and Density

By Dale R. Croes, Philip Pedack and Michael Martin

5.2.1 Introduction

In this section we examine the distribution of the by-products of artifact production, commonly called debitage, which for 35MU4 include wood chips, split wood, basketry waste elements and lithic debitage. These kinds of materials, critical to understanding the functions and general activities at the site, are rarely saved by avocational collectors.

5.2.2 Raw Materials

Over five thousand pieces of debitage were collected during the limited archaeological investigations of Sunken Village, or 59% of the artifactual materials recovered (and 35% of everything recovered if we include charcoal). The frequency of each type of debitage is shown in Figure 5.1.

The majority of debitage from Sunken Village, 67%, consists of wood and fiber elements of wood chips, split wood and basketry waste elements. Lithic debitage, representing 33%, produces a higher percentage than we normally see in wet sites in Puget Sound and northward, reflecting the emphasis on stone tool making at the site. Probably the most striking contrast with sites to the north, and especially the Qwu?gwes wet site on southern Puget Sound (the next well-recorded wet site to the north of 35MU4), is the low amount of basketry waste elements encountered, 2% at Sunken Village (see Section 5.4). This low number leads us to conclude that little basketry was actually being constructed at this site, and lots of wood working and stone tool making was taking place. Ethnographically, woodworking and stone tool

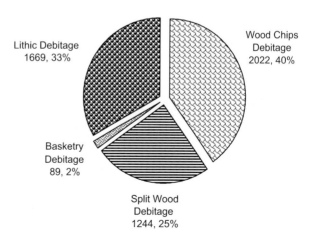

Figure 5.1. Sunken Village lithic, wood and basketry debitage frequencies.

Lithic Debitage 1669, 33%

Wood Chips Debitage 2022, 40%

Basketry Debitage 89, 2%

Split Wood Debitage 1244, 25%

making are generally perceived as men's tasks (Ray 1975, 142), and basketry tends to be considered a women's task, so one could conclude, or at least hypothesize, that men were mostly active at the site, and/or at least that women were not making basketry from the site. One thought, especially if this location is mostly an acorn processing/ leaching location, and not a large village location, men were stationed there to guard the pits during the minimal 4–5 month period of aquifer leaching (see discussion of site function in Section 6.3).

5.2.3 Macroflora, Faunal, Charcoal and Thermally Altered Rock (TAR) Distributions

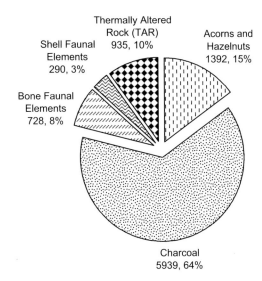

Figure 5.2. Sunken Village debris frequencies for charcoal, bone, shell, thermally altered rock and acorns and hazelnuts.

When considering other waste products that are the indirect results of human activity at the site (not directly manufactured by people), such as acorns, hazelnuts, bone and shell faunal remains, charcoal and thermally altered rock (TAR, or fire-cracked rock, FCR), a strong emphasis on plant foods rather than animal products is seen at 35MU4 (Figure 5.2) as well as an abundance of charcoal at the site, possibly used in the acorn pit leaching process (see Mathews, above), to roast the acorns before placing in the pits, and/or as the result of fires to keep guards warm while they watched over the area, especially at night when raccoons would be active.

5.2.4 Discrete Artifacts

The artifact distribution charts reflect the general emphasis on wood and fiber artifacts (47%) and lithic artifacts (45%), and the less abundant bone artifacts (8%) (during this late period, bone is characteristically a common artifact material in northern Puget Sound sites and those further north). These discrete artifacts will be characterized and reported in separate sections below (Figure 5.3).

5.2.5 Surface Distribution of Cultural Materials

The distribution of *in situ* pits and stakes and surface-collected artifacts (mostly lithics) and faunal remains (mostly animal bones versus shellfish) were mapped with Auto-CADD software. As can be seen in Figure 5.4 this exercise revealed definite cultural boundaries of Transects II and VI, the cultural void between Transect III and IV from the historic era drainage pipe excavated through the site, and the high concentrations of acorn leaching pits found only in Transects II–VI. To make this data accessible even further, we have broken down the transects into 5 meter increments and have given a precise count of artifacts, fauna and/or features within them as a corresponding bar graph (Figure 5.4). The greatest numbers of acorn leaching pits are in Transects III and V which may indicate the acorn leaching process worked best in those two areas.

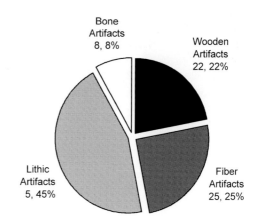

Figure 5.3. Discrete artifacts recorded from Sunken Village (35MU4).

5.2.6 Test Unit (TU) and TU drainage trench excavations creating perpendicular cut-view through Transects IV–VI

In reviewing the horizontal distribution of the debitage and objects of indirect results of human occupation throughout the main site area (Transects IV–VI), and particularly the four Test Units (TU1–4) and excavation of Pit P in Transect VI, one generally sees a void of cultural materials in the three test units (TU1–3) dug in 10 cm levels to as deep as 1 m close to the bank (where the rip rap was placed). Drainage trenches were excavated from the lower end of each Test Unit towards the river, 10 cm wide and 1 m long sections (designated Trench 1, 2, 3, 4…) and dug in 10 cm levels, extend down to the tidal zone from TU 1–3, excavated in case we encountered vegetal mat layers in the excavations of TU1–3, requiring hydraulic excavation and water drainage. Though vegetal mats were not encountered until we opened up TU-4, the 10 cm wide drainage trenches provided a perpendicular 10 cm wide view of the stratigraphy from each TU in the three main 25 m transects (Transects IV–VI) from the TUs (close to the bank) down to the tidal zone.

We established the TUs and the drainage trenches so that at least one acorn leaching pit would be dissected by the drainage trench extending from the TUs. Our objective was to dissect the little understood acorn leaching pits, and to gain a much better understanding of the waterlogged site preservation zone at the site. 100% samples were recovered from a 10 × 10 cm column in the center of each of the five dissected acorn leaching pits for fine water screening and flotation experiments (see above, Diedrich, *et al.*; Figure 4.15).

In this section the artifactual distribution from each Test Unit (TU1–3) down through the 1 m long × 10 cm wide drainage trenches will be reported to document the pattern of increasing amounts of artifactual materials, especially waterlogged wood and fiber items, as one moves from the TU near the bank to the slough channel.

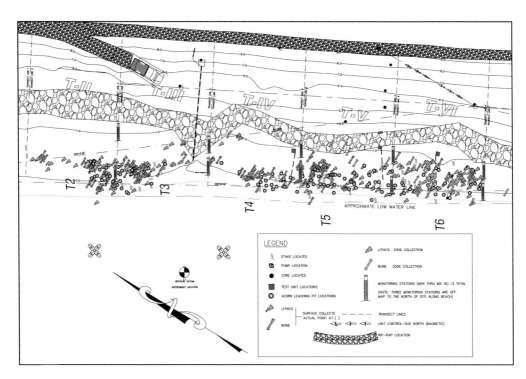

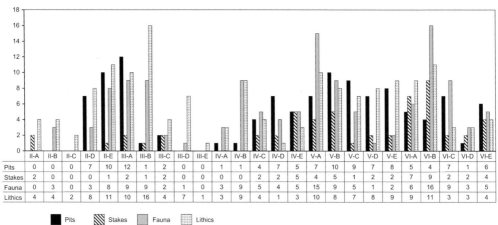

Figure 5.4. Distribution of in situ acorn leaching pits and stakes, and surface collected fauna and lithics in 5 meter sections through the 25 meter transects II–VI at Sunken Village; triangles represent lithics and long bones fauna, see also key to Figures 3.2 and 3.3 (Map by Michael Martin, CAD, SPSCC, 2008).

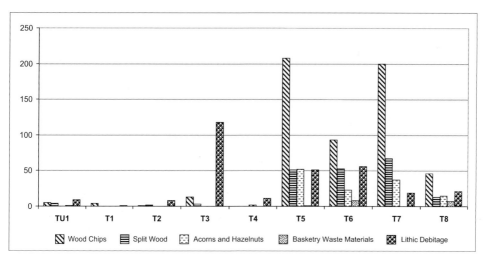

Figure 5.5. Distribution of artifactual materials from TU 1 and along associated Drainage Trenches 1–8 (8 M drainage trench length to slough; note that trenches are 1/10th the volume of the TUs).

5.2.6.1 TU1 and Associated Drainage Trenches 1–8

TU 1 was excavated to a depth of 90 cm and was essentially culturally sterile to this depth (most of the cultural materials indicated were slump materials concentrating in the top 10 cm, Appendix F, Table 1:237; see website: http://www.library.spscc.ctc.edu/crm/JWA9.pdf). We dug a 50 × 50 cm shovel test in the NW corner of TU1 down another meter, until a vegetal mat, aquifer layers were encountered – however the 1.8 m above this zone was essentially culturally sterile silty/sandy beach deposits (see Punke, above). As one moves down the TU1 drainage trench (designated in 1 m lengths, e.g., Trench 1 is first 10 cm × 1 m unit down from the TU, etc.), the waterlogged layers were encountered in Trench 5–8 (5–8+ m towards shoreline from TU1), which dissected two acorn leaching pits (and these pits, as basins, accumulated cultural materials as they filled; Figures 5.4 and 5.5). Wood chips and split wood debitage were particularly abundant in these last four meters of the 10 cm wide drainage trenches (Figure 5.5).

5.2.6.2 TU 2 and Associated Drainage Trenches 1–8

As with TU 1, TU 2 was essentially culturally sterile down to 80 cm, with some cultural materials concentrating in upper levels (Appendix F, Table 1:237; see website: http://www.library.spscc.ctc.edu/crm/JWA9.pdf; Figure 5.6, see also photograph of TU2 and drainage trench, Figure 3.1). The drainage trenches remained culturally sterile until waterlogged matrices and an acorn leaching pit (Pit B) were encountered in Trenches 7 and 8 (Figure 5.6). Again wood chips and split wood contributed to most of the cultural debitage recovered once the waterlogged levels (Trenches 7 and 8) were reached.

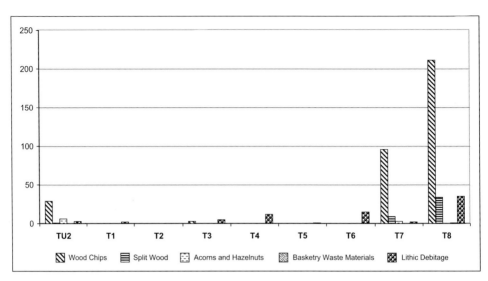

Figure 5.6. Distribution of artifactual materials from TU 2 and along Drainage Trenches 1–8 (8 m drainage trench length to slough; Note that trenches are 1/10th the volume of the TUs).

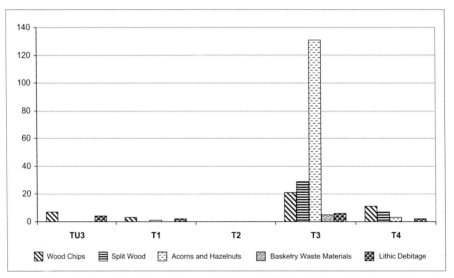

Figure 5.7. Distribution of artifactual materials from TU 3 and along Drainage Trenches 1–4 (5 m drainage trench length to slough; note that trenches are 1/10th the volume of the TUs).

5.2.6.3 TU 3 AND ASSOCIATED DRAINAGE TRENCHES 1–4

TU 3, like TU 1 and 2, was culturally sterile, but only a 35 cm depth was reached before it was discontinued (Figure 5.7; see photograph of TU3 and drainage trench in Figure 3.1). The drainage trenches T1–T2 were also culturally sterile, but we dissected an acorn leaching pit (Pit G) in Trench 3, encountering an abundance of acorns and hazelnuts in this pit (Figure 5.7; see also Figure 4.15, and Appendix F, Table 1:237 on website: http://www.library.spscc.ctc.edu/crm/JWA9.pdf). The main cultural debitage in Trenches 3–4 was wood chips and split wood.

5.2.6.4 TU 4 and Pit P

At the end of the first of two weeks of intensive excavation, we recognized the main remnant beach area containing a series of well-preserved vegetal mats angling down from the waterlogged zone (where the remaining aquifer flow was surfacing from below the natural levee). With a limitation of 4 Test Units, we concluded that the last Test Unit (TU 4) should be explored in the final week of excavation, revealing the nature of these well-preserved vegetal mats in what appears to be the last remnant complete beach surface of a once more extensive aquifer flow and acorn leaching pit distribution. The acorn leaching pits dissected in northerly TU 2 and 3 drainage trenches revealed what appears to be the very bottom of once complete and deep pits (see Figure 4.15). Next to this well-preserved remnant beach area, we also found a pedestaled acorn leaching pit (Pit P, Transect VI (also called Feature 2); Figures 3.4c, 3.12, 4.13, 4.14). As part of our 2006 Scope of Work, we were to dissect these pits to better identify their functions, so we also decided we should cross-section a whole acorn leaching pit to verify their contents and volumes. Pit P was excavated, as were TUs, in 10 cm levels. Following the cross-sectioning of this pit, it was further decided that the AINW crew, especially geomorphologist Michele Punke, would return the third week and take a 10 × 10 cm column sample from the center of the other half of this complete pit and also excavate the exposed, and no doubt endangered (through erosion and vandalism), other half of the pit to conclude investigations.

TU-4 had one down-beach open side on the 1 × 1 m excavation unit, so did not require a drainage trench to hydraulically excavate – the water would drain off the front of the unit as 10 cm levels were excavated and screened (see profile, Figures 3.9 and 3.10). Therefore a full 1 × 1 m by 50 cm deep unit was excavated and recovered through the nested water screens, producing a large sample of cultural debitage and by-products of occupation. The distribution of these cultural materials is reported in Appendix F, Table 1:237 (see website: http://www.library.spscc.ctc.edu/crm/JWA9.pdf), and the overall pattern of results in Figure 5.8. Pit P was not a full 1 × 1 m pit, but instead excavated as an actual pit feature in 10 cm levels (see profile, Figure 3.12). The material culture contents of the first (north) half are shown in Figure 5.8, next to the results of TU4.

The vegetal mats in TU 4 (see stratigraphy in Figures 3.9 and 3.11) reflected the abundance of wood and fiber material culture, especially debitage (split wood and wood chips), that makes up these layers that are probably old point bar beach layers angling down from the bank and where the waterlogging from aquifers running under the natural levee begin surfacing along this beach.

The Pit P cultural debitage and by-products of cultural occupation have a different distribution than TU 4 vegetal mat layers, however variation would be expected since an acorn leaching pit, after final removal of processed acorns, would be expected to have things accumulate rather randomly as they washed into this deep basin from tidal

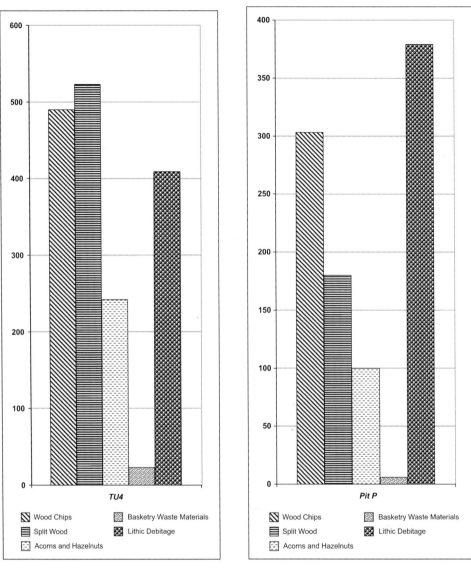

Figure 5.8. Material Culture contents of (left) TU4 vegetal mat 1 × 1 × 0.5 m excavations and (right) Pit P 100% excavations of the first ½ of the preserved acorn leaching pit.

action, beach currents, erosion down the beach and other processes. The hemlock boughs used to line the final use of Pit P were C14 dated to 130±60 years ago, with a range of 1760 to 1880 AD for the final and contact period use of this acorn leaching pit.

5.2.6.5 DISCUSSION

From the distribution of vegetal cultural materials through TU 1–3 trench transects and TU 4 and Pit P, a general beach line of aquifer waterlogging along Transects II to VI can be drawn (see below, Figure 6.5). This is the waterlogged zone along the Sunken Village wet site, as estimated from the 2006 and 2007 site evaluation, and the aquifer zone that worked best as a major acorn leaching station.

We doubt this was a major village location, as will be further discussed in Section 6. However, it is an ideal place for passive leaching of acorns, and was actively used as such to prepare millions of acorns for human consumption. No doubt such a valuable resource would need to be guarded against both four and two-legged raiders. As suggested by Eirik Thorsgard, Cultural Protection Coordinator, Confederated Tribes of the Grand Ronde Community of Oregon "the main village was most likely Cathlahnahquiah located just up the slough on the island, or the Cathlahcommahtups village located on the main land where the Willamette and the channel meet. People were most likely checking this site rather intensively and looking to protect the resources from animals as well as other unaffiliated Tribes" (Eirik Thorsgard, Personal Communication 2008)

5.3 Wood

5.3.1 Introduction

Woodworking appears to be a common activity at the Sunken Village site. The following reports a sample of the abundant wood chip and split wood debris and resulting artifacts found throughout the wet site area.

5.3.2 Split Wood Analysis from TU4

By Jason Channel and Dale Croes

5.3.2.1 SPLIT WOOD DEBITAGE

The excavation of Test Unit 4 (TU4), with numerous vegetal mats and its waterlogged preservation, produced 523 examples of split wood, the vast majority of which appear to be split cedar (*Thuja plicata*). The entire site produced about 947 split wood pieces, with remaining counts (424, 45%) in the drainage trenches of TU1–3 and the Pit P/Feature 2 100% excavation (full data in Appendix G:264, see website: http://www.library.spscc. ctc.edu/crm/JWA9.pdf and artifact distribution patterns, above). Therefore, over 55% of the split wood was recorded from TU4 (an excavation representing only a 1 × 1 × 0.5 m area, or 0.5 cubic m volume), and provides the sample used here to characterize the split wood production.

The measurement of the split-cedar (N=523) debitage illustrates a strong unimodal distribution of length, width and thickness, so did not demonstrate the construction of a distinct series of split wood artifacts types at the site. The only other wet site where split-cedar stick debitage has been similarly reported lies north along the West Coast; it is the considerably earlier Hoko River site (45CA240), where the split wood debitage (sample N=1,414) also is unimodal in its length and width measurements, though multi-modal in distributions for thickness (Croes 1995, 160–165). A contemporary wet site on southern Puget Sound is Qwu?gwes, however split wood debitage is extremely rare, though antler and wooden wedges are found, so probably reflects the lack of a need to process split wood items at that particular location. We will make direct comparisons to the split wood measured at Sunken Village and Hoko River wet sites, as the only two sites where measurements are compiled at this time.

Length
At Sunken Village and Hoko River the split cedar debitage lengths are relatively short, averaging 5 cm, ±4 cm, at both sites (Sunken Village: Mean=4.99, SD=3.55, N=523; Hoko River: Mean=4.97, SD=4.21, N=1,414 (Croes 1995, 160); charts showing the length distribution for both sites are available in Croes *et al.* 2006, 2007a). A number of the Sunken Village examples have burnt ends, possibly reflecting their use as kindling pieces in starting fires (possibly a major purpose for these small split cedar sticks and reason we only get small pieces?). Also these small lengths may in part have been the result of pre- and/or post-depositional breakage, as well as possibly some damage caused in recovery and conservation.

Width
At Sunken Village the average width of split wood is less than a cm, averaging 0.8 cm, ± 0.4, whereas at Hoko River the average at 1cm, ±0.7 cm, being wider by average and a wider range of distribution (Sunken Village Mean=0.77 cm, SD=0.39, N=523; Hoko River Mean=1.04 cm, SD=0.71, N=1,414 (Croes 1995, 160); width distribution charts in Croes *et al.* 2006, 2007a). For one, the average reflects the average cedar "arrow" shaft diameters recovered at Sunken Village (mean =0.76 cm, SD =0.073 cm, N=8), and therefore the cedar board "blank" from which the square arrow "blanks" would be split (probably with an adze as replicated in experiments) to an approximately 0.8 cm square stick. However arrow shaft production is probably not a major industry at the site from the small numbers of split cedar stick debitage that fit this range of width and thickness (approximately 0.8 × 0.8 cm; see below, 5.3.2.2, Arrow Shaft section).

Thickness
Distribution of split cedar debitage thickness at Sunken Village is skewed unimodal and is relatively thin, with an average of 0.4 cm, ±0.2 cm., whereas Hoko River was slightly larger with an average of 0.5 cm, ±0.4 cm (Sunken Village: Mean=0.33, SD=0.19, N=523, Hoko River: Mean=0.47, SD=0.37, N=1,414 (Croes 1995, 160); width distribution charts in Croes *et al.* 2006, 2007a). Hoko River also had a multi-modal distribution of thicknesses, thought to reflect a number of thicknesses sought in making such items as micro-lith fish knives at the site (Croes 1995, 160–163).

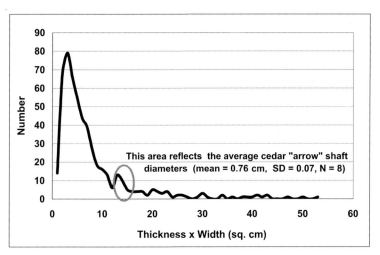

Figure 5.9 Sunken Village split-cedar debitage thickness by width (square cm) measurement distribution (in sq. cm, N=523).

Thickness × Width – Square CM of Split Wood Pieces
To see another dimension of the split wood elements, we ran a thickness by width measure, and found one slightly bi-model blip in the curve where the square cm average for cedar 'arrow' shaft blanks would occur (Figure 5.9). Though not indicative of a major focus on making cedar blanks for shaft production, it probably reflects their production at the site.

5.3.2.2 BROKEN "ARROW" SHAFTS AT 35MU4. (TABLE 5.1)
Eight whittled and formed cedar shafts were recorded in our limited excavations, five being from TU4, two from TU1 lower drainage trenches 5 and 6, and one from a vegetal mat excavation (Feature 1). The shafts were probably whittled with blade-like flakes (see Loffler, below). In Dennis Torresdal's collection from Sauvie Island a notched and formed arrow shaft (and bow end) are seen, documenting that in fact these cedar shafts from our excavations are likely from arrow shafts. The collected arrow shaft has a wide diameter of 0.91 cm, narrow diameter of 0.85 cm and average diameter of 0.88 cm. The 8 broken cedar shafts recovered at 35MU4 have a mean diameter of 0.76 cm (SD=0.07 cm) – similar to the collected arrow cedar shaft
    In the split wood debitage examples of likely 'blanks' split from the ends of approximately 0.8 cm wide boards were recorded and these were replicated using adzes – one example with a cedar split wood ancient blank is shown in Figure 5.10, left.

5.3.2.3 BOX FRAGMENTS?
Some of the cedar split wood was about the right thickness to have been bentwood

Transect	TU/F ea	Trench	Level	Material	Length	Wide Dia	Narrow Dia	Ave. Dia	Bag #
VI	4		10–20	Cedar	8.91	0.70	0.62	0.66	1
VI	4		10–20	Cedar	2.98	0.84	0.82	0.83	2
VI	4		30–40	Cedar	4.20	0.71	0.61	0.66	1
VI	4		30–40	Cedar	14.70	0.78	0.68	0.73	2
VI	4		40–50	Cedar	15.50	0.80	0.84	0.82	1
VI	1	5	10–20	Cedar	5.58	0.83	0.70	0.77	1
VI	1	7	10–20	Cedar	8.53	0.89	0.80	0.85	1
VI	Fea 1			Cedar	4.78	0.81	0.64	0.72	1
Dennis Torresdal Collection				Cedar	25.1	9.05	8.45	0.88	

Table 5.1. Measurements and distribution of carved cedar "arrow" shafts from 35MU4.

Figure 5.10. (left) Example of ancient split wood cedar "arrow" blank and replicated example, split off a 0.8 cm wide split cedar board. (center and right) Example of a cedar split wood piece that appears to have an angle cut at the end which could be a kerf from a bent-wood box fragment.

box pieces, as seen at Ozette and also whole bentwood boxes were recorded in Jacques DeKalb's collection from Sauvie Island (Photo 21, Newman 1990). One example had signs of notching or grooving to create a corner kerf on a box (Figure 5.10, right).

Figure 5.11. Example of split wood timber from Sunken Village (35MU4).

5.3.2.4 SPLIT WOOD TIMBER

One larger split cedar timber was found at the site, measuring in cross-section 9 cm wide × 7 cm thick and 51 cm long (Art No. TV, TU-2, Tr 8, 10–20cm). This timber was no doubt split out using wedges, such as the wooden wedge described above (Figure 4.2, Figure 5.11).

5.3.2 Woodchip Analysis from TU4

By Kathleen L. Hawes and Tyler Graham

5.3.3.1 WOODCHIP CHARACTERIZATION, IDENTIFICATION AND MEASUREMENTS

490 woodchips have been analyzed from the Sunken Village site, Transect VI, Test Unit 4 (TU4; full data in Appendix H:275; see website: http://www.library.spscc.ctc.edu/crm/JWA9.pdf). These woodchips were likely produced using the common stone-bladed adze (or celt) of the Central Northwest Coast of North America – typically an elbow and/or D-shaped wooden handle is used and a nephrite ground stone adze bit/blade (see below). Each TU4 woodchip has been measured by length, width, and thickness; measurements are also taken of the angles of adze blade entry: angle-in, where the adze blade first enters the wood in the cutting process, and angle-out, the point where the opposite end of the wood chip leaves the tree or rest of the wood item (Figure 5.12). The woodchip profiles also were recorded, which is related to the type of cutting tool used. A flat profile tends to be a product of shaving or planing. Triangular woodchips are produced by heavier shaving or light adzing; trapezoidal woodchips result from heavy adzing, chopping or carving. The parallelogram profile is possibly produced

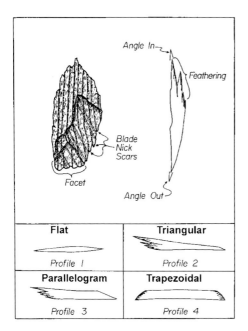

Figure 5.12. Woodchip nomenclature as illustrated by Gleeson 2005:218.

Figure 5.13. Sunken Village Transect V, Stake A, with bark on stake and numerous facets; identified by cellular analysis as Noble fir (Abies procera).

by angle adzing or chisel reduction (Gleeson 2005). Woodchips are also analyzed for feathering, which occurs at the point of blade entry, and also for faceting, which is the result of multiple cuts through the wooden object.

The most frequent profile found from TU4 is trapezoidal, which is produced by heavy adzing, chopping or carving. 78 woodchips (27%) TU4 showed faceting, a result of multiple carving; the majority of faceted woodchips were found (43%) in the 40–50 cm level. Of the discrete artifacts recovered, the wooden yew wedge (Figure 4.2) and the two stakes showed evidence of carving with numerous faceting (Figure 5.13).

A 5% sample of the 490 woodchips was taken from TU4 for cellular analysis and identification. Of the 25 woodchips analyzed, the majority (33%, N=8) were Western yew (Taxus brevifolia); of which 5 were found at the 40–50 cm level (Table 5.2). Half of the yew woodchips revealed faceting, possibly created as debitage from wedge sharpening. Two wooden wedges were excavated in 2006, both showing adzing and identified by cellular analysis as Western yew (Figures 4.2–4.4). Two woodchips from the 30–40 cm level were identified as Pinus species (8%), and one sample each of Western hemlock (Tsuga heterophylla), Sitka spruce (Picea sitchensis), western red cedar (Thuja plicata), Cascara buckthorn (Rhamnus purshiana), willow (Salix spp.) and one woodchip that remained unidentified (Table 5.2). Though a small sample, the results show the considerable diversity of woods used in woodworking from the site.

Level (cm)	Taxus brevifolia	Quercus garryana	Pseudotsuga menziesii	Alnus rubra	Pinus spp	Tsuga heterophylla
0–10 cm	1	1				
10–20 cm		1	1	2		
20–30 cm	1	1		1		
30–40 cm	1		1		2	1
40–50 cm	5		1			
Totals	8	3	3	3	2	1

Level (cm)	Picea sitchensis	Thuja plicata	Rhamus purshiana	Salix spp.	unidentified
0–10 cm					
10–20 cm		1			
20–30 cm			1	1	1
30–40 cm					
40–50 cm	1				
Totals	1	1	1	1	1

Table 5.2. Identification of wood chips through plant cellular analysis, 5% sample from TU4.

Comparisons of woodchip profiles of the four reported wet sites show interesting differences (Figure 5.14). At the Hoko River site, the majority of woodchips analyzed were found to be triangular. At the Ozette Village House 1, the majority were flat; at Qwu?gwes, woodchips were mostly parallelogram. At the Sunken Village site, the woodchips analyzed were trapezoidal in profile. This may reflect different types of tools used.

A composite chart of the woodchips according to angle-in, angle-out, length, width and thickness measurements, demonstrates that the main difference between reported Northwest Coast wet sites is the angle-in and -out measurements (Figure 5.15). Measurements of the width, thickness and length show remarkable similarities, with Hoko River showing a slight difference in length. Sunken Village shows the greatest degree of angle-in and out, again probably reflecting a different kind and/or variety of wood working tools used at 35MU4.

Charts of the actual distribution of Sunken Village site woodchip measurements, and the comparisons of the mean, standard deviation and sample sizes at reported wet sites of Ozette House 1, Hoko River, Water Hazard and Qwu?gwes are illustrated in Croes, Fagan and Zehendner 2006, 2007a). The full data spreadsheets for TU4 woodchips are in Appendix H:275; see website: http://www.library.spscc.ctc.edu/crm/JWA9.pdf.

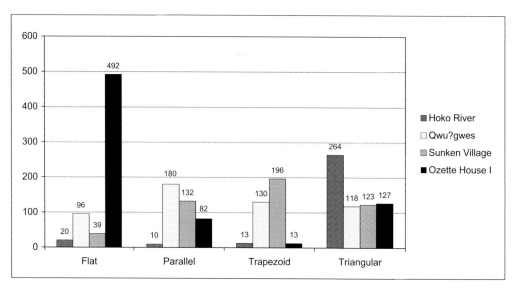

Figure 5.14. Comparison of woodchip profiles from reported Wet Sites on the Northwest Coast.

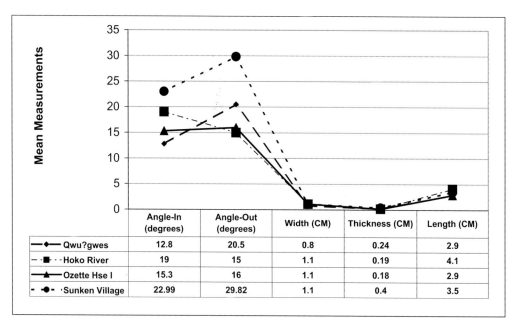

Figure 5.15 Mean woodchip measurements from Northwest Coast wet sites.

Figure 5.16. (above) Adze bits and table of corresponding angles; (below) Replicated elbow adze with nephrite stone bit used in replication experiments.

5.3.3.2 REPLICATING WOODCHIPS

We have used experimental archaeology to replicate woodchips. Four adze blades have been made from nephrite using, in the interest of time, an electric grinder with both diamond and silicon carbide grinding wheels. Adze bit #1 was made by Tyler Graham, who had no woodworking experience at the time. Bit #2 was designed by Michael Ogden, a Squaxin Island Tribal member and apprentice canoe builder. Bits #3 and #4 were based on ancient adze bits excavated from the Qwu?gwes wet site. The angles of the blades were measured from the point of the cutting end and measured for a top and bottom angle (Figures 5.16).

Working with experts in wood working allowed us to gain understanding of how the adzes worked and why. Squaxin Master Carvers Andrea and Steve Sigo along with Michael Ogden examined bit #1 and decided that it was not well formed for adzing, as the bottom angle on the blade was too steep and didn't gently curve into the body of

Fig. 5.17. Two views of an ancient cedar woodchip with splitwood characteristics. In profile view on right, note angle-in (right end) and angle-out (left end).

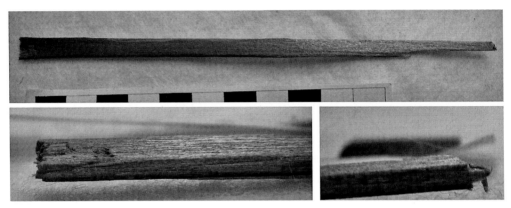

Fig. 5.18. Experimental Western Red Cedar woodchip displaying rectangular profile. In profile view, note the lack of an angle-in or angle-out. Scale in cm.

the bit. When used properly, this causes the blade to hit on the flat length of the bottom angle rather than at the point, which does the cutting. For bit #1 to work the blade had to be held at a steeper angle to wood which changed the motion from adzing to chopping and would mark the wood with chopping marks. Working with Squaxin carvers allowed us to gain understanding of how the adzes should be formed and why.

When adzing Western red cedar, we noticed that not all the woodchips fitted Gleeson's Woodchip Profiles (Figure 5.12). It was first noticed in the heartwood of an old growth piece of cedar which produced woodchips that showed noticeable splitwood characteristics (Table 5.3). We tested a small sample from a piece of cedar that has both the sapwood and heart wood. Split wood characteristics were observed on the sapwood, but to a lesser extent. Some of the heartwood with split wood characteristics produced angle-in and angle-out close to or at 90 degrees which does not fit into Gleeson's Profiles. Tentatively, a 5th profile, named rectangular, has been added to account for these woodchips (compare Figures 5.17 and Figure 5.18; see also Table 5.3). This may account for the high numbers and unimodal distribution of the length, width and thickness of split wood pieces recorded by Channel and Croes (Figures 5.9–5.11), meaning that many of these rectangular profile split wood pieces are actually the result of adzing, creating rectangular profile woodchips, versus intentional splitting. Though both were no doubt occurring, adzing now needs to be considered a likely part of the production of many of these split wood pieces.

Adze	Wood	N =	Percentage with Splitwood Characteristics
2	W. Red Cedar Heartwood	48	65.96%
3	W. Red Cedar Heartwood	17	64.71%
3	W. Red Cedar Sapwood	13	38.46%

Table 5.3. Splitwood characteristics from adzing.

	Adze 1	Adze 2	Adze 3	Adze 3	Adze 4
Wood Type	W. Red Cedar	W. Red Cedar	W. Red Cedar	Western Yew	N/A
Woodchips sampled	54	48	30	76	N/A
Length (cm)					
Mean	3.22	2.56	3.68	5.84	N/A
Standard Dev	2.94	2.90	2.28	5.47	N/A
Thickness (cm)					
Mean	0.22	0.47	0.30	0.24	N/A
Standard Dev	0.10	0.27	0.24	0.23	N/A
Width (cm)					
Mean	0.88	0.96	1.42	1.51	N/A
Standard Dev	0.37	0.44	0.61	0.79	N/A
Angle-In (Degrees)					
Mean	50.17	57.35	39.30	20.20	N/A
Standard Dev	19.72	20.95	16.08	9.09	N/A
Angle-Out (Degrees)					
Mean	22.56	38.00	20.30	13.41	N/A
Standard Dev	23.89	34.24	21.59	8.71	N/A

Table 5.4. Measurements of replicated woodchips. Adze #4 broke before a sample could be obtained.

Measuring the replicated woodchips has not shown a connection between the adzes used and woodchips excavated from sites, especially Qwu?gwes. Adze bit #4 is not represented as there was a flaw in the cutting edge which caused it to break before a sample could be gathered. The high standard deviations of the replicated woodchips may be from having a sample that is more representative of adzing than those that we excavated – which could have been produced by blade-like flake whittling as well (see Löffler, below). The steep angle-in on the cedar could result from an increase in woodchips showing splitwood characteristics as the angle-in drops when sapwood is introduced, which tends to produce more typical woodchips than heartwood. It also may not be accurately reflected in this archaeological record where many woodchips may have been classified as strictly split wood, rather than woodchips with split wood characteristics (Tables 5.3 and 5.4).

5.3.3.3 SUMMARY AND CONCLUSIONS

The analysis of Sunken Village woodchips, when compared to those from all other reported Northwest Coast wet site, reveals that the length, width and thickness of ancient wood chips, regardless of the time period or location, are remarkably similar. The main distinguishing characteristic were: (1) the profiles of the woodchips, being quite different at each site, with Sunken Village profiles diverse, but emphasizing trapezoidal profiles, and (2) the woodchip angle-in and -out measurement, with Sunken Village having the widest degree in both cases.The logical conclusion is that the tools vary among these sites, creating different profiles and angles-in and -out of the woodchips at each site. Before the analyses of Qwu?gwes and Sunken Village, the differences between Hoko River and Ozette Village wet sites were suggested to be the result of using metal tools at the late Ozette site and nephrite adze bits as found at the early Hoko River site (Croes 1995:164–167). Qwu?gwes and Sunken Village may be late enough to have had the presence of metal bits, though Qwu?gwes also has nephrite blades (N=3). Sunken Village has a very limited excavation compared to the other wet sites, but produced a large amount of split wood and woodchips (and some wood working tools in the form of wooden wedges, as well as a corner of a nephrite-like bit).

The use of experimental archaeology has revealed differences in woodchip profiles produced by nephrite adze bits of varying angles, with characteristics unique to each bit. The type of wood also contributed to differences in replicated woodchip angles, with a new category (rectangular) added to document these differences. From this experimental archaeology, we realized that a large amount of the split cedar wood pieces may actually be woodchips of the rectangular profile, and actually helps account for the unimodally distributed length, width and thickness in the split cedar wood so common to the site.

Other sites in the Portland Basin have produced rather rare nephrite adze blades and a thicker cobble celt (Pettigrew 1981, 1990). Possibly nephrite was in low supply in this region, and the larger cobble celts were more often used, producing the widest wood chip angle-in and -out measurements at Sunken Village. Further comparisons with other sites in the Portland Basin and continued excavation of Sunken Village may provide a greater insight into the types of tools used and items created, including possible adzes complete with wooden handles. Until adze bits and other woodworking tools are found, continued experimental archaeology will give insight into common woodworking activities at Sunken Village.

5.4 Fiber – Basketry, Cordage and Binding Curls

5.4.1 Introduction

Fiber artifacts are common from Sunken Village, typically made of roots, sedges, limbs/boughs and barks. In reporting fiber artifacts of basketry, cordage and binding materials, we find a new level of stylistic sensitivity, demonstrating artifact types that can be compared broadly, possibly showing cultural style guarding and sharing throughout the region and possibly north Pacific.

5.4.2 Basketry Types, Cladistic Comparative Analysis, Construction Waste Elements, Native Weavers Perspectives and Experimental Archaeology

By Olivia Ness, Dale Croes, Robert Kentta, Bud Lane, and Pat Courtney Gold

5.4.2.1 BASKETRY TYPES

In our limited two investigations of the Sunken Village site, four distinct types of basketry were recovered: (1) cedar bark checker weave matting, (2) shredded cedar bark capes/skirt fragment, (3) open cross-warp twined cedar root basket, and (4) diamond-plaited fragment (probably a section from a large soft bag). Decades of private collecting have produced many other examples and types of basketry items, but none of these have been recorded *in situ*, so our finds tend to validate those collections as from 35MU4. When analyzing these items, we look at seven different attributes, which are as follows: material, bottom weave, body weave, gauge of weave, lean of twine, shape and selvage (the finished edge of a basketry piece, i.e. the rim of a basket).

In total, seven fragments of **cedar bark checker weave matting** have been recovered from the site (one in 2006 and six in 2007). Their measurements and distributions are recorded in Table 5.5

The construction material of fragments 2006–1 and 2007–6 have been confirmed to be cedar bark based on cellular analysis (see Hawes, above; Figure 4.7). The remaining pieces were identified visually based on comparison of the former two fragments. Since all seven pieces of matting were discovered in fragmented condition, selvage and shape are unknown. However, fragment 2007–6 has a three strand braid (25 cm long × 1.9 cm wide in the middle) extending from one corner (Figure 5.19). This same technique has been found at the Ozette Village Archaeological Site located along the Northwest Pacific Coast, approximately 18 miles south of Cape Flattery, WA (classified as OM2, Croes 1977). The mat, which results in a checker on bias weave, is initiated from the three strand braid extension. This piece also appears to have some decorative grass (genus unknown) overlay (Figure 5.20).

Artifact #	Transect	Pit	Length (cm)	Width (cm)	Gauge of Weave Stitches per 2.5 cm
2006–1	V	AB	25	16.5	3
2007–1	III	F	17.1	13.5	2.5–4
2007–2	III	F	9.2	3.4	4–5
2007–3	III	F	13.8	5.2	2.5–5
2007–4	V	J	13.5	11.7	3–5
2007–5	V	AD	3.8	3.2	4.5
2007–6	VI	D	26	18	2.5–5

Table 5.5. Cedar bark checker weave matting fragments.

Figure 5.19. Cedar bark checker weave matting fragment with 3 strand braid extension on righthand side (2007-basketry #6, Transect VI, Pit D; scale in cm).

Figure 5.20. Close-up of 2007-basketry #6, Transect VI, Pit D checker matting (Figure 5.19) illustrating fine decorative grass overlay (see remnants of grass overlay at arrows).

Figure 5.21. Shredded cedar bark cape or skirt with twined edge (scale mm).

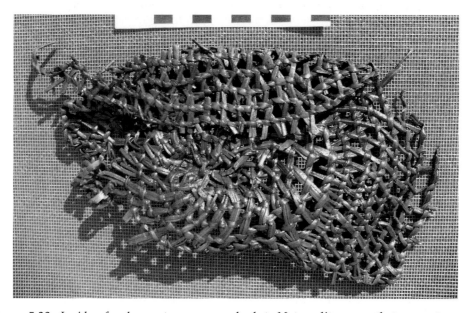

Figure 5.22. Inside of cedar root cross-warp basket. Note split warps that are not crossed creating the transition from base to basket body (cm scale).

The small **shredded cedar bark cape/skirt fragment** was excavated from Transect V, Pit P, BF (Figure 5.21) and measures 7.5 cm wide and 8.5 cm long in area. The selvage consists of plain twined, double strand twisted (Z lay) cedar string, twining together shredded cedar strips with a gauge of 3 stitches per 2.5 cm. The body is comprised of shredded cedar bark. The shape is unknown since only fragments of this piece were found.

The **open twined cross-warp cedar root basket** excavated from Transect V, Pit R, is our best example of ethnographic Chinookan basketry (Figures 5.22–5.24, and see

Figure 5.23. Outside base of cedar root cross-warp basket (cm scale).

Figure 5.24. Close up of cedar root cross-warp basket excavated from 35MU4. Note the Z lay (up to the left – see arrows) and splitting of the warps, which are not crossed, to make the transition between basket base and body (cm scale).

Frontispiece). It measures 11 cm wide and 21 cm long in area. The warp and weft construction material has been confirmed to be split and thinned cedar root, through cellular analysis (see Hawes, above, Figure 4.1). The weave of the bottom and body are classified as open cross-warp twine with a gauge of 6–7 stitches per 2.5 cm. The lean of the twine is up to the left, also known as Z lay. The basket's shape and selvage are unknown since the upper section of the body has been broken off. The intact portion of the body ascends up to seven rows of twining at the highest point from the edge transition of the base. We are referring to the edge of the base as a row in which the warps are split in two and do not cross (Figures 5.22–5.24). This will be discussed further under experimental archaeology.

The ***diamond-plaited soft bag fragment*** (Figures 5.25–5.27) constructed from a sedge material is the most unique basketry artifact from the site, sparking great interest far beyond the Northwest Coast. Upon discovery, the weave technique was unclear due to

Figure 5.25. Hydraulic uncovering of the delicate diamond plaited sedge soft bag from one of the Sunken Village acorn leaching pits (Transect VI, PitG; see Figure 3.4c).

Figure 5.26. The diamond plaiting technique is much clearer after turning over and careful cleaning of sediments from the woven piece (cm scale).

natural erosion of the wefts on the exposed side, which consequently revealed rows of strings serving as warps (there has been debate in regards to which element was used for warp or weft in the weaving process, but for continuity we will refer to the woven elements as aforementioned). However, once the piece was turned over in the lab and the unexposed side cleaned (due to the fragile nature of this soft bag it was removed from the ground with about 2–3 cm of soil still attached to the underside), the wefts were visible, revealing that this weave is a technique known as 'diamond plaiting' (Margaret Mathewson, Personal Communications 2007). The piece measures 42.5 cm long by 35 cm wide. The warps are comprised of twisted two strand Z lay strings with a gauge of 4–5 stitches per 2.5 cm and a diameter averaging 0.38 cm. The string warps are placed approximately 1.2 cm apart, making the gauge of weave about 2 stitches per 2.5 cm. A fragment of selvage discovered still intact has been classified by the technique known as 'turned in' (Croes 1977, 126). The construction material has not yet been identified beyond familial classification, but is in the sedge family (see Hawes above, Figure 4.8).

Figure 5.27. (left) Close up of delicate sedge material woven over 2-strand strings in a diamond plaiting technique to create what appears to be a soft bag; (right) Replication of this weave using Scirpus americanus, a sedge called sweet grass in the Northwest (for additional information on replication see experimental archaeology section below).

Diamond-plaited basketry has been found in a variety of places beyond the North American Northwest Coast. The Sunken Village piece has caught the attention of Great Basin basketry experts Dr. Catherine Fowler (University of Nevada, Reno, Nevada, U.S.A.), Dr. Eugene Hattori (Nevada State Museum, Las Vegas, Nevada, U.S.A). and basketry consultant Dr. Margaret Mathewson. They potentially see this artifact linking to very ancient soft bags examples of the U.S. Great Basin, especially from Spirit Cave (9,400 B.P. examples; Figure 5.28 left), through to museum collections from the Puget Sound (see Figure 5.29). Catherine points out that these diamond-plaited soft bags have interesting similarities with current Japanese Ainu soft bag weaves and also examples from ancient Japanese Jomon sites (Figures 5.28 right and 5.29 left). With this in mind, we contacted our co-sponsor Dr. Akira Matsui who indicated that a Jomon site he is helping to direct, the Higashimyo site on the southern island of Kyushu dating to over 7,000 B.P., has examples of diamond plaiting called *Goza-me-Ori*, referring to a woven rush mat (Ness *et al.* 2007). In Northwest Coast museum collections this kind of distinct flat bag, constructed from sedges similar to sweet-grass, is seen in some Puget Sound assemblages, though some are twined over 2–strand strings. We have recorded some of these examples at the Thomas Burke Memorial Washington State Museum, University of Washington, Seattle, U.S.A. (Figure 5.29 right).

Therefore, this Sunken Village style of a distinct diamond-plaited soft-bag, made with sedge or rush materials, is seen as a potentially linking artifact between ancient Great Basin finds and the Puget Sound. Drs. Fowler and Hattori further point out that this distinct soft bag and weave are seen in Oregon Klamath Indians' ancient

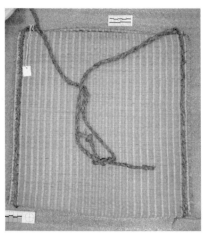

Figure 5.28. (left) Ancient Spirit Cave diamond-plaited rush soft bag from Nevada (dating to 9,400 B.P.; courtesy Nevada State Museum, Carson City; illustrated by Karen Beyers); (right) Japanese diamond-plaited rush soft bag collected in the 1950s (courtesy University of Washington. Thomas Burke Memorial Museum)

Figure 5.29. (left) Ancient Japanese Jomon, twined over cord soft bag (courtesy Dr. Naoto Yamamoto); (right) Puget Sound Salish, vertically twined over cordage rush soft bag.

(approximately 550 BP) and museum basketry (personal communications, 2008). With similar diamond-plaited soft bag techniques found in ancient Japanese Jomon wet sites in addition to current Japanese Ainu collections, this may be one of the few artifact styles that can be traced around the North Pacific Rim. We plan to further explore this possibility through visits between Japanese and U.S. researchers and possibly Ainu and Northwest Coast Tribes. For additional information on diamond plaiting see *Foreword* by Eirik Thorsgard in Section 1.12 above, and conclusion Section 6.2 below.

5.4.2.2 Cladistic Analysis and comparisons to other Northwest Coast Ancient Wet Sites and Ethnographic Collections

We compared the recovered Sunken Village ancient basketry to those from other Northwest Coast Wet Sites (Figure 5.30) using cladistic analysis as done previously for other Northwest Coast Wet Sites by Croes *et al.* (2005). In addition, we added data

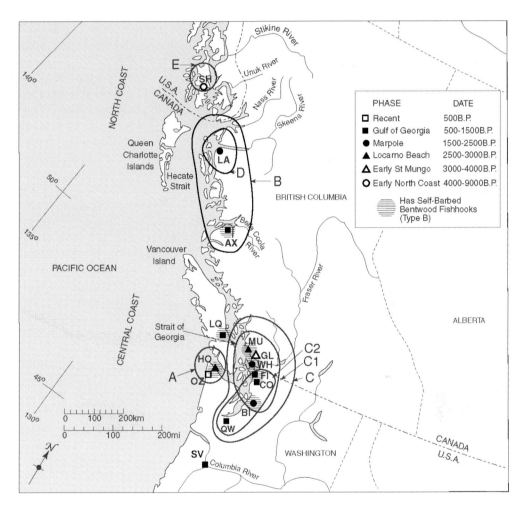

Figure 5.30. Northwest Coast wet site distributions showing major areas A and C of ancient basketry style continuity, and position of the Sunken Village wet site (see Croes, Kelly and Collard 2005 for details of basketry style continuity and also compare with our cladogram below). Site key: SH=Silver Hole (49CCRG433), LA=Lachane (GbTo-33), Ax=Axeti (FaSu-1), LQ=Little Qualicum (DiSc-1), MU=Musqueam NE (DhRt-4), GL=Glenrose Cannery (Dg Rr-6) WH=Water Hazard (DgRs-30), FI=Fishtown (45SK99), CO=Conway (45SK59b), BI=Biederbost (45SN100), QW=Qwu?gwes (45TN240), SV=Sunken Village (35MU4), HO=Hoko (45CA213), and OZ=Ozette (45CA24). (Map adapted from original by Susan Matson).

from ethnographic museum collections, mostly obtained from Joan Megan Jones' M.A. and Ph.D. dissertations (1968, 1976), as well as our own recording of Chinook museum baskets, to see if there was continuity of basketry style and technique from ancient times into post-contact times.

Cladistics defines phylogenetic relationship in terms of relative recency of common ancestry. A pair of taxa is deemed to be more closely related to one another than either is to a third taxon if they share a common ancestor that is not also shared by the third taxon. This exclusive common ancestry is indicated by evolutionary, novel or derived character states. Ultimately, cladistic analysis seeks to find a special similarity rather than overall similarities. Basketry is an ideal artifact for this type of analysis since it is highly culturally sensitive and the knowledge behind it is heavily guarded. With a growing ancient Northwest Coast basketry database, we have conducted several basketry attribute (mode) presence/absence comparative analyses (Croes *et al.* 2005).

When the limited Sunken Village basketry attributes are added to the test, using just ancient Northwest Coast wet sites, we preliminarily see how this Chinookan region compares with others from the ancient past. Cladistically, using an unrooted cladogram, Sunken Village basketry is a branch all its own, associating with other wet sites that do not easily exhibit ancestry with other sites (Figure 5.31). The best ancestral clustering remains with the 3,000 year old series in ancient Coast Salish sites and Wakashan sites (which are polar opposites for 3,000 years).

Private collections from the Sunken Village site and museum collections of Chinook origin have recently been recorded and added to this database along with previously recorded attributes of museum collections spanning twelve decades and ten cultures along the Northwest Coast of North America (Jones 1976). In an attempt to focus on relatively frequent attributes, therefore demonstrating distinct cultural styles, we have only included weave attributes of a given culture that have a frequency greater than five spanning all twelve decades. It should be noted that Jones' data includes 2,840 baskets, therefore making our exclusion of specimens with a frequency of five or less a relatively marginal proportion. However, we did include all of the Chinook museum collections since we have only had access to 35 baskets to record so far. Additionally, we split Jones' ethnographic data into two temporal blocks (1820–1879 and 1880–1939) per culture. In the decades that this data spanned, many changes took place in Northwest Coast Native life. Basketry forms no doubt reflected these vast and largely post-contact transformations. Basketry became less of a necessity for daily functions and more of a commodity to be traded with settlers and tourists in exchange for money or credit, a new necessity. Between the 1880s and the 1930s this trade flourished which in turn sparked innovation from weavers as well as an emphasis on design opposed to function (Wray in prep. 2009). Despite these changes, we hope to demonstrate a continuity of transmitted cultural knowledge from the very ancient sites through to both the early and late ethnographic eras.

Furthermore, we decided to concentrate on base and body weaves since these attributes appear to be the most flexible in terms of innovations through time and space, and possibly best represent cultural evolution that is less affected by function. Croes, who worked with Makah basket weavers for about thirty years, witnessed some changes in base and body weaves over that time period, often with no functional consequences (a

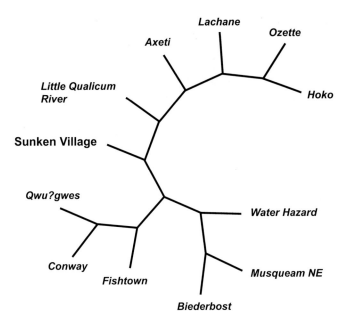

Figure 5.31. Unrooted cladogram derived from Northwest Coast wet site basketry attributes. The Sunken Village Site lies on a branch along with a series of other sites that are spatially and temporally not related – indicating Sunken Village basketry really did not fall into a good branching series. The best ancestral series shown is the bottom series of sites (Coast Salish basketry for 3,000 years, area C in map, Figure 5.30) and the top branch (Wakashan basketry for 3,000 years, area A in map, Figure 5.30). For details and discussion of all the sites, besides Sunken Village, see Croes et al. 2005, 137–149.

form of transmission change as seen in 'gene flow'). In one case there was an intentional style change amongst weavers from plaited cedar bark checker weave basket bases to plaited twill weave. One master weaver, Isabell Ides (74 at the time), wanted to make the change, and depended on her husband, Harold, to make her basket bases with twill weave, eventually taking over after a couple of years. In another case a weaver in training, Kibby (Vivian) Lawrence, made a mistake in applying the duck design on her body weave, placing the bill 'dot' on the back of the head – making the duck look backwards. The weaving group found great humor in this mistake ('mutation') and Kibby was encouraged to carry it on as her trademark weave pattern. These changes involved innovation versus direct functional impact – the basket was really the same kind of basket.

Our cladistic analysis of ancient and museum basket, both body and base weaves, resulted in 22 possible unrooted cladograms (using the software program PAUP with the following commands: *parsimony* as the criterion, the Silver Hole wet site as the *outgroup* – being the oldest site dating to approximately 6000 BP, and *random* as the addition

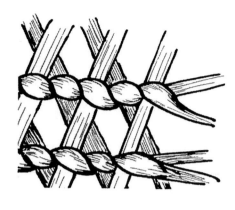

Figure 5.32. Chinook twined wallet and diagram to show cross-warp twining with a Z lay, from 1904 publication by Otis Mason (1904:234, Plate 166). This style of basket is unique to this southern region, and almost all twined baskets from ancient Northwest Coast wet sites from Puget Sound north have an S lay twining.

sequence under the **heuristic search**). Each of these cladograms is an equally valid outcome possibility based on the base and body weaves compared. All 22 cladograms kept Sunken Village and Chinook Museum basketry as their own and separate branch, demonstrating their cultural affiliation from ancient to recent times, and their separation from other Northwest Coast ancient and museum basketry, undoubtedly showing a distinct Chinookan basketry transmission in this region. A distinct form of Chinookan basketry from Sunken Village, found in our excavations, recorded several times in artifact collections from the site, and also common in Chinook Museum collections, is the cross-warp twined, spiral base, conical baskets (Figure 5.32).

We next generated a **strict consensus** tree generated from all 22 cladograms (Figure 5.33). Like all of the cladograms, this one shows a relatively good affiliation of ancient Northwest Coast basketry with their counter-parts in the museum collections. The 6,000 year old Silver Hole basket from the Prince of Wales Island links with Tlingit and Haida museum baskets (area E in the map, Figure 5.30). The 3,000 year old Hoko River basketry links in with a branch leading to Nootkan Museum baskets (area A in the map, Figure 5.30). The one unexpected divide is between the ancient and museum Salishan basketry. Most of the ancient Salishan basketry (Musqueam NE, Biederbost, Water Hazard and Conway) is displayed in a fanning cluster in the center of the cladogram which links across to the other two ancient Salishan sites (Qwu?gwes and Fishtown, area C in the map, Figure 5.30).

The museum Salishan basketry clusters together on the lower left and consistently includes the ancient Ozette baskets (a distinctly Makah/Nuu-chah-nulth/Nootkan late

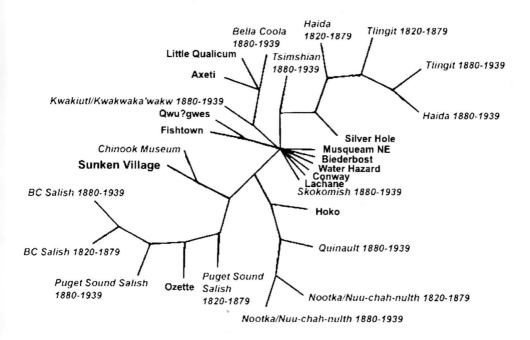

Figure 5.33. Strict consensus unrooted cladogram derived from Northwest Coast wet site and ethnographic museum collection basketry body and base weave attributes. Sunken Village and Chinook Museum basketry lie on their own separate branch, demonstrating their cultural affiliation from ancient to recent times. Their separation from other Northwest Coast ancient and museum basketry undoubtedly shows a distinct Chinookan basketry transmission in this region.

wet site, area A in the map, which typically links to Hoko River, Figures 5.30 and 5.31). In trying to understand this ancient and museum Salishan split, it is noted that *coiled* or sewn baskets are not seen in the ancient Salishan wet sites, although it is present in the late Ozette Village wet site (dated to about 300 years old) and has been characterized as an introduced form of basketry from further east, out of late Salishan areas by Croes (1977, 2001, 2003). In fact, the separation of ancient Salishan wet sites and museum Salishan basketry could very well be the result of a late innovation and introduction of coil basketry from further east, upriver, Plateau Salishan regions. Coil basketry has also been recorded in private collections from Sunken Village as well as Chinookan museum collections, which may explain why this cluster consistently branches out from the same internal node as the Salishan museum cluster.

The fanning cluster of ancient Salishan basketry also includes Skokomish museum collections (a Salishan tribe) and Lachane, a non-Salishan, Tsimshian area ancient site. In previous studies that have additionally included basketry shape and construction material, Lachane has strongly associated with ethnographic Tsimshian museum baskets

(Croes 1989; 1995, 132; 2001). The absence of shape and construction material attributes in our test may be the cause for a split between Lachane and Tsimshian museum basketry, though they are in close proximity in the branching. Additionally, there is a cluster including the ancient Axeti and Little Qualicum along with the Bella Coola and Kwakiutl museum basketry. Although Little Qualicum is farther south than the others, this area is known historically as transitional between Wakashan and Salishan areas (Barnett 1955, 26; Bernick 1983, 154–155; Boas 1888, 201; 1890, 840; Croes 1995, 131). Axeti, in Bella Coola territory, is also in a cultural area completely surrounded and no doubt influenced by Wakashan cultures, and therefore this overall clustering may be due to this transitory condition.

Therefore, based on our comparison of base and body weave techniques (which are proposed to be more closely linked to innovation as opposed to function), we can fairly say that the ancient Northwest Coast wet site baskets generally link through millenniums to their ethnographic counterparts. We believe this shows some of the analytical power of basketry in observing cultural evolution and the guarding of cultural styles in different Northwest Coast regions for thousands of years. After learning of the perceived associations of the distinct diamond plaited soft bags at Sunken Village with those from ancient U.S. Great Basin (at least 9,400 years old) and equally early time periods of the Japanese Jomon (at least 7,000 years old), we now need to expand our systematic testing of shared ancestry into these regions. If these styles follow an ancient continental shelf Pacific Rim, and possibly the entire Pacific Basin distribution, we will demonstrate the first connecting artifacts shared by the original Circum-Pacific cultural area.

5.4.2.3 Observations and Analyses from Regional Master Basketweavers

Pat Courtney Gold, Wasco Master Basket-weaver and member of the Confederated Tribe of Warm Springs, analyzed the Sunken Village cross-warp basket soon after recovery. She made these observations about what she identified as an acorn basket:

> *Touching the Ancestors*
> I had a very emotional and spiritual experience touching a basket remnant dating to 700 years old, approximately. I looked at the basket with awe; the beauty of the basket as if it were woven just a week ago. The cedar warps were approximately ¼ inch wide, the basket was a cross-warp, twined with ⅛ inch wide cedar bark (or root). This technique is exactly the same that I use in my cattail cross-warp baskets. As I touched the basket, handling the warps and wefts, I felt that I was touching the hands of the weaver while she twined and crossed each weft. Her spirit and my spirit connected. I was blessed by an ancient weaver.
> The basket was found in a Chinook Village site along the Lower Columbia River. Sauvie Island (Wapato Island) was a popular trade site. Wapato and acorns grew abundantly on the island. Historically, there were hundreds of Chinook villages in this area. The Chinook Nation stretched along the Columbia River from the mouth to Celilo Falls (near The Dalles, OR). They were a wealthy Nation trading internationally and inter-Tribally. The River provided salmon and steelhead that was processed for consumption and trade. Some goods that were traded included

European beads, cloth, metal objects such as hammers, fish hooks, and cooking pots. Other food sources included deer, elk, wapato, acorns, hazelnuts, root crops, and berries. Unfortunately, in the late 1700s, and again in the 1830s, small pox and malaria epidemics spread along the Columbia River. It is estimated that 85 to 90% of the Chinook population died. The descendants of the survivors continue to live along the Columbia River.

Bud Lane, Vice Chair of the Confederated Tribes of Siletz Indians and Master Basketweaver had these observations about the cedar root basket:

> The wet site work that was done this last fall by Dale Croes and his team at the Sauvie Island Sunken Village site was for us, the members of the Confederated Tribes of Siletz, probably the most valuable site work done on any of our ceded lands to date. Many, many artifacts were found. One in particular really made a connection for me. A twined cedar root basket was found at the site and it looked to me as if it could have been used yesterday, but it was actually in the neighborhood of 700 years old. I am a basket-maker and I use similar materials (spruce root) for my baskets. Cedar and Spruce are very similar.
>
> For me to look at and hold in my hands this very precious basket is something that is not easy to explain. Everyone obtains their knowledge from others and from experience. I teach basketry, and I always tell my students, "no one comes into this world knowing it all, everyone learns and is taught by others, what they know". The processes that we use in gathering, preparing, storing and weaving Siletz baskets have been handed down to us over thousands of years. The process may seem new to a student, but in fact what they are learning is very ancient.
>
> It was probably used for carrying a number of things from acorns to roots, etc. These types of baskets are of a class that we call 'Khee-lu' or openwork and are considered work baskets. They range from large 'burden baskets' we call 'tulh', to smaller openwork baskets, sometimes cross-twined baskets of the Khee-lu class.

Robert Kentta, Member and Councilmember of the Confederated Tribes of Siletz Indians, has been searching throughout the country for baskets said to be either from Sauvie Island or of Chinookan origin. He located one in particular from the Smithsonian Natural History Museum that is said to be Chinook or Quinault. It is constructed of spruce root and bear grass. Robert points out that this basket has a different start (bottom weave) than the Sauvie Island cedar root basket "but it may be very similar in design… (once the sides turn up)" giving us an idea as to how the selvage may have been woven on the Sauvie Island basket.

These cultural experts have significantly aided in our research and added greatly in explaining the Sunken Village artifacts and site. This information cannot be gained from books and, as Lane indicates, is the result of knowledge transmitted through the millennium. These cultural experts have breathed life into what most scientists/ archaeologists consider inanimate objects, changing the way we analyze and appreciate them. We use tools such as cladistics analyses to see the transmission of styles through time, the Tribes carry and transmit that knowledge from these past times.

5.4.2.4 Sunken Village Basketry Waste Materials

When constructing or repairing a basket, waste materials are left behind that may be the product of perfecting the preferred length, thickness, or width of a basketry element, or the result of finishing the selvage of a basketry item (edge clippings).

The basketry construction debris discussed here consists of cedar bark strips, and cedar bough or root splints. Analysis of the distributional patterns and measurement of the debris, have contributed to our understanding of the amount of basketry construction taking place at the site. In addition, analysis of the variations in width and thickness of the debris have contributed to an understanding of the preparation of the basketry elements, and of the types of basketry being made.

The examples of basketry waste materials found at Sunken Village include thinned strips of cedar bark and splints that are presumably edge clippings discarded during manufacturing or repair of basketry items. However some of the bark pieces were not worked to the extent that the splints were. Also unearthed were withy (or withe) remnants and strips with crimp marks suggesting they were at one time basketry elements.

The Hoko River archaeological site located approximately 19 miles east of the northwest tip of the Olympic Peninsula, and the site known as Qwu?gwes located on the Eld inlet of Mud Bay in Olympia, WA, are the only wet sites in which basketry waste elements have been analyzed, therefore they serve as our only sites for comparison (Figure 5.34). The large quantities of waste materials at Hoko (n=1,495) and Qwu?gwes (n=1,119) suggest that basketry manufacturing was a common activity among the inhabitants of these sites. In contrast, the Sunken Village site (n=53) has revealed a much smaller amount of basketry waste materials (Figure 5.34). One suggestion made above in considering all the site debitage (split wood, woodchips, lithics and basketry waste elements) may be that this debitage, especially all the wood working and lithic debris,

Figure 5.34. Varying emphases on cedar bark versus splint basketry waste elements at three recorded Northwest Coast wet sites.

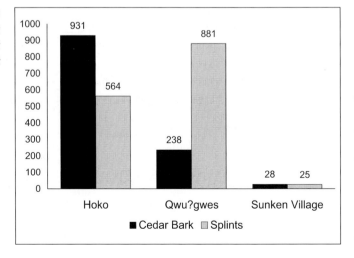

reflects men's activities, as they were guarding acorn provisions, therefore women, who have historically been the primary basket weavers on the Northwest Coast, did not congregate in large numbers at this site over long periods of time. Women were probably primary in collecting and setting up the acorn leaching pits for the processing – an activity intense focus – whereas some men may have been there long-term, guarding the area while doing other things. Alternatively, our results may be due to the limited time of excavation at 35MU4 (roughly three weeks) compared to several full summers of basketry waste materials excavated from Hoko and Qwu?gwes, or we may not have excavated areas of intense basketry production at the Sunken Village site.

Basketry waste materials emphases differ between Qwu?gwes and Hoko River, with a major emphasis on splint (bough or root) material at Qwu?gwes (79%) and a heavier emphasis on cedar bark at Hoko River (62%). These proportions tend to reflect the kinds of basketry production emphasized at these two wet sites. The preliminary and low numbers of basketry waste elements recorded from Sunken Village reflect a relatively equal use of splints (47%) and cedar bark (53%). It will be interesting to see if this pattern continues as basketry waste materials from 2007 are taken out of preservation and recorded (for additional information on specific measurements of basketry waste elements from these wet sites and distribution charts, see Croes *et al.* 2006, 2007a).

5.4.2.5 EXPERIMENTAL ARCHAEOLOGY

Replicating artifacts is an invaluable practice in our approach and has given us a more comprehensive understanding of the artifacts at hand, not to mention an infinitely greater appreciation for the time, effort, and care that went into creating these impressive cultural items. Experimental archaeology has aided in the comprehension of the basketry artifacts studied, as well as helped in the identification process of basketry waste materials, and what possible stage of basketry production they may have resulted from.

Olivia Ness attempted to replicate the open cross-warp twined cedar root basket in an effort to obtain what can only be gained by 'doing'. She dug up the cedar roots, stripped them of their bark and rootlets, split them into halves or quarters depending on their girth, then proceeded to remove their piths to achieve an ideal thickness – a process almost as time consuming as the basket weaving itself. Once the roots were processed and ready for weaving, Dale Croes helped her start the base. After cross-warp twining seven rows in a clockwise spiral formation, she split the warps in two and did not cross them for one row in accordance with the ancient basket. When we started this process we did not understand if there was a purpose behind this splitting or if it were simply decorative. As she twined further around the basket, it began to curve upwards from the split section. These split uncrossed warps appear to act as a sort of hinge that brings the body of the basket upwards giving it shape (Figure 5.35).

Additionally, she attempted to replicate the diamond-plaited soft bag, though on a smaller scale. Before the cellular analysis was conducted by Kathleen Hawes (above), she tried out a few different materials. This piece was obviously made from a rather pliable material, ruling out boughs or roots. First she tried cedar bark but quickly discovered that this material was not spongy enough, resulting in a loose weave that

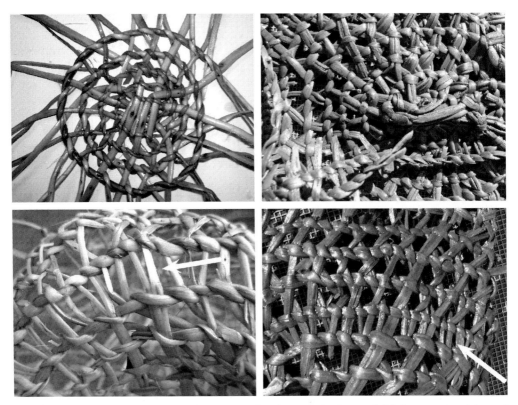

Figure 5.35. (left upper and lower) Replicated cedar root basket and (right upper and lower) ancient cedar root basket showing (upper) the start and (lower) the split warp 'hinge' transition into the body of the basket (see arrows).

did not have the same appearance as the ancient piece. Next she tried the sedge *Scirpus lacustris*, commonly known as tule. This material worked far better than the cedar bark but had too much spring in its structure, making it also difficult to weave as tightly as the ancient piece. Last she used *Scirpus americanus*, a sedge commonly referred to as sweet grass in the local region by Native basket weavers. This material worked superbly in twisting the two strand string needed for the warps as well as weaving the wefts in the diamond-plaiting technique. This choice of material is now further supported based on Kathleen Hawes' Cellular Analysis section above (see Figure 4.8). Per Dale Croes' instructions, she made two replicas, one with a frame and the other woven around a thin wooden form (Figure 5.36). Both worked rather well, however it was easier to achieve the tight weave present in the ancient piece when she used the frame. Further research will need to be conducted in order to accurately say what construction technique was likely used on the Sunken Village diamond-plaited fragment.

Figure 5.36. Replicated pieces of diamond-plaited weave with Sweet Grass sedge, using a form (left) and frame (right). Notice that in the form version the string warps can be seen in between the wefts, whereas in the frame version they are not visible.

5.4.2.6 SUMMARY AND CONCLUSIONS OF BASKETRY ANALYSIS

These basketry artifacts have given us a new cultural glimpse of the ancient Multnomah People who occupied the Sunken Village site. The master basket weavers that we work with have furthered our cultural understanding of these essential artifacts. The ancient basketry from wet sites throughout the Northwest Coast are the most sensitive measure of ethnicity of any archaeological artifact, and the unique styles, now actually excavated *in situ* from 35MU4, demonstrate a consistent and ancestral association of Chinook Museum baskets to those from Sunken Village. We plan to continue our recording of private and public collections from the Sunken Village site, as well as Chinookan museum basketry. This will greatly assist in testing the ancient roots of this distinct regional style, providing potential support of long-term Chinookan cultural identity through ancient and current basketry.

5.4.3 Cordage

By Dale Croes

As has been the case at other Northwest Coast wet sites, cordage artifacts are recorded for the Sunken Village site (N=14). In some wet sites such as Hoko River (45CA213), Little Qualicum River and Axeti, cordage represents a large percentage of the artifacts recovered (55–65% of all artifacts found at these three wet sites (Croes 1995:143)). Sunken Village cordage, like basketry, does occur (Figure 5.37) but does not represent the main categories of artifacts at the site (obviously acorn leaching pits, as features, and wood working debitage reflecting wood working are emphasized from 35MU4).

Cordage is defined as "any line, commonly categorized as a rope, cord or string, that is twisted, braided or a plain thin strip of bark, limb, twig or root" (Croes 1980, 4). This definition includes the general categories of rope, cord and string, as well as the cordage

Figure 5.37. Varied examples of cordage from Sunken Village (with site artifact numbers for reference).

forms of lines and wedge collars, as seen at Sunken Village. Two of the cordage pieces at SunkenVillage have knots represented, and both are overhands, with one being an overhand whip (Cordage No. 12; Table 5.6).

With only fourteen examples recorded, we will first generally characterize Sunken Village cordage and then describe each example in Table 5.6. Cordage from the site has been observed as made of cedar bark, cedar bough and what appears to be a layered grass. Construction techniques include multi-strand twisting and three-strand braiding.

Most examples are of a string (N=5; 0.1–0.5 cm) and cord (N=8; 0.51–1.3 cm) gauge, though a rope gauge wedge collar and cedar bark braid (0.31–2.3 cm) were recorded (gauge categories defined in Croes 1980, 20). With the twisted cordage, eleven examples had a Z lay or twist, and one had an S lay or twist. Though a small cordage sample, a wide variety of construction materials, techniques, lays and gauges are seen at Sunken Village. The examples described in Table 5.6. (below) are characterized by cultural attributes used to define Stylistic/Technological classes/types of cordage from other Northwest Coast wet sites (Croes 1980, 47–54; 1995, 150).

5.4.4 Cherry Bark Curls

By Jason Channel and Nola Nahirnick

Northwest Coast people use cherry bark (*Prunus emarginata*) as a binding element, as well as for medicine, basketry, and as a fuel source. Cherry bark is resistant to decay, and it doesn't expand or contract when moving from wet to dry. Fresh bark is slightly elastic, making it a superior binding material. When whipped for making tools, it makes a smooth union. With ancient wet site contexts, ethnographic studies and experimentation we can explore the long-term use of this product.

Coiled strips of cherry bark (*Prunus emarginata*) have been found at Sunken Village (N=29) and most other reported Northwest Coast wet sites (Figure 5.38). All Sunken Village examples are plain strip pieces, often curled in a watch-spring like fashion. At Sunken Village, and most other Northwest Coast wet sites, these cherry bark curls occur as independent coils of bark, probably examples that were stored for later use, unwound from artifacts or discarded surplus from the ends of strips. Only two Northwest Coast wet sites have recorded lengths, widths and thicknesses of their cherry bark specimens – Sunken Village and Qwu?gwes (Table 5.7)

Sunken Village, with a limited excavation, has a typical sample of cherry bark strips when compared to sites that have had much larger volumes of site excavated, and, therefore, probably would have a higher percentage if more extensively explored (Figure 5.38). The one Northwest Coast wet site with a noticeably large number of cherry bark curls, even when compared to the extensively excavated Ozette Village Site, is Qwu?gwes. Since few cherry bark curls were found binding artifacts or in basketry at Qwu?gwes, it is felt that this site may have served as a good source for this raw material, like a quarry, where it was collected for later uses.

In comparing measurements from cherry bark curls from Sunken Village and Qwu?gwes (Table 5.7), the length and thickness are comparable, and probably the least culturally controlled dimensions. The width can be culturally selected and in fact this is the one dimension that appears to have variation between Sunken Village and Qwu?gwes, with Sunken Village having a tighter standard deviation and smaller width than the typical Qwu?gwes examples.

Only the Hoko River, Biederbost, Conway, Ozette Village, and Qwu?gwes wet sites have examples of cherry bark elements in a functional context. Therefore a description of their uses may help us suggest how it was used at Sunken Village and other wet sites. Ancient cherry bark strips have been found as binding fishhook shanks (Hoko River, see Croes 1995) and binding otherwise unmodified anchor stones (Conway,

Cordage ID	Transect	TU/Trench /Pit	Material	Technique	No. of Strands	Lay/ Twist	Gauge Diameter (cm)	Length (cm)	Knots
1	V	Pit M	Grass?	Twist	2	Z	0.677 (cord)	6.47	
2	VI	TU-4/40–50	Cedar bark	Twist	2	S	0.234 (string)	4.50	
3	VI	TU-4/40–50	Cedar bark	Twist	2	Z	0.176 (string)	6.58	
4	V	Pit Y	Grass?	Braid	3	n/a	0.873 (cord)	4.37	
5	VI	TU-4	Cedar bark	Braid	3	n/a	1.042 (cord)	29.0	
6	VI	TU-1/Trch 7 /20–30	Cedar bough	Twist	2	Z	1.78 (rope)	16.0	
7	V	Pit K	Cedar bark	Twist	2	Z	0.707 (cord)	9.61	
8	IV	B-CH	Cedar bark	Twist	2	Z	0.657 (cord)	10.58	
9	VI	B-FG	Cedar bark	Twist	2	Z	0.670 (cord)	19.0	
10	V	Pit AF	Cedar bark	Twist	2	Z	0.416 (cord)	6.57 (2 pcs)	
11	III	Pit O	Cedar bark	Twist	2	Z	0.193 (string)	3.40	
12	II	Pit C	Cedar bark	Twist	2	Z	0.212 (string)	31.50 (6 pcs)	Overhand whip
13	II	Pit B	Cedar bark	Twist	2	Z	0.292 (string)	just a knot	Overhand
14	V	Pit AQ	Cedar bark	Twist	2	Z	0.925(cord)	8.66 (2 pcs & frags.)	

Table 5.6. Cordage recovered from Sunken Village Site 2006–2007.

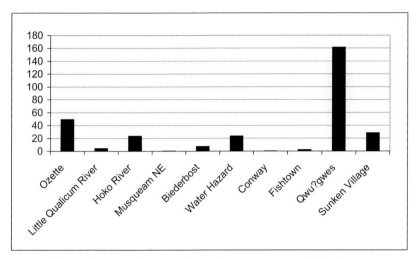

Figure 5.38. Number of curled cherry bark strips from reported Northwest Coast wet sites. Sunken Village has, with a limited excavation, about the numbers seen at most other sites. Qwu?gwes has a particularly common occurrence – possibly collected for later use or trade.

see Munsell 1976b, 121; Biederbost, see Nordquist 1961, 3–4; 1976, 200). The most common use of cherry bark at Ozette Village is in the construction of the whale harpoon equipment, an unlikely function at the upriver Sunken Village site, however seal harpoons may have been made and used in this ancient Columbia River setting (one harpoon inset bone point was found, see Pagel, below). Other general uses observed at Ozette include bindings for projectile or spear points, binding elements for anchor stones, wrapping elements in lattice work, imbrication on coil basketry, and weft wrapping elements in open wrapped west coast burden baskets (Croes 1980). The Qwu?gwes wet site has a small toy war club (less than 5 cm long), with a pebble wrapped onto the end of a cedar stick using cherry bark binding – providing

Sunken Village	Qwu?gwes[O1]
Length	*Length*
M=71.17mm	M=87.76mm
SD=43.79mm	SD=85.94mm
N=29	N=92
Thickness	*Thickness*
M=0.76 mm	M=0.73 mm
SD=0.23 mm	SD=0.28 mm
N=29	N=162
Width	*Width*
M= 5.12 mm	M= 6.23 mm
SD=2.37 mm	SD=5.71 mm
N=29	N=162

Table 5.7. Length, thickness and width measurements of Sunken Village and Qwu?gwes cherry bark strips.

a unique example of using cherry bark binding elements (Figure 5.39).

Wet site research is the only way to develop a clear picture of bitter cherry use by early people of the Northwest Coast of North America. The many unique qualities

Figure 5.39. Example of cherry bark binding on a miniature toy war club from Qwu?gwes wet site (cm scale).

of cherry bark binding elements need to be recognized as part of the archaeological record.

5.5 Bone Artifacts

By Tressa Pagel

Well preserved bone artifacts (n=10) were uncovered at the Sunken Village site (35MU4). This accounts for 8% of all discrete artifacts found at the site. This percentage is low when compared to northerly Northwest Coast sites of the late period. For example, the Hoko River Rockshelter (45CA21) has an abundance of bone artifacts (n=1,137, 66%) (Croes 2005, 117). This may be attributed to the limited excavation that took place at Sunken Village and with further excavation in different activity zones of the overall occupation area a higher percent of bone artifacts may be discovered.

Although few in number the bone artifacts found at Sunken Village has a range of tool types. Bone was grooved and sectioned using a chipped stone. The splinters were then sharpened and smoothed on an abrader, such as sandstone. Northwest Indians used these raw materials for "tools, weapons, personal adornment and many household and ritual objects" (Stewart 1973, 110). Those found at 35MU4 are chisel tips (n=3) which would have been used in wood working (Table 5.8, Figure 5.40). Chisels are sectioned and placed into wooden handles with a grommet on the end to keep it from breaking. A half beaver tooth chisel was also identified and was sharpened at the tip for fine carving. The lower incisors were used because they are very strong and could be re-sharpened. A wedged based harpoon point (n=1) was compared with artifacts from the Hoko Rockshelter (45CA21, type SIIc1) to assist in the identification of the artifact. Wedge based harpoon points are defined by McKenzie "as points with wedge-shaped base" (McKenzie 1974, 92; Croes 2005, 149). Awls (n=3) have been identified and "are made of split and ground mammal leg bones ... and usually unfinished accept for the tips" (Croes 2005, 128). Unfinished worked bone artifacts (n=9) have also been identified from 35MU4 site in 2007 and show signs of grinding. The final artifact located at the

Artifact	Description	Length (mm)	Width (mm)	Thickness (mm)	Weight (g)
1	chisel	34.62	25.03	8.90	4.6
2	chisel	18.62	9.08	4.10	0.4
3	harpoon	41.25	8.32	5.55	1.7
4	dull point	27.01	8.65	6.86	1.3
5	chisel	26.67	20.62	7.68	1.5
6	Beaver tooth chisel-haft	46.49	9.13	4.27	1.5
7	awl	81.85	14.61	4.3	5.5
8	awl	56.09	15.86	5.8	5.4
9	awl	83.69	15.07	5.6	6.0
10	Worked bone	8.35	13.58	3.38	0.1

Table 5.8. Discrete bone artifacts from 2006–2007 Sunken Village explorations.

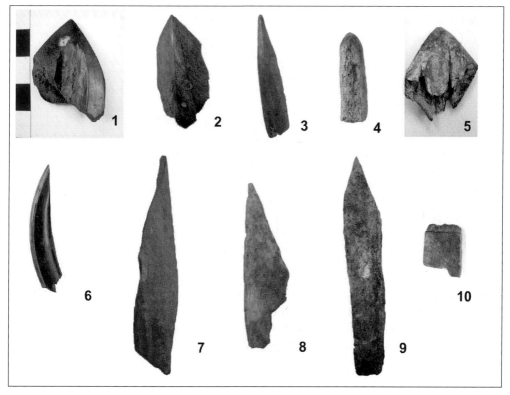

Figure 5.40. Examples of bone artifacts from 35MU4, with bone chisel tips (1 and 2), a wedge based harpoon point (3), a dull bone point (4), and a half beaver tooth chisel (6). Artifacts from 2007, bone chisel tip (5), awls (7–9) and ground bone artifact (10).

site was a dulled bone point (n=1) that had been charred and is rounded on the sides and tip.

5.6 Lithics

Archaeology in the Portland Basin region of the Sunken Village wet site, and in most parts of the world, is mostly define by lithic artifact analyses. Here we place lithic artifacts into this wet site context, with an examination of (a) an in situ dry exposure of an upper cutbank exposure above the intertidal aquifer waterlogged layers, within the natural levee and beach occupation area (the Half Test Unit (HTU)), (b) half of the complete acorn leaching pit (Pit P) excavation in the wet site, (c) in terms of use-wear analyses of the blade-like flakes to explore their uses in cutting softer materials of wood, fiber, leather and for butchering, and (d) a Sunken Village wet site projectile point typology to see how this site relates to similar classifications within the Central Northwest Coast of North America.

5.6.1 Analysis of lithics from HTU 1 and south half of Pit P
By John Fagan and Maureen Zehendner

5.6.1.1 LITHICS RECOVERY FROM HTU-1

Half Test Unit 1 (HTU1) was located above the wet site surface within the cutbank exposure of the natural levee and within exclusively dry deposits at 35MU4 (Figures 3.1–3.4b–c). The unit extended 1 meter north-south along the upper cutbank, above and near TU 2 on the intertidal surface and extended east-west into the bank for a distance of 0.5 m (Figures 3.7–3.8). Prior to commencing excavation work, a profile of the exposed cutbank was prepared. The profile on the cutbank revealed a fire-cracked rock (FCR) feature that was visible at *ca.* 65–75 cm below the surface. Underlying the FCR feature were visible charcoal layers at approximately 80 cm and 90 cm below the surface (see Figures 3.7–3.8).

The excavation was undertaken using arbitrary 10 cm levels. The FCR was exposed and left in place. Once the level was excavated, the FCR was collected prior to beginning the excavation of the level below. The two distinct charcoal layers that were identified in the profile were exposed and mapped in place prior to removal. Both arbitrary level 8 and level 9, containing the charcoal layers, were removed entirely as bulk samples for more controlled processing. A radiocarbon sample obtained from the charcoal layer, in arbitrary level 9 produced a radiocarbon date of *ca.* 500 years before present (BP) (Figure 3.5). The calculated date range for the sample was 1400 to 1450 AD.

Material excavated from HTU1 was water-screened through ½, ¼, and ⅛ inch screen in the field, except for levels 8 and 9 which were removed entirely as bulk samples. The bulk samples comprising all of the soil for each of these excavation levels, were returned to the AINW laboratory, Portland, Oregon, U.S.A. to be water screened using a 1 millimeter mesh fabric. Once the samples were water-screened they were air-dried in the laboratory and removed from the 1 mm mesh. Dry samples were sorted to identify lithic debitage and tools, fire-cracked rock, charcoal, botanical and faunal remains. Charcoal samples for radiometric dating were collected from the bulk samples from level 8 and level 9.

Cultural materials collected during excavation of HTU1 included lithic debitage and tools, fire-cracked rock and faunal remains. In total, 422 pieces of lithic debitage were recovered (Appendix I:287; see website: http://www.library.spscc.ctc.edu/crm/JWA9. pdf). Lithic material included cryptocrystalline silicate (CCS) 96.4% (n=407), obsidian 2.1% (n=9) and basalt 0.9% (n=4).

The FCR feature consisted of *ca.* 9 angular basalt rocks clustered at the west edge of the unit at the cutbank, extending approximately 20 cm north-south and 10 cm west-east (see Figure 3.7). A dense concentration of charcoal, and bisque (burned earth) occurred throughout the level increasing in density below the feature in level 8.

5.6.1.2 Lithics recovery from South half of Pit P

Pit P occurred within the wet deposits on the beach near TU-4 (Figure 3.4c). The acorn leaching pit was exposed during surface clearing during low water and the north half of the unit, was excavated during the regular field session. The excavated sediments were water-screened in the field. The southern half of the pit was removed in 10 cm levels as bulk samples following the two week intensive excavations in 2006 and were taken to the AINW laboratory for processing and analysis.

Prior to removal of the pit fill, a column of 10 × 10 cm, 5 cm deep sediment samples was collected from the center of the south half of the pit (see Figure 3.12). The northern half of the pit fill was excavated with hydraulic excavation techniques during the field session by excavators from SPSCC. AINW returned to the field on September 20, 2006 to remove the remaining southern half of the pit.

The excavated portion of the pit extended east-west approximately 70 cm, and the half section extended *ca.* 50 cm north-south. While the portion of the pit removed was defined by the pit diameter determined during the earlier excavations, there was evidence that suggested the pit had been excavated through and into other pits (see Figure 3.12). Thus not all edges were easily defined, and the layering within the pit walls gave the appearance of possibly intersecting pit edges. Additionally, cultural materials continued beneath the twigs lining the bottom of Pit P, indicating that possible pit fill from earlier uses of the pit was deeply buried (see Figure 4.14).

Artifacts recovered from the south half of Pit P, included 1,156 pieces of lithic debitage and 2 bone flakes as well as tools, and the faunal remains of both mammals and fish. A large obsidian biface was recovered in level 3 during excavation of the bulk sample (Figure 5.41). The recovered artifacts included 1,110 CCS flakes, 40 obsidian flakes, 6 basalt flakes and 2 bone flakes (Appendix I:287, see website: http://www.library.spscc. ctc.edu/crm/JWA9.pdf).

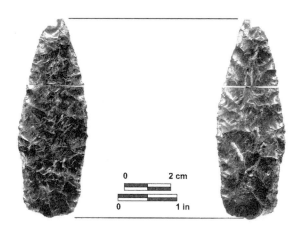

SV-B-24 Pit P Type: XXI

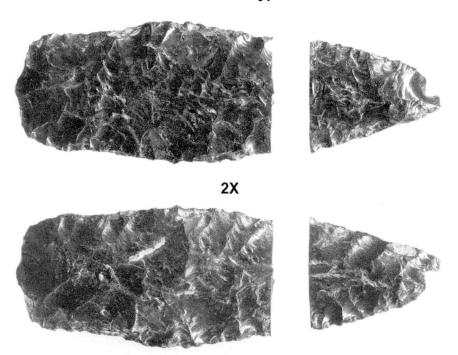

2X

Figure 5.41. Obsidian biface found in Pit P, views of both faces. The enlarged views below show the clean nature of the break. This point is classified in the Projectile Point Analysis below as a Type XXI example.

5.6.1.3 Lithic Debitage Analysis

Though derived from different site contexts, one from a dry upper and *in situ* levee beach occupation area and one from a wet site pit fill, the lithic debitage recovered from HTU1 and the south half of Pit P exhibited several similarities in the types of raw materials present (Table 5.9) and the reduction technologies used in their production (Table 5.10). Over 95 % of all of the debitage in both units was comprised of CCS. Obsidian was the second most abundant type of stone and accounted for just over 2% of the debitage in HTU1, and 3.5% in Pit P. Basalt, although representing less than 1% of the debitage for each excavation unit, was the third most abundant type of stone represented in the debitage assemblage for these two units. Basalt accounted for 0.5% of the Pit P debitage, and 0.9% of the HTU1 debitage. In addition to the CCS, obsidian, and basalt, 2 bone flakes were recovered from Pit P, while 1 petrified wood flake and 1 other type of stone flake were recovered from HTU1.

Diagnostic lithic debitage from HTU1 and Pit P reflect an overwhelming emphasis on pressure flaking. Pressure flakes represent over 57% of the debitage from Pit P, and over 65% of the debitage from HTU1 (Table 5.10). In both cases, there were a greater number of late-stage pressure flakes than early-stage pressure flakes. The relatively small size of the pressure flakes and the number of early-stage pressure flakes that exhibit remnant ventral surfaces (43 for Pit P, and 45 for HTU1) indicate that flake blanks were used for the manufacture of pressure flaked tools, presumably, projectile points (see projectile point analysis, below). Differential luster and differential color on early-stage pressure flakes indicates that heat-treated flake blanks were pressure flaked into tools on site, presumably for the production of arrow points. The emphasis on late-stage pressure flakes indicates that completed points were being sharpened, maintained, and most likely repaired at 35MU4. The pressure flakes from level 6, 7, and 8 of HTU1 represent 28 different types of stone and suggest that minimally 28 arrow points are represented by these pressure flakes from this provenience. Likewise, the 51 different types of stone pressure flakes from all five levels from the south half of Pit P, suggest that minimally 51 different arrow points were manufactured and/or sharpened in this portion of the site.

Percussion flakes representing early- and late-stage biface and core reduction combined represent a relatively small percentage of the debitage from HTU1 (n=28 or 6.6%) and Pit P (n=108 or 9.3%). The debitage from Pit P contains slightly more early-stage than late-stage biface thinning flakes, but contains twice as many late-stage as early-stage core reduction flakes. A similar pattern is evident in the HTU1 percussion debitage. These trends suggest that bifaces were being made, used, and sharpened at the site, while cores were being more extensively reduced, probably for the production of flake tools and flake blanks for the production of other tools such as arrow point preforms and arrow points.

The presence of primary geologic and incipient cone cortex on CCS debitage indicates that raw materials were quarried from bedrock outcrops and were also obtained from alluvial sources. Both obsidian and basalt debitage with incipient cone cortex indicates that these raw materials were obtained from alluvial sources.

South half of Pit P

Unit	Level	BAS	BON	CCS	OBS	OTH	PET	Total	%
SOUTH 1/2 PIT P	1	1		109	5			115	9.9%
SOUTH 1/2 PIT P	2			173	12			185	16.0%
SOUTH 1/2 PIT P	3	2		163	6			171	14.8%
SOUTH 1/2 PIT P	4	2		363	10			375	32.4%
SOUTH 1/2 PIT P	5	1	2	302	7			312	26.9%
Total		6	2	1110	40			1158	100.0%
%		0.5%	0.2%	95.9%	3.5%			100.0%	

HTU 1

Unit	Level	BAS	BON	CCS	OBS	OTH	PET	Total	%
HTU 1	2			1				1	0.2%
HTU 1	3					1		1	0.2%
HTU 1	6	1		1			1	3	0.7%
HTU 1	7			26				26	6.2%
HTU 1	8			81	5			86	20.4%
HTU 1	9	3		288	3			294	69.7%
HTU 1	10			1	1			2	0.5%
HTU 1	11			6				6	1.4%
HTU 1	12			3				3	0.7%
Total		4		407	9	1	1	422	100.0%
%		0.9%		96.4%	2.1%	0.2%	0.2%	100.0%	

Table 5.9. 35MU4 Lithic Debitage by Composition (HTU1 and southern ½ of Pit P). Key: BAS=basalt, BON=Bone, CCS=Cryptocrystalline Silicate, OBS=Obsidian, OTH=Other, PET=Petrified Wood.

South half of Pit P

Unit	LEV	BIFE	BIFL	CORE	CORL	PERC	PREE	PREL	THE	UNK	Total	%
South half Pit P	1	3		2	4	24	33	34	1	14	115	9.9%
South half Pit P	2	4	5		9	13	52	69	1	32	185	16.0%
South half Pit P	3	2	3	7	10	19	46	46	2	36	171	14.8%
South half Pit P	4	4	4	7	12	26	84	117	7	114	375	32.4%
South half Pit P	5	6	5	8	13	23	84	100	6	67	312	26.9%
Total		19	17	24	48	105	299	366	17	263	1158	100.0%
%		1.6%	1.5%	2.1%	4.1%	9.1%	25.8%	31.6%	1.5%	22.7%	100.0%	

HTU 1

Unit	LEV	BIFE	BIFL	CORE	CORL	PERC	PREE	PREL	THE	UNK	Total	%
HTU 1	2							1			1	0.2%
HTU 1	3				1						1	0.2%
HTU 1	6	1				2					3	0.7%
HTU 1	7				2		5	7		12	26	6.2%
HTU 1	8	1	1	1	4	1	22	36	1	19	86	20.4%
HTU 1	9	1	4		6	11	77	126	4	65	294	69.7%
HTU 1	10			1				1			2	0.5%
HTU 1	11			3	2	1		2			6	1.4%
HTU 1	12						1	2			3	0.7%
Total		3	5	5	15	15	105	173	5	96	422	100.0%
%		0.7%	1.2%	1.2%	3.6%	3.6%	24.9%	41.0%	1.2%	22.7%	100.0%	

Table 5.10. 35MU4 Lithic Debitage by Technology (HTU 1 and southern ½ of Pit P). Key: BIFE=Biface Percussion Early Flake, BIFL=Biface percussion Late Flake, CORE=Core ercussion Early Flake, CORL=Core Percussion Late Flake, PERC=Undetermined Percursion Flake, PREE=Pressure Early Flake, PREL=Pressure Late Flake, THE=Thermal Flake (Potlid) or Thermal Break, UNK=Undetermined Flake, Pressure or Percussion.

5.6.1.4 HTU-1 AND SOUTH HALF OF PIT P: LITHIC TOOL ANALYSIS

Ten tools were recovered from HTU1 and 45 tools were recovered from the south half of Pit P. Most of the tools were fragments and most were made from CCS (See Appendix J:292, website: http://www.library.spscc.ctc.edu/crm/JWA9.pdf).

The 10 tools from HTU-1 included 7 fragments of arrow point preforms that had been broken in manufacture, 2 arrow point fragments that had been broken in use (see Projectile Point Analysis, 5.6.3, below), and 1 bipolar core. All of these items were made from CCS. Remnant dorsal or ventral surfaces on 6 of the preforms indicated that they had been made on late-stage core reduction flakes. Differential luster on 4 of the arrow point preforms indicated that the flake blanks had been heat-treated prior to shaping by pressure flaking.

The 2 arrow point fragments included a stem fragment with a bending break and a slight finial indicating that the point had been broken in use on impact. The nearly complete arrow point was a stemmed point with shoulders. The tip had sustained a bending break from use and the blade had been re-sharpened.

The bipolar core was a small piece of CCS with percussion flake scars on one surface. The specimen appears to have been a thick percussion flake that had been used as a bipolar core, presumably as a means of recycling the piece for the production of useable edges or smaller flakes.

The 45 tools from the south half of Pit P included 16 CCS arrow point preform fragments that were broken in manufacture, 8 flake tools (7 CCS and 1 obsidian), 7 arrow points (1 compete, 1 broken in manufacture, and 5 broken in use (5 CCS and 2 obsidian), 5 ground stone fragments of basalt, 4 CCS cores, 1 obsidian core, 1 CCS bifacial blank fragment, 1 CCS scraper fragment, 1 heat treated flake broken during initial pressure flaking, and 1 large obsidian knife found in two pieces.

Remnant dorsal or ventral surfaces on 7 of the preforms indicated that 6 had been made on late-stage core reduction flakes and 1 had been made on an early-stage core reduction flake. Differential luster on 6 of the arrow point preforms indicated that the flake blanks had been heat-treated prior to shaping by pressure flaking. Most of the arrow point fragments were broken in use, several included tips that exhibited bending breaks. One base-notched point fragment had been made on a thin obsidian flake that was broken during shaping of the distal end. One base-notched CCS point was complete and appeared not to have been used.

The 5 ground stone fragments were pieces of larger tools that had been used for pecking and/or grinding, but had been recycled and used as cooking or heating elements resulting in their fragmentation and classification as pieces of fire-cracked rocks. The fragments were too small to assign a former function.

The 4 CCS cores were blocky chunks of raw material that had been brought to the site for the production of flakes. One CCS core exhibited primary geologic cortex and was presumably obtained from a bedrock source. One obsidian core exhibited incipient cone cortex indicating that it had been procured from an alluvial source.

A CCS bifacial blank that was broken in manufacture was recovered from Pit P. The blank had been made on a heat-treated early-stage core reduction flake and it was broken by an overshot flake that removed the distal end of the blank. A CCS scraper was recovered from Pit P and 8 flake tools, 7 of which were of CCS, and one of obsidian. One CCS heat-treated flake had been broken during the initial stages of pressure flaking.

A large obsidian bifacial knife was found in two pieces in Pit P (Figure 5.41). The damage may have occurred during excavation. The biface had been shaped by percussion flaking and finished and sharpened by pressure flaking.

5.6.1.5 DISCUSSION

Comparison of the debitage and tools from HTU1 and the south half of Pit P indicates a similar emphasis on the use of CCS for the production of flakes and flake blanks for use as flake tools and as flake blanks for projectile points. Heat treatment of flakes is evident in the number of arrow point preforms exhibiting differential luster. The large number of arrow-point preform fragments and the number of projectile points broken in use indicates that the site was heavily used for the manufacture, repair and replacement of broken and worn out arrow points. Most of the arrow points were either shallowly basally notched, or were stemmed with short barbs or shoulders (see Projectile Point analysis, below).

The types of tools recovered suggests a wide range of activities associated with hunting, food processing, and the manufacture of other types of tools that required the use of sharp stone cutting and scraping edges. The amount of fire-cracked rock and charcoal suggests the extensive use of heating and cooking, as well as the formal heat treatment of lithic material for the production of projectile points. In addition, the splitting of cedar arrow shaft blanks and shaping of arrow shafts (Section 5.3.1.2, Figure 5.13) and the cherry bark curls for binding fletching and arrow points (Section 5.4.7) demonstrate the full combination of arrow production at this wet site. Vocational collections observed also reveal broken ends of bows and slotted arrow shaft ends.

5.6.2 Analysis of lithic tools from Sunken Village Wet Site (35MU4) and comparison with those from Qwu?gwes Wet Site (45TN240)

By Germán Löffler

A site survey and the equivalent of four 1x1 meter test excavations at 35MU4 over a two week span in September 2006 and a one week surface survey during September 2007 recovered 174 lithic tools (see Appendix K:297, website: http://www.library.spscc.ctc.edu/crm/JWA9.pdf), 287 proximal flake debitage (Appendix L:301, website: http://www.library.spscc.ctc.edu/crm/JWA9.pdf), and 1,357 pieces of angular and flake shatter debitage (see Appendix M:306, website: http://www.library.spscc.ctc.edu/crm/JWA9.pdf) as defined by a generalized morphological typology (following Andrefsky 2005).

5.6.2.1 LITHIC TOOLS

Most of the lithic tools found at the Sunken Village wet site are flake tools (n=111, 63.8%, Table 5.11). Bifaces are second in frequency (n=34, 19.5 %, see Projectile Point analysis, Section 5.7, below). Hammer stones, 'scrapers', abraders, multi-directional cores, ground-stone, and an awl were also recovered (Table 5.11). The diverse lithic

Tool Type	Frequency	Percent
Flake Tool	111	63.8
Biface	34	19.5
Hammer Stone	12	6.9
"Scraper"	8	4.6
Abrader Stone	4	2.3
Multi-directional Core	3	1.7
Groundstone	1	0.6
Awl	1	0.6
Total	174	100

Table 5.11. Frequency of lithic tools recovered.

Material	Frequency	Percentage
Obsidian	1	1
Siltstone	1	1
Basalt	2	2
Quartz	2	2
Rhyolite	2	2
Chalcedony	3	3
Jasper	3	3
Metamorphic	3	3
Quartzite	6	5
Agate	9	8
Chert	11	10
CCS	68	60
Total	111	100

Table 5.12. Raw materials used for flake tools.

tool assemblage represents a large range of tool types reflecting a wide range of activities undertaken in the vicinity of the site.

The frequent flake tools and bifaces at Sunken Village (83.4% of the lithic tools) probably reflect both a need for woodworking and/or hide processing tools and bifaces as hafted projectile tips (Churchill 1993; Peterkin 1993), though studies also indicate that bifaces served multiple functions, including sawing, cutting, scraping, whittling and boring (Ahler 1971; Andrefsky 1997; Goodyear 1974; Greiser 1977; Nance 1971).

5.6.2.2 LITHIC FLAKE TOOLS EXPERIMENTAL EDGE-WEAR ANALYSIS

To better understand what the most numerous Sunken Village lithic tools were likely used for, a method of wear analysis was developed via microscopy analysis using wear attributes obtained from replicated flake tools used in three distinct ('whittling', 'scraping', and 'cutting'), controlled activities (following Löffler 2007, 2008). The wear analysis left on the replicated flake tools are compared to the wear attributes on the archeological flake tools to see which activity they most closely resemble. From the comparison of the replicated flake tools' wear attributes to the wear attributes of the archeological flake tools some guesses can be made to what the archeological flake tools were most likely used for.

To begin, one hundred flake tools of Edwards Plateau chert were replicated by direct percussion on a unidirectional core with a hard hammer-stone. Edwards Plateau chert was chosen as the lithic raw material for comparison because of its high quality (high silicate concentrations), and because it most proxies the majority of the archeological flakes lithic materials at 35MU4 (Table 5.12). For comparative purposes, morphological similarities are juxtaposed between the replicated flake tools, the Sunken Village wet site flake tools and the Qwu?gwes wet site (45TN240) flake tools in Table 5.13 and Figure 5.42. Overall the replicated flake tools cover the morphological range of the artifact assemblages.

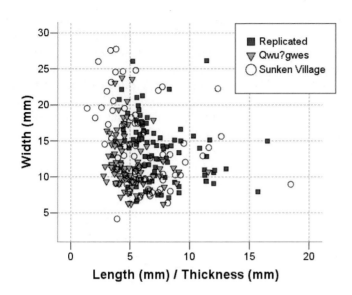

Figure 5.42. Morphological attributes comparison between Sunken Village, Qwu?gwes, and replicated flake tools.

	Minimum			Maximum			Mean			Std. Deviation		
	Sunken Village (SV)	Qwu?gwes (Q)	Replicated (R)	SV	Q	R	SV	Q	R	SV	Q	R
	(n = 111)	(n = 82)	(n = 100)									
Length (mm)	6.71	9.13	14.96	59.00	44.72	53.37	22.34	23.37	27.24	9.15	7.13	7.73
Thickness (mm)	1.00	1.79	1.48	19.10	11.44	8.33	4.18	5.00	4.17	2.69	2.12	1.52
Width (mm)	4.17	6.22	6.34	43.00	23.76	26.12	14.92	12.05	13.58	7.01	3.86	4.17
Weight (g)	0.1	0.2	0.2	13.6	9.0	6.1	1.7	1.6	1.6	2.7	1.7	1.3

Table 5.13. Morphological similarities among Sunken Village, Qwu?gwes, and replicated flake tools.

Three actions – cut (n = 44), scrape (n = 28), and whittle (n = 28) – were undertaken with the 100 replicated flakes on cherry bark (*Prunus emarginata*) and the wood of western red cedar (*Thuja plicata*). 'Cutting' is defined as: "insertion of an edge using bidirectional or unidirectional strokes with the working edge parallel to the direction of use" (Keeley 1980, 18; Odell 1981). 'Scraping' is the action of a tool which is held at a very high angle to the worked surfaces; the edge is held approximately at a right angle from the direction of use with the contact edge and worked material. The tools is 'pulled' rather than pushed as might be done in 'whittling' (Keeley 1980). 'Whittling' is the shaving off of material from the parent piece with the working edge of the tool moved at a right angle with the direction of use; the contact edge of the lithic tool is held at a low angle to the worked material; the tool 'pushes' the worked material rather 'pulls' it as is done with scraping (Keeley 1980; Odell 1981).

Three wear attributes – striation direction, polish intrusion, and edge morphology – are observed and used to identify the action's wear pattern on a flake edge after 'whittling', 'scraping', and 'cutting' activities of the replicated flake tools on the cherry wood bark and western red cedar (following Löffler 2007, 2008). Wear attributes were observed on the experimental and archeological flake tools utilizing a Hitachi S-570 model Scanning Electron Microscope running at 20 Kilo Watts at Washington State University's Electron Microscopy and Imaging Center. Additional close up images were observed under 60–85 magnification with a Nikon C-PS light microscope at one of Washington State University's Anthropology Department's lithic laboratories. Each attribute observed after the flake is used in cutting, scraping, and whittling activities shows a different wear pattern on the flakes edge. Combining the replicated flake tools different wear attributes via a discriminant function analysis (DFA) allows us to make a prediction of what the archeological flake tools were likely used for.

Striation Direction
The first attribute observed after cutting, scraping and whittling activities, striation direction, was assigned an ordinal measurement following Löffler's (2007, 2008) methodology: The edge of the flake tool is used as a base line of an imaginary protractor. The striations' closest point to the worked edge is followed to its further distance from the worked edge. The line the two points make form an angle on the protractor which is measured. The striation direction is then given a value of '1' if the angle formed is between 1°–22.5°; a value of '2' if the angle formed is between 22.5°–45°; a value of '3' if the angle formed is between 45°–77.5°, or a value of '4' if the angle is 77.5°–90° respectively.

The microwear striation directions are graphed by percentages of used-flake tools per task (Figure 5.43). A Chi-squared shows high statistical significance of the data patterning, while a Cramers' V shows its strong association (X^2 = 71.31, df = 6, p ≤ 0.001, Cramer's V = 0.64.8). The Chi-squared test should be taken at face value as more than 20% of the cells had values less than '5' frequency – a violation of the Chi-square parameters. Nevertheless, the patterning of striation per action is apparent. Cutting actions microstriation directions are most often less than 45 degrees. Scraping and whittling actions most often leave striations whose angles are higher than 45 degrees. On striation direction alone scraping and whittling actions are difficult to distinguish apart because they are both transverse actions to the worked surface and consequently both actions leave higher than 45° striations on the tools edge.

Polish Intrusion
The second attribute recorded was polish intrusion and it was measured from the working edge of the flake tool to its uppermost visible mark again following Löffler's (2007, 2008) methodology. This method of polish intrusion measurement works well on the experimental flake tools because their used edges are known. However, this schema

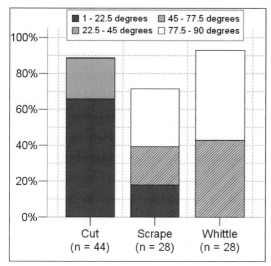

Figure 5.43. Staked column chart illustrating percentage of replicated flake tools, striation direction after cutting, scraping and whittling activities. For the most part, cutting actions tend to leave striation directions smaller than 45° while scraping and whittling actions tend to leave striation directions greater than 45°. The patterning is statistically significant: $X^2 = 71.31$, df = 6, $p \leq 0.001$, Cramer's V = 0.64.8.

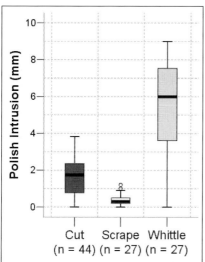

Figure 5.44. Box plot illustrating the range, interquartile range and median of polish intrusion on replicated flake tools after cutting, scraping and whittling activities. The circles indicate outliers greater than twice the interquartile range of polish intrusion for that action.

should be applied to the archeological record with caution and with the analyst's best judgment as the extent of the used edge on the archeological record is unknown.

The polish intrusion was graphed by the action undertaken (Figure 5.44). There is an evident difference in patterning of the polish intrusion per activity. A Students T-Test procedure compares the means of polish intrusion per cutting, scraping, and whittling activities to demonstrate that polish intrusion after each activity are statistically different from each other. The Students T-Test between cutting and scraping indicates the difference in polish intrusion is not due to chance ($t = 6.913$, $F = 25.052$, df = 69, $p \leq 0.001$.). The Students T-Test between cutting and whittling also indicates that the difference in polish intrusion is also not due to chance (t = -8.592 F = 40.206, df = 69, p ≤ 0.001). Lastly, a Students T-Test between scraping and whittling polish intrusion also indicates their difference is not due to chance (t = -9.845, F = 56.265, df = 52, p ≤ 0.001).

Edge-Morphology
Edge morphology was the last attribute observed. The used-edge-morphology was classified into one of four categories: (1) dilapidated, (2) smooth, (3) lunate, or (4) worn (after Löffler 2007, 2008). 'Dilapidated' used-edge-morphologies were often associated with flake edges that were not snapped off, but where noticeably 'used' up; rough asymmetrical and non-patterned dulling effect of the used edge morphology. 'Smooth' used-edge-morphology has minimal morphological alteration after the flake has been used: microchipping is small – less than 0.2 mm in width – mostly shallow with feathered termination. 'Lunate' used-edge-morphologies are evident by 'half-moon' crescent shaped breakages along the edge after use; sometimes the edge is snapped off. 'Worn' used-edge-morphologies have much morphological alteration after the flake is used; the flakes' edge is snapped off and/or severely crushed. 'Worn' use-edge-morphologies also have large microchipping scars – larger than 0.2 mm in width – which are often deep and step terminated.

Used-edge-morphology was tallied and graphed by the percentage by activity (Figure 5.45). A Chi-squared test on the data reveal the pattern is highly significant and a Cramers' V measures its association (X^2 = 35.97, df = 6; p ≤ 0.001, Cramer's V = 0.42). The patterning of the used-edge-morphology is varied by action as illustrated in Figure 5.45. However, overall, cutting actions' used-edge-morphology after the flake is used tend to be either 'smooth' or 'dilapidated'. Scraping actions tend to leave 'lunate' used-edge-morphology after they are used for scraping. Lastly, whittling actions leave a mixture of 'smooth' and 'worn' used-edge-morphology types after use.

Discriminate Function Analysis
The three attributes observed striation direction, polish intrusion, and used-edge-

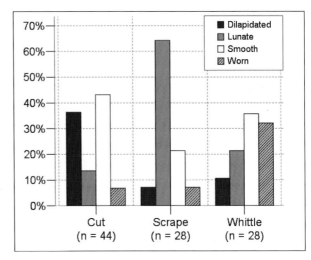

Figure 5.45. Column chart illustrating the percentage of replicated flake tools, used-edge morphology after cutting, scraping and whittling actions. The patterning is statistically significant X^2 = 35.97, df = 6; p ≤ 0.001, Cramer's V = 0.42.

morphology each individually demonstrate that each wear signature can be utilized to better guess what a tool was used for. A discriminant function analysis (DFA) was applied to combine the three usewear attributes observed from the experimental activities with the replicated flake tools to model the use of flake tools from the archeological record (following Löffler 2007, 2008). A discriminate analysis is helpful for this situation as the procedure generates a discriminant function based on linear combinations of the predictor variables – striation direction, polish intrusion and used-edge-morphology – which provide the best discrimination between the groups. The linear combinations of the predictor variables are generated from cases for which group membership is known – the 100 replicated flake tools and the experiments – and are then applied to different cases with measurements for the three predictor variables but whose group membership is unknown – the archeological record. (Baxter 1994; Drennan 1996; Shennan 1997). The DFA attempts a more 'objective' methodology in identifying the function of stone tools which does not rely on the 'expertise' of a lithicist.

The DFA applied to the experimental flake tools after 'whittling', 'cutting', and 'slicing' actions demonstrates that each activities wear attributes in combinations can be utilized to teased apart each action (Figure 5.46). When applying the DFA to the Sunken Village sites flake tool assemblage the DFA demonstrate that the majority of the flake tools were most likely utilized for 'scraping' and 'cutting' activities (Figure 5.47). When applying the DFA to other sites in geographic proximity like Qwu?gwes, the flake-tools DFA also suggest similar activities – 'cutting' and 'scraping' (Figure 5.48).

5.6.2.3 DEBITAGE

There were 287 diagnostic debitage (proximal flakes) collected during the 2006 and 2007 explorations. The proximal flakes include 219 (~76%) examples of cryptocrystalline

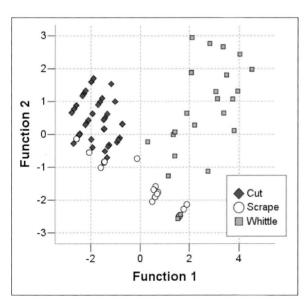

Figure 5.46. Scatter plot illustrating the DFA grouping for replicated flake tools after cutting, scraping and whittling activities (see Appendix N:315, website: http://www.library. spscc.ctc.edu/crm/JWA9.pdf).

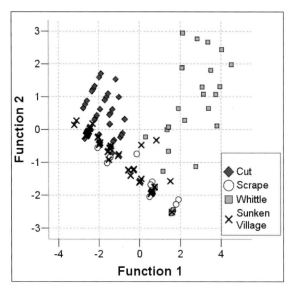

Figure 5.47. Scatter plot illustrating the DFA grouping for the Sunken Village (35MU4) flake tools as projected on the replicated flake tools after cutting, scraping and whittling activities (see Appendix N:315, website: http://www.library.spscc.ctc.edu/crm/JWA9.pdf).

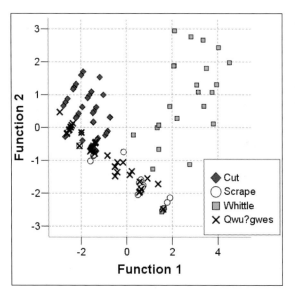

Figure 5.48. Scatter plot illustrating the DFA grouping for the Qwu?gwes (45TN240) flake tools as projected on the replicated flake tools after cutting, scraping and whittling activities (see Appendix N:315, website: http://www.library.spscc.ctc.edu/crm/JWA9.pdf).

silicates (CCS). There are 15 (~6%) agate, 15 (~6%) jasper, 9 (~3%) quartzite, 8 (~3%) metamorphic, 4 (~1%) chert, 4 (~1%) rhyolite, while 4 basalt, 3 chalcedony, 3 quarts, 1 obsidian, 1 petrified wood, and 1 siltstone make up approximately 5 percent of the raw materials represented in the proximal flake debitage assemblage (Table 5.14).

The two most abundant raw materials used for the production of stone tools and represented in both the debitage and tool assemblages are CCS. This indicates that several types of stone and stone tools were brought to the site as unprocessed resources and were likely acquired nearby. Raw materials were likely brought to the site as alluvial cobbles of CCS or other types of stone that were used for the production of flakes for expedient tools or as blanks for the production of flaked tools such as scrapers or projectile points. The alluvial cobbles source of raw material is particularly clear in the obsidian "scraper" as it has cortex reminiscent of obsidian cobbles (as well as other debitage with large amount of cortex remaining) which have been churned by water forces (following Andrefsky 'dorsal cortex' ordinal scale for cortex identification (2005, 106)).

The debitage assemblage also indicates that finished tools were brought to the site where they were used, sharpened, and possibly carried away for use elsewhere. That some tools were brought in finished is particularly clear from the finished obsidian biface found in Transect VI, Pit P (Figure 5.41), whose debitage representation (if manufactured at the site) remains undetected by the projects' initial excavation.

The stone tools indicate that several different tool production and resource processing tasks were performed at the site. The 287 pieces of proximal flake debitage make up approximately 20% of the total debitage assemblage recovered

Material	Frequency	Percent
CCS	219	76.3
Agate	15	5.2
Jasper	15	5.2
Quartzite	9	3.1
Metamorphic	8	2.8
Chert	4	1.4
Rhyolite	4	1.4
Basalt	4	1.4
Chalcedony	3	1.0
Quartz	3	1.0
Obsidian	1	0.3
Pet-wood	1	0.3
Siltstone	1	0.3
Total	287	100.0

Table 5.14. Flake debitage lithic material.

Platform	Frequency	Percent
complex	141	49.1
flat	106	36.9
abraded	32	11.1
cortical	8	2.8
Total	287	100.0

Table 5.15. Flake debitage platform type frequencies.

at 35MU4 so far. However, from these, the 8 (~1.5%) cortical, and 32 (~11%) abraded platforms from the diagnostic debitage suggests little early stage manufacturing of tools. In a similar vein 106 (~37%) of platforms were flat while 141 (49%) of platforms were complex (Table 5.15). This indicates several reduction technologies for late stages of reduction were represented in the artifact assemblage; late stages of core reduction, biface reduction, and possibly pressure flaking reduction technologies are represented in the debitage assemblage.

The proximal flake debitage includes many more late-stage core reduction flakes than early-stage core reduction flakes, suggesting that flakes were produced at the site, possibly for use as expedient flake tools. The possibility that the flakes were intended for the manufacture of bifacial tools and/or unifacial tools seems unlikely as most sizable flakes indicate usage. Possibly biface reduction flakes suggest that bifaces could have been initially manufactured on-site, but most likely represent thinning, re-sharpening, or reworking activities after the bifaces were transported into the site. The number of impact fractured bifaces 11 (~33 %) suggests that the bifaces were likely used as projectile points and that they broke in the hunted animal on impact; when the carcass was brought back to 35MU4 the fractured biface was discarded during butchering activities.

The 981 pieces of angular and flake debitage collected during the limited excavation during 2006 weighted 636.54 grams and are left unexplored at this juncture. With the 2007 surface survey debitage, the number increases to 1,353 pieces of debitage in total.

5.6.2.4 INTERPRETATION

Based on an analysis of the tools from the 35MU4 site inhabitants engaged in the production and maintenance of flaked stone tools probably used in hunting and butchering – as suggested by the bifaces. The lithic assemblage from 35MU4 exhibits a wide range of flint knapping activities associated with the production of flakes as expedient tools. The edge-wear analysis of the flake tools suggest cutting and scraping activities, such as preformed on wood and plant fiber processing activities. These flakes would be ideal for cutting leather/basketry elements and cutting/scraping the surface of cherry bark binding elements, in the process of removing the bark in a spiral fashion from the tree limbs and scraping the bark to create the polished surface sheen as seen at the site. Possibly too, the flake tools could have been used in cutting open and removing the shell from the potentially huge numbers of acorns leached at this site.

5.6.3 Projectile Points

By Dale Croes, Mark Collard and Carolyn Dennler

At present, the stylistically most sensitive ancient artifact in the Portland Basin, occurring in large numbers, are projectile points. Richard Pettigrew, who has done some of the most extensive analyses of artifacts in this region, provides this definition: "formed bifaces significantly broader than they are thick, with a relatively sharp tip, sufficiently small, and with bases formed in such a way as to make them adaptable for hafting on the end of a projectile shaft" (1981, 13). Thousands have been archaeologically reported from throughout the basin (Ames and Maschner 1999; Pettigrew 1981, 1990).

As in other parts of the Northwest Coast of North America, when more wet sites such as Sunken Village are investigated in the Columbia River region, basketry will prove to be even more sensitive in terms of determining ancient ethnicity and its cultural evolution. However, until that time, projectile points are most available for this region, and provide the data for attempting to establish chronological frameworks and culture histories as they do further north in the Puget Sound/Gulf of Georgia region. We will attempt to compare this well-known northern neighboring region to what we find in the Portland Basin (see map, Figure 5.51).

The documented ancient cultural sequence of the Portland Basin has two main phases: the Merrybell, 600 BC to 200 AD; and the Multnomah, 200 AD to contact (Pettigrew 1977, 1981, 1990). As mentioned, the sequence is based primarily on projectile point types, as well as some stone implements including net-weights. Pettigrew developed the chronology after testing nine sites in the Sauvie Island-Scappoose area, and studying private collections (documenting 996 projectile points, 300 from archaeological testing and 696 from collections). Currently, no sites date to before 3,000 years B.P. in the Portland Basin, whereas the Puget Sound/Gulf of Georgia region has evidence dating back to 13,000 years ago, from Clovis Tradition time periods on. Pettigrew suggests that evidence of the earliest occupations of the area has been inundated with water and alluvial deposits on the floodplain (1990). Most of the sites investigated in the Portland Basin are floodplain sites. Pettigrew's work in the late 1970s was the first intensive testing work done by any professional archaeologists. These test excavations were the basis for his chronology.

Pettigrew also developed one of the earliest explicit definitions of projectile point types for this region, establishing 15 types with some sub-types (1981, 13–18). His classification is an attempt to define a limited number of types that are chronologically sensitive. The attributes used can be considered a series of binary oppositions, mainly depicting 'three important attribute distinctions' involving whether the points were: I. (a) broad-necked or (b) narrow-necked, II. (a) barbed or (b) shouldered, and/or III. (a) diverging stem or (b) non-diverging stem, as well as a number of other attributes to create final type and/or sub-type definitions (1981, 13–18). This established the 16 main types that we can use to identify Sunken Village projectile point types and to compare to types found further north.

We also defined explicit projectile point types for the northern and neighboring Puget Sound/Gulf of Georgia region using a different set of attribute characters, mostly qualitative in nature: (a) body shape, (b) blade edge outline, (c) shoulder type, and (d) stem type (Croes et al. 2008). Details of these characters and their states are given in Figure 5.49 and example illustrations with type designations in Figure 5.50. To standardize our labeling of the characters and states, we used Gumbus' (1999) lithic attribute designations. In examining 5 well recorded sites in Puget Sound, we established 28 projectile point types that became the basis of a cladistic analysis, testing the ancestral sequencing of the sites by their projectile point types (Croes et al. 2008). One of the main Puget Sound sites, Hartstene Island, was a large surface collected site with 250 projectile points, and, since it was undated, we wanted to see how it temporally fit into the cladogram, suggesting its date and possibly its cultural affiliation. The cladistic analysis, using presence/absence of projectile point types, did establish a temporal sequence that placed Hartstene into a position following dated sites of Duwamish No. 1 and branching with the dated Qwu?gwes site (Croes et al. 2008). Hartstene was further associated with the earlier Duwamish No. 1 site through comparisons of the actual frequency of types from the sites and the stone materials emphasized (a character not used in type definitions).

Cladistics is the dominant method of phylogenetic reconstruction used in zoology, botany, and paleontology. In recent years, it has also begun to be used by archaeologists and anthropologists to investigate cultural evolution (see Croes et al. 2008 for a full discussion of the approach).

To make the two projectile point type classifications consistent between the Puget Sound/Gulf of Georgia and Portland Basin regions, and therefore have comparable and

Figure 5.49. Definition of Portland Basin projectile point types corresponding with the 15 projectile point types defined by Pettigrew (1981, 13–18; Types 1–15). For example of type XXI see obsidian biface, Figure 5.41. The roman numeral type designations in parentheses are Portland Basin types that correspond to the 28 types (I–XXVIII) defined for the Puget Sound and Gulf of Georgia regions to the north (see Figure 5.51; for definitions see Croes et al. 2008)

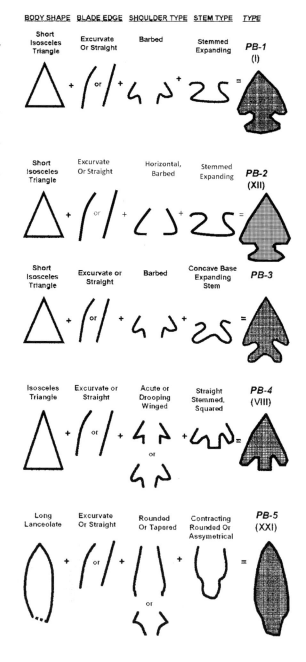

BODY SHAPE	BLADE EDGE	SHOULDER TYPE	STEM TYPE	TYPE	BODY SHAPE	BLADE EDGE	SHOULDER TYPE	STEM TYPE	TYPE
Long Lanceolate	Excurvate	Weak or None	Stemless, Flat, to Rounded Point to Sloped	PB-6 (XVIII)	Isosceles Triangle	Excurvate or Straight	Rounded	Side-notched, Convex Pointed	PB-11 (XXIII)
Isosceles Triangle	Excurvate Or Straight Or Incurvate	Barbed	Stemmed Expanding	PB-7 (XXVII)	Short Isosceles Triangle	Straight	Side Notched Expanding	Concave	PB-12
Long Isosceles Triangle	Excurvate	Tapered	Side-notched Expanding	PB-8	Short Isosceles Triangle	Straight	Not Applicable	Concave	PB-13
Short Isosceles Triangle	Excurvate or Straight	Barbed	Contracting	PB-9 (XVII)	Short Isosceles Triangle	Straight	Not Applicable	Stemless "Flat" to Convex to Base	PB-14 (II)
Long Isosceles Triangle	Straight or Excurvate	Tapered or Horizontal or Slightly Barbed	Stemmed Straight	PB-10 (III)	Short or Long Isosceles Triangle	Straight	Barbed out	Contracting	PB-15

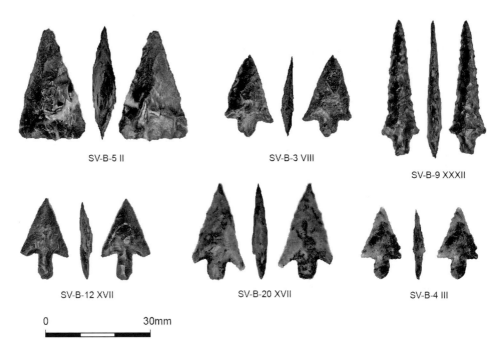

SV-B-5 II

SV-B-3 VIII

SV-B-9 XXXII

SV-B-12 XVII

SV-B-20 XVII

SV-B-4 III

0 ⎯⎯⎯⎯ 30mm

Figure 5.50. Examples of Sunken Village projectile points and their type designations from 2006 excavations.

explicit units of comparison, we converted Pettigrew's projectile point typology into our typology, defining his 16 types using the additional attribute characters of: (a) body shape, (b) blade edge outline, (c) shoulder type, and (d) stem type (Figures 5.49–5.50).

Our analysis of five well reported sites in southern Puget Sound had to be compared with the better know projectile point typologies and cultural sequences in the Gulf of Georgia and San Juan Island areas (known as the Central Coast Salish region in map, Figure 5.51; our southern Puget Sound area has had limited archaeological investigations in comparison to work in southern British Columbia and the San Juan Islands (northern Puget Sound)). Recognize spatially our the sites of reference, Qwu?gwes and Hartstene, are equally distant from the Portland Basin as they are to the Gulf of Georgia in British Columbia, Canada (Central Coast Salish, Figure 5.51). However our region is better linked to the north through waterways of Puget Sound, and linguistically as a major contact period Southern Coast Salish, Lushootseed, region (Croes *et al.* 2008).

Using our cladistic analysis, based on the presence and absence of the projectile point types at the various sites (Table 5.16), the analysis was run in the widely used phylogenetics program PAUP* 4 with the commands of *parsimony* as the criterion and *random* as the addition sequence under the *heuristic search* (Swofford 1998). The collection of points from West Point was used as an outgroup on the grounds that West Point is the oldest of the sites studied (over 4,000 years B.P.) and therefore its projectile points can be expected to retain the largest number ancestral character states. Our cladistic analysis resulted in 10 possible unrooted cladograms, and each would be equally valid outcome possibilities. To predict the best linkages, we next generated a *strict consensus* tree generated from all 10 cladograms (Figure 5.52). Like all of the cladograms, this one shows a relatively good affiliation of ancient Portland Basin sites and Puget Sound sites based on defined projectile point types (with the

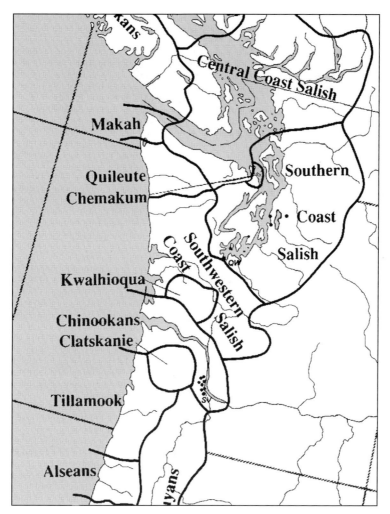

Figure 5.51 Map showing locations of sites compared in the projectile point study: eight sites are in the Chinookan cultural region, with Sunken Village at the bottom (SV), and five sites are in the Southern Coast Salish, Puget Sound cultural region, with Qwu?gwes wet site at the bottom (QW) (Base map adapted from Suttles, W. (ed.) 1990 Handbook of the North American Indians, Volume 7: The Northwest Coast. Smithsonian Institution, Washington, D.C.).

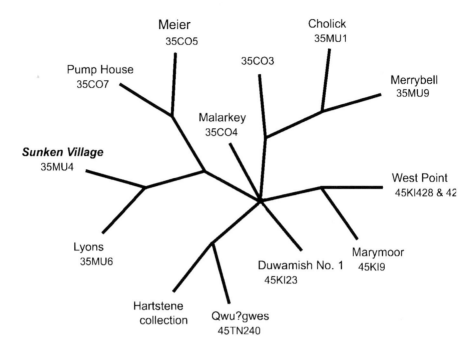

Figure 5.52. Strict consensus unrooted cladogram of projectile point types for Puget Sound region (lower cluster) and Portland Basin, including Sunken Village 35MU4 (upper branching).

exception of the Portland Basin site 35CO4, which equally links to the Puget Sound Duwamish No. 1 site).

Therefore the strict consensus unrooted cladogram generally demonstrated a distance between the collections from the two geographic regions, supporting considerable antiquity in separate cultural evolutions between the two regions (Figure 5.52). In other words, the cultural evolution, at least in terms of projectile point styles, seems to be on its own separate and distinct cultural trajectories in the two relatively well known regions, by at least 3,000 years ago. In Puget Sound we would suggest the lower clustering to be a Coast Salish (possibly even Lushootseed language group) cultural pattern, and it is fully supported by 3,000 years of ancient basketry data from six wet sites in this Puget Sound/Gulf of Georgia region (Ness, above; Croes *et al.* 2005). The one Portland Basin site that appears to link in the Puget Sound grouping, could easily have included some introduced points through contact, similar to the suggestion in the basketry strict concensus cladogram that Ozette had introduced coiled baskets through trade, and since this is based on presence/absence data, Ozette links to historic Salish museum collections (Ness, above).

Further the Portland Basin projectile point clusters reflect the known temporal pattern, with older sites branching together on the upper right branch in the cladogram

Type / Site	I	II	III	IV	V	VI	VII	VIII	IX	X	XI	XII	XIII	XIV	XV	XVI	XVII	XVIII	XIX	XX	XXI	XXII	XXIII	XXIV	XXV	XXVI	XXVII	XXVIII	XXIX	XXX	XXXI	XXXII	XXXIII
Puget Sound																																	
Qwu?gwes	1	1	1	1	1	1	1	1	1	1	1	0	0	0	0	0	0	0	0	0	0	0	0	0	0	0	0	0	0	0	0	0	0
Hartstene	1	1	0	1	1	1	1	1	0	0	1	1	1	1	1	1	1	1	1	1	1	1	1	0	0	0	0	0	0	0	1	1	0
Duwamish No. 1	0	1	1	1	0	0	0	0	0	1	1	0	0	1	0	1	1	0	1	0	0	0	0	0	0	0	0	0	0	0	0	0	0
West Point	0	1	1	0	0	1	0	0	0	1	0	0	0	0	0	1	0	1	1	0	0	0	0	1	1	1	0	0	0	0	0	0	0
Marymoor	0	1	1	1	0	0	0	0	0	0	0	0	0	0	0	0	1	1	1	0	0	0	0	1	1	1	1	1	0	0	0	0	0
Portland Basin																																	
35MU6	0	0	1	1	1	0	0	0	0	0	0	0	0	0	0	0	1	1	0	0	0	0	0	0	0	0	0	0	1	0	0	1	1
35CO7	0	0	1	1	1	0	0	1	0	0	0	0	0	0	0	0	1	0	0	0	0	0	0	0	0	0	0	0	0	0	1	1	1
35CO5	0	1	0	1	1	0	0	0	0	0	0	1	0	0	0	0	1	0	0	0	0	0	0	0	0	0	0	0	1	0	1	0	1
35CO4	0	1	1	0	0	0	0	0	0	0	0	0	0	0	0	0	1	1	0	0	0	0	0	0	0	0	0	0	1	0	0	0	0
35CO3	1	1	0	0	0	0	0	1	0	0	0	0	0	0	0	0	1	1	0	0	0	0	0	0	0	0	0	0	1	0	0	0	0
35MU1	1	1	1	0	0	0	0	1	0	0	0	1	0	0	0	0	1	1	0	0	1	0	0	0	0	0	0	0	1	1	0	0	0
35MU9	1	0	1	0	0	0	0	1	0	0	0	0	0	0	0	0	1	1	0	0	1	0	1	0	0	0	0	0	1	1	0	0	0
35MU4	0	1	1	0	0	0	0	1	0	0	0	0	0	0	0	0	1	1	0	0	0	0	0	0	0	0	0	0	0	0	0	1	1

Table 5.16. Presence/absence of defined projectile point types found at each of the five main Puget Sound and seven main Portland Basin sites in this study (0=absence, 1=presence).

(Figure 5.52) and more recent sites, including Sunken Village (35MU4) clustering together on the upper left branch in the cladogram, with the exception of the late Malarkey site.

As with Puget Sound/Gulf of Georgia, this general pattern does not necessarily reflect ancient ethnicity, though probably a culturally different trajectory between this area and the Portland Basin, and this correlates with culturally and linguistically very different peoples, Coast Salish and Chinookan. However, as seen in the Western Washington region, ideas of stone (and bone) tool manufacture and these styles appear to cross-cut differences seen in ancient basketry styles between the West Coast (Wakashan areas today) and Puget Sound/Gulf of Georgia (Coast Salish Areas today, see Figure 5.31).

The stone, bone and shell artifacts help establish well known phases in this region of Locarno Beach, Marpole and Late Period, but Croes has argued elsewhere that these phases are broad economic evolutionary phases that Western Washington, U.S.A./Southern British Columbia, Canada peoples all went through, and it is reflected in the diffusion of subsistence and manufacturing related stone, bone and shell artifacts (see Croes 1995; 2005; Croes et al. 2005). However ancient basketry (from eight wet sites) does separate regions through the 3,000 years (see Figure 5.30) and patterns differently than the phases defined by stone, bone and shell artifacts, and ancient basketry (like pottery in the Southwest U.S.A.) is proposed to be far more sensitive to the evolution of ethnicity than are typical stone, bone and shell artifacts (Croes et al. 2005). The Sunken Village basketry further demonstrates a distinct and ancient Portland Basin/Chinook style area (Ness, above).

Therefore the projectile point patterns shown generally separating the Portland Basin from neighboring Puget Sound/Gulf of Georgia regions appear to be real, useful for showing a separate patterning of cultural trajectories through antiquity, and probably reflects the considerable cultural difference through millennium in these two major Northwest Coast cultural areas. Therefore these lithics analyses, like those of basketry, contribute to the understanding of regional cultural trajectories, as will be explored in the final section.

6 Assessing the Results of the 2006 and 2007 Investigations at Sunken Village Wet Site

6.1. Site context overview

The Sunken Village site is situated in a major flood plain basin, at the confluence of the Willamette and Columbia rivers – a geographical position that made it highly attractive as a cross-roads for ancient and current human occupation – known as a trade center supporting large populations for millennia. Major paleoenvironmental events formed the current Portland Basin, including Holocene floods 13–15,000 year ago, scouring the Columbia River channels from massive releases of glacial ice dams in Missoula, Montana, U.S.A., and more recently, a directly upriver release of the massive Bonneville Landslide floods through the Portland Basin region approximately 700 years ago. This last, and no doubt catastrophic event for the ancient Multnomah Peoples, probably sheared and/or buried earlier sites throughout the Portland Basin, and may account for the earliest dates of approximately 700 years BP for the Sunken Village site.

The site is located on the Multnomah Channel/Slough which may have once been a main channel of the Willamette River as it flowed northward into the Columbia River, but currently the main Willamette River discharge moves northeastward into the Columbia River, forming Sauvie Island. The Multnomah Channel/Slough forms the west side of the island (see Figures 2.2 and 3.6). As a slough the channel has limited current flow, explaining the fine silt clay matrix of the Sunken Village beach, and its flow is influenced by the tidal action (though it is fresh water at this location). The site is on the outer convex curved edge of the channel point bar, therefore the depositional side, contributing to a slow build up of the original point bar levee at this location (see Figure 2.2). Therefore the beach deposits were progressively accreting out, with organic debris mats being deposited, along with the discarded cultural debris, in vegetal layers along the lee slope of the ancient bar, as revealed in TU4 excavations and deep-cores 5 and 6 at the site (see Punke, above).

Two paleoenvironmental conditions no doubt contributed to the ideal conditions at the Sunken Village location for its primary use as an acorn leaching pit station: (a) the non-aggressive currents of this protected slough, forming dense silt/clay point bar deposits for secure construction of hemlock bough-lined pits for the acorn harvest, and, more importantly, (b) the shallow aquifer flow from the island under the natural levee and surfacing along this section of the point bar, creating the underground water flow needed to affectively leach the potentially millions of acorns processed at this prime location.

The excavation of Test Unit 4 (TU4) in the second week of 2006 field work revealed the outside edge of the best remnant beach surface. TU4 revealed thick and shoreward-sloping vegetal mat beach surfaces in 2006, and over 4 meters depth of vegetal mat layers by coring in 2007, representing an *in situ* deposit of discrete cultural materials, concentrated in Transect VI (see Punke, above). That's not to understate the 125 meters of intertidal *in situ* features; the 114 acorn leaching pits and 55 wooden stakes that were driven into the beach in ancient times. However, much of their contents following their last use were cultural and non-cultural material that entered these low lying basins through natural processes. The intertidal zone for most marine peoples is where broken or worn items are discarded. Broken baskets, capes/skirts, mats, cordage, wooden wedges, arrow shafts, bentwood box pieces etc can all be expected to be thrown or swept into the intertidal zone and rapidly become waterlogged and naturally captured in the emptied acorn leaching pits. Material found in Test Unit 4 is probably the result of movement of cultural debris down the beach, creating vegetal mat layers which were occasionally covered by flood sands and silts as part of a river point bar expansion. This preservation of vegetal mat layers is probably assisted by the more aggressive aquifer discharge flowing through this section (Transect VI) of the site. In 2006 we were only able to excavate 50 cm down into TU 4 vegetal mat layers. In 2007 we excavated two cores; Core 5 in TU4 and Core 6 six meters west of it. The latter revealed cultural vegetal mat layering to over 4 meters depth (see Punke, above).

Sauvie Island was given the name 'Wappato Island' by the first overland American expedition lead by Lewis and Clark in 1805, and they called the whole Portland Basin "Wap-pa-too Valley from that root or plants growing Spontaniously in this valley only" (Clark, in Thwaites 1969, 3, 202). This leads to the question: where are the wapato tubers at Sunken Village wet site? The site must have been close to wapato beds/fields, either across the slough where ponds today have *Sagittaria latifolia* growing, or behind the natural levee where the island had ponds and seasonal ponding before the dike was built (Newman 1991, Figure 6.1; also see Figure 2.2). Wapato had to be a major food product and trade item for this location and the entire Portland Basin (Darby 2005). It does not require extensive processing such as is needed to leach acorns, and could be stored for long periods (Darby 2005). However our limited excavations failed to produce any recognizable wapato tubers in the waterlogged deposits (though PSU augering appears to have produced wapato corms (Appendix A:204; see website: http//www. library.spscc.ctc.edu/crm/JWA9.pdf).

It could be that this site was not where wapato was typically processed; 35MU4 was mainly used as an acorn processing area because of the environmental conditions described above (also note the limited focus on fishing at this location, discussed in Section 4.6). Possibly we did not reach levels with better conditions for wapato preservation. We did find tubers in the 1987 augering close to TU-4, and the augering revealed vegetal mats extending to a depth of 250 cm, but we never reached the bottom of these mats. In June 2007 our SPSCC researchers visited PSU and examined items recovered from Pettigrew's 1987 augers and found nothing that resembled tubers in the collection (see Pettigrew and Lebow 1987). Following our visit, Dr. Ken Ames found the notes for Auger #8 that indicated that tubers were found at 80–100 cm; Melissa Darby re-visited the collection but found no tubers in the samples from this horizon.

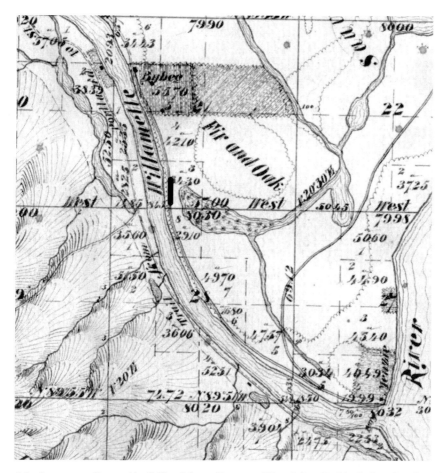

Figure 6.1. Surveyor General's Office Map, Oregon, City, May 5, 1854 showing location of the Sunken Village site (black block along natural levee) with a large wetland behind it and a fir and oak grove on ridge above. This wetland corresponds to the LIDAR map image of the Kruger Subbasin, Figure 6.5.

Recent excavations at the Katzie First Nations wet site DhRp52 near the lower Fraser River east of Vancouver, BC, Canada, has produced abundant wapato tuber shells, showing that they do preserve well in wet sites (Homan 2008).

6.2 Overview of the Sunken Village Artifact Assemblage

The Sunken Village (35MU4) artifact assemblage produced from a limited two fall seasons of low water (equivalent to a month of field work) demonstrates one of the richest heritage assemblages ever explored on the Northwest Coast of North America and validates its designation as a landmark site.

The acorn leaching pits can be considered the most abundant discrete artifacts found at the site, and, like most archaeological features, could not be extracted intact for laboratory analysis. Most of these pits had been heavily eroded during 150 years of abandonment, no doubt through wave action following increased motor boat movement through this slough over the past 80+ years. In fact several reports exist of boats being backed up to this section of slough to create accelerated erosion for artifact collecting (Newman 1991). Many of the acorn leaching pits dissected in the northern end of the site (north of TU4) were only 5–20 cm deep, though the hemlock bough bottom lining and whole acorns remain evident (see Figure 4.15). With a remnant beach remaining in Transect VI, and where TU4 and Pit P were explored, we were able to reconstruct the general depth and volume of whole acorn leaching pits (see Mathews, above), though more could be done to examine full pits in this well-preserved and possibly last surviving remnant beach area. Many of the *in situ* wooden stakes were round or split square/rectangular stakes averaging 5 cm in diameter. Some were driven into the south side of the acorn leaching pits, no doubt providing above-ground markers for silted-over pits (see Figure 4.5).

Following acorn leaching pits and stakes, the most common Sunken Village material culture assemblages are debris from making things: wood chip, split wood, lithic and basketry waste elements. Basketry waste appears to be very limited in numbers, especially when compared to other Northwest Coast wet sites such as Hoko River and Qwu?gwes; therefore it appears that wood working and lithic tool construction were more common tasks at Sunken Village. As mentioned above, these tasks ethnographically tend to be associated with men's work (Ray 1975, 142; though not exclusively, similar to basketry not being considered exclusively women's tasks). This may reflect a more predominantly male occupation of the site.

Major discrete artifacts were both of perishable (basketry, cordage, stakes, 'arrow' shafts, 'box' pieces) and more durable materials (projectile points, blade-like flakes, scrapers, bone tools). The bone artifacts are rare, but show a considerable variety of wedges, awls, beaver teeth chisels and projectile/harpoon points. The stone flake tools, projectile points and scrapers are common, considering the limited excavations. Slicing and scraping wear on the flake tools may associate with leather and hide work at the site, and may be important for slicing off the acorn skins in processing the large number being leached, and possibly for working on fiber artifacts such as basketry, cordage and many other tasks (no doubt multi-tasked, see Loffler, above). The projectile points are common, being made in large numbers at the site (see Fagan and Zehendner, above), and stylistically reflect a late-period assemblage when compared to other sites in the region. More importantly, comparisons with other sites in this area and around Puget Sound/Gulf of Georgia to the north, show a pattern of differing cultural style evolution, which probably reflects a deep-rooted and separate evolution of cultural ethnicity, Chinookan and Salishan, for a millennium (see Croes, Collard and Dennler, above).

The basketry assemblage reflected matting, baskets and clothing, with a fragment of a shredded cedar bark cape/skirt. The cedar root cross-warp basket is of a distinct contact-period Chinookan style, quite different from basketry styles seen from northern wet sites on the Northwest Coast of North America. After conducting cladistic analyses with ancient and museum baskets, we found that indeed Sunken Village and

Chinook museum baskets linked on a separate branch, and other Northwest Coast ancient and museum baskets linked in their own regions (see Ness *et al.*, above). No doubt basketry will be the most sensitive artifact on the Northwest Coast of North America in demonstrating who, ethnically, the people represent. We continue to track down artifact collections said to be from Sunken Village, and, now that we have *in situ* examples of basketry from Sunken Village, we can confidently associate similar basketry in collections said to be from 35MU4. In so doing, we can greatly increase the understanding of the cultural affiliation for this ancient site.

The following narrative of a 2007 basketry discovery shows just how significant the waterlogged context of our work at Sunken Village is, and what the preservation of organic materials can add to the interpretation of cultural histories through artifact studies. This recovery also demonstrates a snap-shot of the community involvement in these discoveries:

> On Wednesday September 19th, 2007 we found a far more important piece of basketry than we realized at the time of removal by our joint U.S. Tribal, U.S./ Canadian and Japanese archaeological team. In one of the acorn leaching pits in Transect V an extremely delicate soft material weave began to be exposed. We could see 2-strand string 'warps' or 'sewing' elements running through a very soft sedge/rush/tule-like material. It was too delicate to hydraulically float by our process of spraying water under the basketry piece until it releases from the basal matrix (though we tried), so we decided we would have to use a number of long stainless steel spatulas to lift it out on a 2–3 cm silt pedestal. That afternoon we returned to our tent lodging at the Native American Rehabilitation Association facilities (NARA) for dinner and borrowed all their large spatulas to be sure we had enough. We also were joined by a song group from the Grand Ronde Tribe (who were on their way to perform a welcoming for the Nike Corporation release of athletic shoes designed for Native Americans) and the President of our College, Dr. Gerald Pumphrey and Dean of Student Life, Dr. David Rector, who had driven up for dinner and to thank Dr. Akira Matsui and his team for sponsoring our project. We all returned to the site after dinner with a large board provided by NARA to place the basketry onto. The spatulas worked well and we were able to carefully lift out the soft basketry (Figure 6.2).
>
> With the successful recovery, the drum-group from Grand Ronde recognized the event and the international teamwork in songs, and speeches were given by all parties (Figure 6.3). However, we still had no idea of the particular importance of the actual basketry discovery.
>
> When this soft basketry reached the SPSCC conservation laboratory, we knew it would take weeks to fully turn-over and clean. Once we revealed the other side, we realized that the exposed weave had eroded through to the string 'warps', probably from long-term exposure of its surface at the site, and that it was actually constructed with a wicker plaiting [see Figures 4.8 and 5.25–5.27]. We sent pictures of the preserved side and weave to all the Tribes and principle archaeologists, and that's when the true importance began to be recognized.
>
> After sharing the photographs sent, Eirik Thorsgard, Cultural Protection

Figure 6.2. Crew running spatulas under soft basketry and carefully lifting it on a thin pedestal of silt onto a plywood platform covered with wet towel paper. (left) Eirik Thorsgard, Cultural Protection Coordinator, Grand Ronde Tribe with crew member Vanessa Chang (center, SFU, Canada) and others getting ready to lift; (light) lifting under way.

Figure 6.3. (left) Grand Ronde song-group recognizes the recovery of the soft basketry (Eirik Thorsgard with eagle feather); (right) The Tribe gave gifts to all, including wrapping Dr. Akira Matsui with a Confederated Tribes of Grand Ronde Pendleton blanket in thanks for his sponsorship of the 2007 joint work, while South Puget Sound Community College President Dr. Gerald Pumphrey (standing right) was honored and witnessed too.

Coordinator, Grand Ronde Tribe, got us in touch with Dr. Margaret Mathewson, a basketry consultant they regularly employ. She was very excited by the discovery, referring to it as the 'Lucy of basketry'. Generally Margaret saw this example linking very ancient soft bags examples of the U.S. Great Basin, especially from Spirit Cave (9,400 BP examples) through to museum collections of the Skokomish and Duwamish in Puget Sound. She called the weave 'Diamond Plaiting', as the distinct technique, and these soft bags from other sites are often woven with a soft sedge-like construction material such as tule or bulrush. Our example is a sedge material and possibly what is commonly called sweet grass in our region (see Hawes, above). Drs. Catherine Fowler and Eugene Hattori, basketry specialist from the State of Nevada, U.S.A, confirmed these associations and further pointed out that this distinct soft bag and weave also are seen, for one, as ancient (approximately 550 BP) and museum basketry of the Klamath Indians of Oregon. Catherine pointed out they have seen interesting similarities with Japanese Ainu soft bag weaves and examples from ancient Japanese Jomon sites. With this in mind, we contacted Dr. Akira Matsui who indicated that a Jomon site he is helping to explore, the Higashimyo site on the southern island of Kyushu and dating to over 7,000 BP, has examples of diamond plaiting called *Goza-me-Ori*, referring to a woven rush mat (Akira Matsui, personal communication 2008)[see Figures 5.28–5.29].

Therefore we realized that we have been too limited in conducting cladistic analyses of only Northwest Coast of North America ancient wet site and museum basketry (Ness *et al.*, above), but must, like our Japanese colleagues, look at these materials in a complete Pacific neighborhood/region perspective, and may have found an artifact category that can be used to inter-connect the Pacific Basin as a result of cultural sharing of styles for 7–9 millennia or more (see Ness *et al.*, above). Certainly this discovery is a unique outcome of our joint Tribe/U.S.-Canada/Japan collaboration.

The Sunken Village cordage, wooden wedges, 'arrow' shafts, and 'box' pieces also provide evidence of a diverse perishable material culture, reflecting the full inventory of kinds of perishable artifacts seen from major Northwest Coast wet site such as the Ozette Village wet site (Croes 2003; Kirk and Daugherty 2007). The considerable variety of wood and fiber artifacts from a limited two-season exploration demonstrates the likely richness of the remaining wet site at 35MU4.

6.3 Interpretation of Site Function

Site function at Sunken Village has been a topic of debate for at least eighty years, with the common name implying that it may be a village that was somehow submerged, possibly through seismic subsidence. Though geological faults may be in the vicinity (see Figure 3.6), we found limited indication of submergence, or, for that matter, of a major village. As a regional expert in excavating large ancient houses and villages in the Portland Basin, Dr. Ken Ames, who served as a panel discussant in a symposium we presented on Sunken Village (March 15, 2007 at the 60th Annual Northwest Anthropological Conference, Washington State University, Pullman, Washington, U.S.A.), stated that he did not see this site as a major village. Ancient houses in the region, for example Meier (35CO5; Ames, *et al.* 1998) and Cathlapotle (45CL1; Ames 1999), do have pits throughout the house floor area that are thought to have been covered with planks. This is not a pattern seen to the north; for example, at the Ozette Village wet site few pits are dug into the house floors (Samuels 1991).

However the pits at Sunken Village are not in deeply layered house floors or surrounded by signs of house walls or large posts as at Ozette (Samuels 1991). In fact, no signs of house floors or posts are reported on the intertidal beach or observed for the upper eroded beach cutbank of the natural levee. Some charcoal layers and possible steaming oven features are seen (see Fagan and Zehendner, above), but not in large numbers. In discussing the importance of wapato tubers in this region, Melissa Darby recently reported that:

> Throughout the Greater Lower Columbia region, aboriginal settlements appeared in two forms, including villages, containing several houses, and hamlets with only one or two permanent houses. These villages and hamlets in the Wapato Valley swelled with visiting friends and relatives during resource collecting times. People came in the fall for elk hunting and wapato seasons, and again in the spring for fish and wapato harvests (Lewis, in Thwaites 1969, 4, 223). Chinookan consultants reported to Lewis and Clark that many houses along the Lower Columbia were only occupied during the wapato harvest (2005, 210).

Based on the interpretations presented in Sections 6.1 and 6.2, it appears that 35MU4 was most likely a hamlet, with possibly a house or shelter or two on the natural levee, that was used for seasonal resource production and processing, possibly for wapato, but more likely for acorn processing in leaching pits, which would need to be guarded through the months of leaching. The only shelter construction material found during our surface mapping was a 'bark board', such as were often used on temporary shelters on the Northwest Coast as shingle materials (Stewart 1984:119). These are cedar bark un-thinned sections reinforced through their sides with split cedar sticks (Figure 6.4). This single piece of shelter construction material would tend to support the use of temporary hamlet-like shelters at the site.

Besides other people who might raid these valuable carbohydrate food resources, local ethnographic stories emphasize how 'Raccoon' wanted to get into Grandmothers acorn pits and, once successful, would reach "into the pit, under the dirt covering" to get to her acorn cache (Hunn 1990:183–187; Mathews, above). Raccoons are nocturnal and omnivorous and have human-like hands capable of nimble manipulation. Millions of acorns being stored and processed along a beach would be in constant threat from this potential visitor, especially at night.

This suggests a need to have guards overnight, probably by fires for warmth. This scenario could account for some of the abundant charcoal along the beach and the construction of arrow shafts and abundant projectile points at the site. In part, this may have mostly been a male task in the community, reflecting debitage frequencies that emphasize woodworking and flintknapping, and not basketry construction. We had hoped to see abundant raccoon bones in the faunal analysis, but only three elements were found. Therefore either the hypothesis is challenged, or the guards were affective in convincing them to stay away!

As with all Northwest Coast aquifer wet/waterlogged archaeological sites, this section of beach appears have been the main avenue of underground water flow, creating a low-oxygen, waterlogged zone with wood and fiber preservation. Dr. Curt Peterson's Portland State University student, Fiona Seifert, conducted tests on parts of this Sunken

Figure 6.4. Cedar bark board or shingle reinforced with cedar sticks run through the edges. Such boards were commonly used as roofing shingles for temporary shelters on the Northwest Coast, supporting the idea of shelters being present at Sunken Village on top of the natural levee.

Village aquifer and found the water flow in the aquifer seepage to be 5 ml/second (5 gallons/hour). Also the dissolved oxygen in the aquifer seepage measured 2.8 parts per million (ppm) versus the surface and adjacent river water content of 10.1 ppm, demonstrating the low oxygen leading to preservation of wood and fiber in this wet site (see Appendix R, in website: http://www.library.spscc.ctc.edu/crm/JWA9.pdf).

Therefore, as pointed out above, only this section of beach would function well for acorn leaching pits as a result of aquifers pumping waters out from behind the site, and, in this case, under the natural levee. Dr. Curt Peterson and his students also conducted a ground-penetrating radar and locational geological analysis of this site area (Waibel, *et al.* 2007; see Appendix R, website: http://www.library.spscc.ctc.edu/crm/JWA9.pdf), including LIDAR Paleo-Landscape Analysis. The LIDAR images best reflect how these aquifers would have come through only this section of natural levee deposits:

> The LIDAR images for the Sunken Village study area indicate the presence of an abandoned paleochannel meander track that left a terrace and underfilled depression on the east side of the present Multnomah channel…. The artificial drainage channel that bisects the acorn leach pit site takes advantage of the natural axial channel that drained the Kruger subbasin (Figure 6.5). The subbasins represent ponding features that could have served as a seasonal hydraulic head for elevated groundwater flow towards the lower Multnomah channel bank site. Any percolation through floodsilts to the underlying sand aquifer would have driven groundwater flow out to the channel bank, possibly as a confined aquifer below the channel bank mud layer (Waibel, *et al.* 2007; see alsoAppendix R in website: http://www.library.spscc.ctc.edu/crm/JWA9.pdf, and early 1854 map, Figure 6.1).

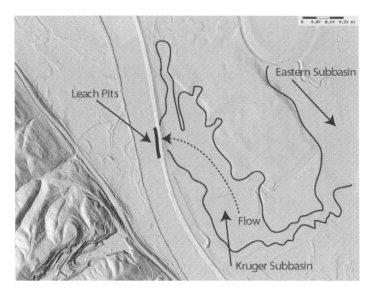

Figure 6.5. LIDAR image with outline (bold line) of Kruger and Eastern subbasins connected by the overflow discharge channel. Ponding, surface flow, and subsurface groundwater flow would have been concentrated in the axial discharge channel (dotted line) that leads to the acorn leaching pit site (from Waibel et al. 2007:19, see Appendix R, website: http://www.library.spscc. ctc.edu/crm/JWA9.pdf; see similar area in 1854 map, Figure 6.1).

The fact that we have wood and fiber preservation only along this stretch of beach (Transects II–VI), and not in Transects I and VII–XII (or 175 of the 300 meters explored), indicates that these north and south transects were beyond the aquifer movement and therefore not suited for acorn leaching pits. Dr. Peterson and his students have presented a 3–D illustration of the aquifer movement through this area of the site with a broader description provided in their caption (Figure 6.6).

As emphasized to us by California archaeological researcher, Wendy N. Pierce (Archaeological Research Center, Institute of Archaeology and Cultural Studies, California State University, Sacramento), who is familiar with both passive and aggressive acorn leaching, even with water moving through the acorns, it takes from 4–5 months for them to become completely sweet or tannic acid-reduced (Pierce, Personal Communications 2006). Ground-water flow is therefore essential, and the fact that aquifers only pump through this area of the beach was no doubt noticed by the ancient Multnomah People. The fact that this is a protected slough with low discharge also provides the ideal mud cap (Figure 6.6) for processing pits that are thus less likely to erode. Once lined with flat hemlock boughs, the 100+ pits recorded would potentially contain 2.5 million acorns, if all in simultaneous use (see Mathews, above). The aquifer movement through the hemlock needles and acorns would eventually and effectively remove the tannic acid. Some pits were marked on their south side with

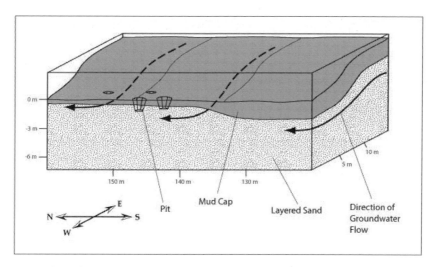

Figure 6.6. A three dimensional view of east-to-west groundwater flow following topography from the low relief basin in Sauvie Island interior into the Multnomah channel. The sandy mud cap provides a possible upper confinement to the (stippled) lower muddy sand aquifer. The acorn leaching pits are located where the mud cap is at its thinnest, being better exposed to the flow of the aquifer. The pit tops were stabilized by cohesive sandy mud. The scenario shown above demonstrates possible groundwater flow (arrows) from the seasonally flooded interior basin through the zone of acorn leaching pits (from Waibel et al. 2007:21, see Appendix R, website: http://www.library.spscc.ctc.edu/crm/JWA9.pdf).

a wooden stake and no doubt capped with a layer of boughs and matrix (Figure 6.7 and see Figure 4.5).

It is thought that the Sunken Village site is the largest passive acorn leaching pit site so far identified along the West Coast of North America. Pits have been recorded in California, but only a few at a time; certainly not an entire beach covered with over 100 pits capable of containing millions of acorns. Not only is this level of processing acorns a major discovery for Northwest Coast researchers, but is equally significant to researchers in California, where the heart of acorn subsistence exists along the North American Pacific Coast. Arguably this facility for passive acorn leaching in bulk, and possibly others in the Portland Basin area, helped sustain what is often considered the highest population density north of Mexico (Darby 2005:194). It may be that the acorn processing technologies spread south from here, rather than in the opposite direction, enhancing acorn use thoughout Oregon and perhaps parts of California.

As indicated by Mathews (above), the technique of passive leaching is remembered in northwest tribes today: "the Siletz of western Oregon call acorns that are leached in stream banks for several months to a year 'tus-xa', and acorns are still gathered, stored and eaten by people living there" (Bud Lane, personal communications 2007). Siletz, Grand Ronde and Warm Springs Tribal members often speak of acorns mashed and used as a common soup or stew stock with meals.

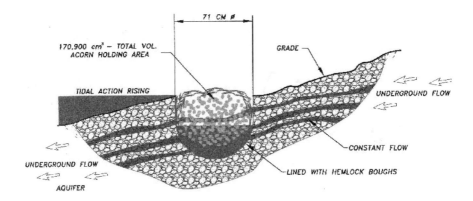

Figure 6.7. Schematic diagram of acorn leaching pit, showing aquifer pumping water through the acorns in the pits (drawing by Professor Michael Martin. CAD, SPSCC). See also End-piece.

In summary, this National Historic Landmark site seems to have functioned for several centuries as a place where people exploited ideal conditions for acorn leaching. Sunken Village (35MU4) certainly adds a unique new dimension to our understanding of Northwest Coast subsistence practices, resource intensification, probable ownership and no doubt management of oak grooves and acorn leaching pits, predicted surplus production for trade, and the importance of plant foods in an area best known for its fisheries focus. All these practices were argued for wapato in the Portland Basin ('Wapato Valley') by Melissa Darby (2005). If we combine the dual potential of wapato and acorn for this unique region, the influence of the Chinookan Peoples throughout the Northwest Coast and beyond becomes easier to explain. Unlike wapato, however, acorns require months of oversight while they leach. This considerable labor probably reflects a unique value attached to acorns as a product worth the time and energy to process; perhaps as a delicacy of considerable value in trade as well as consumption. The Multnomah family or families owning this particular prime section of aquifer leaching beach would no doubt have greatly enhanced their wealth through exchange of this high cost food. Trade is a particularly well developed and recorded activity amongst the Chinookan Indians.

With the discovery of basketry that links both very ancient and modern techniques in the U.S. and Japan, we also need to explore how this site reflects a complete Pacific Basin cultural association. Sunken Village (35MU4), after 2 limited low-water seasons of archaeological exploration, truly reflects a distinct and well-preserved acorn leaching station, no doubt of huge value to its ancient Multnomah owners. This wet site exploration has rapidly and forever expanded the cultural understanding of our overall and rich Pacific region heritage.

6.4 The wider significance of Sunken Village

When Principle Investigator, Dale Croes, began to realize during the 2006 fieldwork that the 'baskets' pits (as they were referred to by researchers in the past) dug into the beach at Sunken Village were acorn pits, he recalled a plenary talk by his friend and colleague, Dr. Akira Matsui (Chief Archaeologist, National Institute for Cultural Heritage, Nara, Japan), at the 2005 Wetland Archaeology Research Program (WARP) meeting in Scotland, UK. Matsui presented a major new discovery of wet site research in Japan: the 7,000 year old Higashimyo shellmidden and wet site on the southern island of Kyushu, with numerous examples of Jomon basketry, often in *acorn pits*. Following the 2006 Sunken Village field season Croes sent Matsui pictures and the report of the basketry and acorn pits found at Sunken Village. Matsui was keen to bring his researchers to see the site for themselves, and offered to sponsor an expanded recording of these features and additional deep coring of the site, which we accomplished in this international and intertribal effort in 2007.

Wet/wetland sites around the world provide a new dimension for understanding past cultures through their preservation of a major component often missing in other sites: wood and fiber artifacts and plant food resources. In this case, insights on the previously unknown (to archaeologists) value of oak products, both wood for fuel and acorns for food, on the ancient Northwest Coast of North America. Now we are observing ancient acorn use on the lower Fraser River east of Vancouver, BC, in Canada at the Katzie First Nations wet site (DhRp52; Homan 2008), on Washington State's Puget Sound at the Qwu?gwes wet site (45TN240), as well as at Sunken Village. We need to also look south to similar passive acorn pit leaching practices in California, U.S.A., where acorns are seen in macrofossils dating to 7–10,000 years ago and increase sharply between 2500 and 3000 years ago, when use is believed to intensify (Bettinger and Wohlgemuth 2006, 274–283). Bettinger and Wohlgemuth find that all California groups had access to several of the nine oak species deemed most important (2006, 274). Acorns are considered the most important California staple, helping to support one of the largest populations in ancient North America (Baumhoff 1978), who subsisted without any agricultural production as seen in the ancient U.S. Southwest, Southeast and Northeast.

Oaks are found on every continent that humans inhabit, and no doubt were a valuable resource throughout the ancient world. Almost 20% (31 of 165) of the cultures in the Human Resources Area Files (eHRAF) are referred to as either using acorns or lacking acorns in relation to their neighbors who make use of them. Twelve of these are on the American continent – Moerman lists 45 species and variations of oak (*Quercus* and *Lithocarpus*) that are used in North America alone for food, medicine and technology (Moerman 2003; Mathews, personal communications 2008; http://www. yale.edu/hraf/index.html). Besides North America and East Asia, acorn use is seen in paleoethnobotanical studies in many parts of Europe and Southwest Asia (Renfrew 1973). Also a closer review is needed of the potential for management of oak woodlands by ancient peoples throughout the world, as has been initiated in Northwest Europe (Mason 2000).

The focus of our particular work remains the Pacific Basin, and we plan to conduct expanded research into similar acorn pit sites in ancient Jomon, Japan, though these may be for storage, rather than processing, of acorns. Basketry used in acorn processing also provides a fertile area for Pacific Basin joint research and comparisons. The ancient Jomon wet site that Dr. Akira Matsui has been helping to explore on the southern island of Kyushu (the Higashimyo site), has over 700 recorded examples of basketry, including diamond plaited woven rush basketry (Akira Matsui, Personal Communications 2008).

6.5 Project support

In an overall world context we recognize we have much still to do in comparing our well-preserved data from the National Historic Landmark wet site of Sunken Village. We are pleased to have been able to begin exploring this rich site in 2006 and 2007, even with a very limited budget; the actual financial expenditure for two years of fieldwork and report writing is under $100,000 US, and largely possible through volunteer support from agencies, Tribes, college administrators, fellow researchers and a lot of donated time and facilities. We are pleased to see the broad interest provided by the avocational public, invaluable Tribal support and research involvement and assistance, and the regulatory agencies, and especially the Oregon State Historic Preservation Office and U.S. National Park Service and Army Corps of Engineers.

Even with this interest wet sites fieldwork sometimes never gets published, possibly because of the sheer volume of preserved data. We are please that the Wetland Archaeological Research Project (WARP) recognizes the need for interim reports on new discoveries to be published speedily (regardless of its sometimes rough shape) in order to quickly reach international researchers through their *Journal of Wetland Archaeology*. Currently wet site researchers are limited in numbers, and this journal is an invaluable means to communicate their work to all researchers and new students entering wetland site research. The Northwest Regional U.S. National Park Service, the agency that designates sites as National Historic Landmarks, provided the main part of the subsidies needed to assure the speedy publication of our current results. Our South Puget Sound Community College Anthropology Club, with 13 of our faculty and research students involved in the volume, provided the additional subsidy. Our partners, research specialists and authors from the Archaeological Investigations Northwest, Inc., were ever available to help, even to subsidize the work, with donated time, including this volume's graphics needs.

6.6 Recommendations for the future

Twenty years ago, following his assessment of Sunken Village through auger testing, Pettigrew concluded:

> The availability of the very large quantities of perishable cultural debris believed to be present at the Sunken Village Site, combined with the paleoenvironmental evidence no doubt associated with it, places this among the most scientifically valuable archaeological sites in North America and the world at large (1987:19).

We hope that, through this report on our two seasons of evaluation at the site, we have demonstrated the validity of Pettigrew's assessment, and conclusively vindicated its designation as a National Historic Landmark site. It is rightly one of the most famous such sites in the Western United States.

However, and typical of wet sites throughout the world, Sunken Village is at risk (Olivier 2004; see concluding statement below). The Sunken Village wet site appears to have progressively eroded away, as is often mentioned by persons who have visited the site through the past fifty or more years, so what is left becomes increasingly more important as a landmark cultural resource. Through this critical and timely field work at Sunken Village we found a few large remnant areas that are better preserved and remain fairly intact; these are in Transect VI, through TU-4, Pit P and Cores 5 and 6. Fortunately these critical areas were identified despite the short period of time we had to observe the entire 300+ meter beach area. These are the areas that require particularly strong protection, and this will be most effective within a strategy that recognizes the importance of the surrounding context.

We also need to compare our work with what has been done to protect and manage wet/wetland sites in other parts of the world. A process we need to pursue in evaluating Sunken Village and its future was well outlined by Bryony Coles in evaluating three European wetland sites (Coles 2004, 183–198). She explored their (a) physical context and existing means of exploitation, (b) archaeological profiles, (c) economic aspects, and (d) links with nature conservation programs. Some of these areas have begun to be explored here (a and b), but much more needs to be done with the Sunken Village site in exploring the last two (c and d).

Recommendations for the heritage management of Sunken Village wet site.

As a site of national importance, we strongly believe that the remaining areas of Sunken Village need to be carefully and systematically monitored for vandalism. In order to pursue any future field sampling or investigations of this National Historic Landmark site, the main areas of the site must remain protected from any further vandalism and/or erosion, and from any risk of de-watering. The following assessment is offered as a means of protecting and managing this unique and important National Historic Landmark archaeological site.

The limited 2006 rock facing, following placement of cloth and sand, allows protection of the immediate bank from vandalism, but still leaves the front waterlogged areas vulnerable. We also need to actively monitor the *indirect effect* of this rock facing on erosion along the exposed beach area, and especially the carefully mapped, photographed, and drawn 114 acorn leaching pits and 55 wooden stakes – these are unique *in situ* cultural features that are the main existing cultural resources and they are the most vulnerable to the indirect affects of future erosion, so must be directly and individually monitored. Therefore we highly recommend:

- Careful monitoring and annual evaluation of the specifically mapped, photographed, and drawn 114 acorn leaching pit surfaces and 55 in situ wooden stakes to determine any amount of erosion or damage done to these ancient cultural features – and the addition to the data base of any newly exposed acorn leaching pits or wooden stakes for future monitoring. (This would be in addition to the monitoring plan developed by consulting parties to regularly assess potential impacts of erosion/siltation near the rip-rap cover for a period of 5 years).

- The site should be patrolled on a regular basis during times of low water to deter vandalism.
- Use of surveillance cameras and signage indicating that the area is being monitored by cameras are suggested.
- A barrier should be constructed along the edge of the site between the dolphins to break the wave action from wind and passing boats. Log rafts stored in the area in the past reduced the wave action erosion and deterred the use of private boats to use propeller-wash to erode the bank.
- Measures for site protection and/or emergency recovery of sensitive deposits should be put into place in the event that the deposits are found to be threatened by erosion, construction impacts, or vandalism.
- A long-range plan for the curation, analysis, and interpretation of artifacts and environmental data from the site should be developed.
- Funds for site stewardship and interpretation should be sought by international, federal, Tribal, state, county, and local public agencies for site protection, interpretation, and enhancement.

Recommendations for future research at Sunken Village:

- Conduct detailed recording of Sunken Village site (35MU4) public and private collections (this has been initiated through support of the Confederated Tribe of Siletz Indian's Community Fund Award).
- Seek support for more fine screening of the 100% samples recovered.
- Continued diatom analyses of the deep cores will help to better define the depositional history of the site and the landform.
- Expanded plant identification of the wood and fiber artifacts and charcoal through microscopic plant cell analysis.
- Continued detailed analysis of the acorns, hazelnuts and other plant food materials found in the 114 acorn leaching pits that were mapped, tested and photographed, better defining the contributions of these plant resources to regional diets.
- When conducted, future systematic wet site excavation should minimally investigate the TU4 area (Transect VI), representing probably the last remnant beach surface at the site.
- Explore feasibility of a joint Tribes, U.S., Japanese limited exploration/excavation of Transect VI area to better understand the overall site and to compare wet site field excavation and analysis techniques among the participants to learn from each other.
- Further regional and cladistic comparative analyses of Sauvie ancient basketry, cordage, projectile points, bone artifacts and microblades, especially between the Portland Basin, Puget Sound, and Pacific Basin sites.
- Advanced computer aided 3–D mapping and modeling of the 114 acorn pits and overall site area.

- Examine economic aspects of future research with all involved communities (local, tribal, and scientific).
- Explore linkages with natural and/or archaeological conservation programs.

When discussing English Heritage's approach to wetland management, Adrian Olivier emphasized that a wetland site "tells us about all aspects of the past much more vividly than equivalent dryland sites", however "this evidence is particularly fragile and vulnerable to change and we must make common cause….to preserve and manage what survives for the benefit of present and future generations" (Olivier 2004, 115–168). Olivier's paper outlines four strategies for English Heritage wetland management, all of which apply to Sunken Village: management strategies, education and outreach, policy and procedures, and research and understanding. Many of these issues were addressed by one of the co-authors here, Maureen Newman-Zehendner, in her M.A. thesis and long professional involvement with Sunken Village, especially in her successful registration of this wet site on the U.S. National Register of Historic Places and the U.S. National Historic Landmark (NHL) status (Newman 1991). Olivier's and Newman's proposals and strategies need to be followed into the future.

When Principle Investigator Dale Croes participated in the 1987 limited auger testing of the Sunken Village site, he recognized that this was certainly one of the most important Northwest Coast wet sites known, and one that needed some professional attention. Croes and fellow co-editors Maureen Newman-Zehendner and John Fagan have watched for opportunities over the past 20 years to initiate this professional attention. The opportunity finally came when the U.S. Army Corps of Engineers required a cultural resource evaluation before considering a permit application to place protective stone rip-rap above the NHL wet site area.

As Olivier (2004) pointed out, these fragile and vulnerable wetland sites require special attention, including specialized archaeological techniques and research approaches, and we are beginning to see students and Tribes recognize the need to make sure these skills are learned and these heritage sites properly evaluated. In our case, the consulting Tribes all knew that the basketry and wooden artifacts were of particular value to their own heritage, identity and futures, and were ever-present at key meetings with agencies to be sure this site received the careful evaluation that it deserved. As for a new generation of students, we are also seeing their interest in making sure wet site excavation and preservation are part of their archaeological learning, something slow in coming but critical to wetland archaeology's future. Our colleagues in Japan also stepped forward to make sure these fragile and vulnerable cultural resources are recognized in their broad comparative context. We hope this is another step in moving archaeological research in that direction, and that the Sunken Village wet site will provide another point of reference in the evolution of that critical heritage research.

References

Ahler, Stanley A. 1971. *Projectile Point Form and Function at Roger's Shelter, Missouri.* Columbia: College of Arts and Science, University of Missouri-Columbia and the Missouri Archeological Society.

Agee, James K. 1993. *Fire Ecology of Pacific Northwest Forests.* Washington, D.C.: Island Press.

Aguilar, George W. Sr. 2005. *When the River Ran Wild!: Indian Traditions on the Mid-Columbia and the Warm Springs Reservation.* Portland, Oregon: Oregon Historical Society Press.

Alt, David D. and Donald W. Hyndman 1981 *Roadside Geology of Oregon.* Mountain Press Publishing Co., Missoula, Montana.

Alt, David D. and Donald W. Hyndman 1984. *Roadside Geology of Washington.* Mountain Press Publishing Co., Missoula, Montana.

Ames, Kenneth M. 1994. *Archaeological Context Statement: Portland Basin.* Wapato Valley Archaeological Project Report No. 4, Department of Anthropology, Portland State University, Portland, Oregon. Submitted to the Oregon State Historic Preservation Office, Salem.

Ames, Kenneth M. 1999. *Archaeological Investigations at 45CL1 Cathlapotle (1991–1996), Ridgefield National Wildlife Refuged, Clark County, Washington.* A Preliminary Report prepared for U.S. Fish and Wildlife Service, Portland, OR. Department of Anthropology, Portland State University.

Ames, Kenneth M., William L. Cornett, and Stephen C. Hamilton 1998. *Archaeological Investigations (1991–1995) at 45CL1 (Cathlapotle): Clark County, Washington: A Preliminary Report.* Wapato Valley Archaeology Project Report Number 6, Department of Anthropology, Portland State University and U.S. Fish and Wildlife Service.

Ames, Kenneth M. and Herbert D. G. Maschner 1999. *Peoples of the Northwest Coast, Their Archaeology and Prehistory.* London: Thames and Hudson.

Andrefsky William Jr. 2005. *Lithics: Macroscopic Approaches to Analysis.* Second edition. New York: Cambridge University Press.

Andrefsky William Jr. 1997. Thoughts on stone tool shape and inferred function. *Journal of Middle Atlantic Archaeology* 13:125–44.

Atwater, Brian F. 1994. *Geology of Holocene Liquefaction Features Along the Lower Columbia River At Marsh, Brush, Price, Hunting, and Wallace Islands, Oregon and Washington.* June U.S. Department of the Interior. U.S. Geological Survey. Open File Report 94–209. U.S. Geological Survey, Department of Geological Sciences, University of Washington, Seattle, WA 98195.

Bagley, C. B. 1930. *Indian Myths of the Northwest*. Seattle, Washington: Lowman and Hanford Company.

Bainbridge, David A. 1986. Use of Acorns for Food in California: Past, Present and Future. Paper presented at Symposium on Multiple-Use Management of California's Hardwoods, San Luis Obispo, California, November 12–14.

Balsillie, J. H., and G. T. Benson 1971. Evidence for the Portland Hills Fault. *The ORE BIN*. 33(6)109–118.

Barnett, Homer G. 1955. *The Coast Salish of British Columbia*. Eugene: University of Oregon Press.

Baumhoff, Martin A. 1978. Environmental Background. In R. F. Heizer (ed.) *Handbook of North American Indians, Vol. 8, California*, 16–24. Washington DC: Smithsonian Institute Press.

Basgall, Mark E. 1987. Resource Intensification Among Hunter-Gatherers: Acorn Economics in Prehistoric California. *Research in Economic Anthropology* 9, 21–52.

Baxter, Michael J. 1994. *Exploratory Multivariate Analysis in Archaeology*. Edinburgh University Press.

Beeson, M. H., Tolan, T. L., and Madin, I. P. 1991. Geologic map of the Portland quadrangle, Multnomah and Washington counties, Oregon and Clark County, Washington, Oregon Department of Geology and Mineral Industries Geological Map Series GMS-75, scale 1:24,000.

Bernick, Kathryn 1983. A Site Catchment Analysis of the Little Qualicum River Site, DiSc 1: A Wet Site on the East Coast of Vancouver Island, BC. *National Museum of Man Mercury Series* 118.

Bernick, Kathryn 2005. *Research Options for Archaeological Investigations at Sunken Village National Historic Landmark, 35MU4: A Planning Document*. Report Submitted to the National Park Service, Seattle, Washington

Bernick, Kathryn 2007. Identifying Anthropogenic Deposits in Alluvial Settings on the Northwest Coast. From proceedings from the WARP 2005 Conference. In *Archaeology from the Wetlands: Recent Perspectives*, National Museum of Scotland, Edinburgh, Scotland.

Bettinger, R. L. and E. Wohlgemuth 2006. California Plants. In Douglas Ubelacker (ed.) *Handbook of North American Indians, Vol. 3, Origins, Ecology, and Population*, 274–283. Washington DC: Smithsonian Institute Press.

Blakely, R. J., R. E. Wells, T. S. Yelin, I. P. Madin, and M. H. Beeson 1995. Tectonic Setting of the Portland-Vancouver Area, Oregon and Washington – Constraints from low-altitude aeromagnetic data. *Geological Society of America Bulletin* 107(9)1051–1062.

Boas, Franz 1888. Myths and legends of the Catloltq of Vancouver Island. *American Antiquarian and Oriental Journal* 10

Boas, Franz 1890. First general report on the Indians of British Columbia. *Report of the 59th meeting of the British Association for the Advancement of Science* 801–855. Newcastle-upon-Tyne, September 1889.

Boas, Franz 1894. *Chinook Texts*. Bureau of American Ethnology Bulletin 20. Washington D. C.

Boggs, S. Jr. 2001. *Principles of Sedimentology and Stratigraphy, Third Edition*. Prentice-Hall, Inc. New Jersey.

Borden, Charles E. 1975. Origins and Development of Early Northwest Coast Culture to About 3000 B.C. *National Museum of Man Mercury Series*. Archaeological Survey of Canada, Paper No. 45. National Museum of Canada.

Bourdeau, Alex 2003. Excerpts from: "Geologically Complex" The Flood Plain of the Lower Columbia River. December 25, 2003. U.S. Fish and Wildlife Service. 20555 SW Gerda Lane, Sherwood, OR 97140.

Boyd, Robert 1985. *The Introduction of Infectious Diseases Among the Indians of the Pacific Northwest, 1774–1874*. Ph.D. dissertation, Department of Anthropology, University of Washington, Seattle. University Microfilms, Ann Arbor.

Boyd, Robert 1990. Demographic History, 1774–1874. In Wayne Suttles (ed.) *Handbook of North American Indians. Vol. 7. Northwest Coast*. Smithsonian: Washington, D.C.

Boyd, Robert 1995. *Kalapuya Disease and Depopulation*. Symposium: What Price Eden? The Willamette Valley in Transition 1812–1855. Mission Mill Museum Association: Salem, Oregon.

Boyd, Robert and Yvonne P. Hajda 1987. Seasonal Population Movement Along the Lower Columbia River: The Social and Ecological Context. *American Ethnologist* 14(2), 309–326

Bretz, J. Harlen 1913. *Glaciation of the Puget Sound Region*. Washington Geological Survey. Henry Landes, State Geologist.

Burke Museum of Natural History and Culture 2006. *WTU Herbarium Image Collection*. Seattle, WA. http://biology.burke.washington.edu/herbarium/imagecollection.php

Butler, B. Robert 1965. Perspectives on the Prehistory of the Lower Columbia Valley. *Tebiwa*. Journal of the Idaho State University Museum. Pocatello, ID.

Cameron, K. A. and Patrick T. Pringle 1986. Postglacial lahars of the Sandy River basin, Mount Hood, Oregon. *Northwest Science* 60(4), 225–237.

Cameron, K. A. and Patrick T. Pringle 1987. A detailed chronology of the most recent major eruptive period at Mount Hood, Oregon. *Geological Society of America Bulletin* 99(6), 845–851.

Carey, Charles 1971. *General History of Oregon*. Binford and Mort Publishers: Portland, OR.

Carver, D. H. and Carver, G. A. 1996. Earthquake and thunder: Native oral histories of paleoseismicity along the southern Cascadia subduction zone. *Geological Society of America, Cordilleran Section, 92nd annual meeting, 1996 abstracts with programs* 28, 54.

Church, J. A., J. M. Gregory, P. Huybrechts, M. Kuhn, K. Lambeck, M. T. Nhuan, D. Qin, and P. L. Woodworth 2001. Changes in Sea Level. In J. T. Houghton, Y. Ding, D. J. Griggs, M. Noguer, P. van der Linden, X. Dai, K. Maskell, and C. I. Johnson (eds), *Climate Change 2001: The Scientific Basis*, 639–694. Contribution of Working Group 1 to the Third Assessment Report of the Intergovernmental Panel on Climate Change. Cambridge University Press.

Churchill, Steven E. 1993. Weapon technology, prey size selection, and hunting methods in modern hunter-gatherers: implications for hunting in the Paleolithic and Mesolithic. In Gail Larson Peterkin, Harvey M. Bricker, and Paul Mellars (eds), *Hunting and Animal Exploitation in the Later Paleolithic and Mesolithic of Eurasia*, 11–24. Archaeological Papers 4. Arlington, Virginia: American Anthropological Association.

Cleaver, J. D. 1986. *Island Immigrants: The Bybees and The Howells*. Oregon Historical Society Press. Portland, OR.

Clynne, M.A. 2005. *Pre-1980 Eruptive History of Mount St Helens, Washington. Vancouver, WA*. U.S. Geological Survey, David A. Johnston Cascades Volcano Observatory. USGS Fact Sheet, 2005–3045.

Conner, Glen 1865. Kentucky's Climate During the Civil War. *Kentucky Climate Center: Fact*

Sheet. 2005. Department of Geography and Geology, Western Kentucky University, 1906 College Heights Blvd., Bowling Green, KY 42101.

Coles, Bryony 2004. Steps towards the Heritage Management of Wetlands in Europe. *Journal of Wetland Archaeology* 4, 183–198.

Cox, Ross 1957. *The Columbia River.* Jane R. Stewart (ed.). University of Oklahoma Press.

Crandell, Dwight R. 1980. Recent eruptive history of Mount Hood, Oregon, and potential hazards from future eruptions. *U.S. Geological Survey Bulletin 1492*. pp. 1–75.

Crandell, Dwight R. 1987. Deposits of pre-1980 pyroclastic flows and lahars from Mount St. Helens volcano, Washington. *U.S. Geological Survey Professional Paper 1444*, 1–91: 1 plate.

Croes, Dale R. 1977. *Basketry from the Ozette Village Archaeological Site: A Technological, Functional and Comparative Study.* Ph.D. dissertation, Washington State University. Pullman, Washington.

Croes, Dale R. 1980. Cordage from the Ozette Village Archaeological Site: A Technological, Functional and Comparative Study. Washington State University, Pullman, Washington. *Laboratory of Archaeology and History* Project Report 9.

Croes, Dale R. 1987. *Sunken Village Site (35MU4) Archaeological Potential as a Northwest Coast Wet Site.* Prepared for Infotech Research, Inc., R. Pettigrew, and C. Lebow. Report No. PNW 87–10.

Croes, Dale R. 1989. Prehistoric ethnicity on the Northwest Coast of North America, an evaluation of style in basketry and lithics. In R. Whallon (ed.), *Research in Anthropological Archaeology*, 101–130. Academic Press, New York.

Croes, Dale R. 1995. *The Hoko River Archaeological Site Complex: The Wet/Dry Site (45CA213) 3,000–1,700B.P.* Washington State University Press. Pullman, WA 99164–5910.

Croes, Dale R. 2001. North Coast Prehistory—Reflections from Northwest Coast Wet Site Research. In Jerome S. Cybulski (ed.), *Perspectives on Northern Northwest Coast Prehistory,* 145–171, *Mercury Series* Paper 160. Canadian Museum of Civilization, Hull, Quebec.

Croes, Dale R. 2003. Northwest Coast wet-site artifacts: a key to understanding resource procurement, storage, management, and exchange. In R. G. Matson, G. Coupland and Q. Mackie, *Emerging from the Mist, Studies in Northwest Coast Culture History*, 51–75. UBC Press, Vancouver, BC.

Croes, Dale R. 2005. *The Hoko River Archaeological Site Complex: The Rockshelter (45CA21), 1,000–100 B.P., Olympic Peninsula, Washington.* Washington State University Press.: Pullman, Washington

Croes Dale R., Katherine Kelly and Mark Collard 2005. Cultural historical Context of Qwu?gwes (Puget Sound, USA): A preliminary Investigation. *Journal of Wetland Archaeology* 5, 137–149.

Croes, Dale R., John L. Fagan and Maureen M. Zehendner (eds) 2006. *Testing the National Historic Landmark Wet Site, 35MU4, The Sunken Village Archaeological Site, Multnomah County, Oregon.* Prepared for Sauvie Island Drainage Improvement Company, Portland, OR., Report No. 4, Department of Anthropology, South Puget Sound Community College and Archaeological Investigations Northwest, Inc.

Croes, Dale R., John L. Fagan and Maureen M. Zehendner (eds) 2007a. *A U.S. National Historic Landmark Wet Site, the Sunken Village Site (35MU4), Portland, Oregon – the First Explorations*, Report No. 5, Department of Anthropology, South Puget Sound Community College and Archaeological Investigations Northwest, Inc. Submitted as 2007 report to the Oregon State Historic Preservation Office.

Croes, Dale, Rhonda Foster, Larry Ross, Melanie Diedrich, Nea Hubbard, Katherine Kelly,

Mandy McCullough, Tom McCullough, Karen Myers, Cassandra Sharron, Barbara Vargo, Rebecca Wigen, and Lauren Valley 2007b. Qwu?gwes A Squaxin Island Tribal Heritage Wet Site, Puget Sound, U.S.A. In (edited by SWAP, compiled by Catherine Green), *Archaeology from the Wetlands: Recent Perspectives, Proceedings of the 11th International Wetlands Archaeological Research Project Conference, Edinburgh, Scotland*, 135–156.

Croes, D. R., S. Williams, L. Ross, M. Collard, C. Dennler and B. Vargo 2008. The Projectile Point Sequences in the Puget Sound Region, In Roy Carlson and Martin P. R. Magne, (eds), *Projectile Point Sequences in Northwestern North America.* SFU Archaeology Press: Burnaby, BC.

Crosby, Alfred W. 1994. *Germs Seeds and Animals: Studies in Ecological History.* M. E. Sharpe Inc.: Armonk, New York.

Danielopol, Dan L., Janine Gibert, and Jack A. Stanford 1994. *Groundwater Ecology.* Academic Press: San Diego CA.

Darby, Melissa 2005. The Intensification of Wapato (*Sagittaria latifolia*) by the Chinookan People of the Lower Columbia River. In Deur, Douglas and Nancy J. Turner (eds), *Keeping It Living, Traditions of Plant Use and Cultivation on the Northwest Coast of North America*, 194–217. University of Washington Press: Seattle.

DePuydt, Ray 1994, *Data Recovery Excavations from Site 45PC101, North Nemah River Bridge Site, Pacific County, Washington.* Eastern Washington University.

Deevey, Edward S. and Richard Foster Flint 1957, Postglacial Hypsithermal Interval. *Science* New Series, 125 (3240), 182–184.

DeVoto, Bernard (ed) 1997[1953], *The Journals of Lewis and Clark.* Boston/New York: Houghton Mufflin.

Diedrich, Melanie M. 2007a. *Setting the Stage – The Environment at Sauvie Island.* Paper presented at Northwest Anthropological Conference, Washington State University, Pullman, Washington, March 15–17.

Diedrich, Melanie M. 2007b. Location and Setting. In Croes, D. R., Fagan, J. L., and Zehedner, M. N. (eds), *Testing the National Historic Landmark Wet Site 35MU4, the Sunken Village Archaeological Site, Multnomah County, Oregon*, 6–16. Archaeological Investigations Northwest, Inc., Portland, Oregon, and South Puget Sound Community College, Olympia, Washington, Report No. 4. Prepared for Sauvie Island Drainage Improvement Company, Portland, Oregon.

Dodds, Walter K. 2002. *Freshwater Ecology: Concepts and Environmental Applications.* Academic Press: San Diego CA.

Drennan Robert D. 1996. *Statistics for Archaeologist: a Commonsense Approach.* Plenum Press. New York.

Drooker, Penelope B. and Laurie D. Webster (eds) 2000. *Beyond Cloth and Cordage: Archaeological Textile Research in the Americas.* University of Utah Press: Salt Lake City, Utah.

Dunnell, Robert C., J. C. Chatters, and L. V. Salo 1974. *Archaeological Survey of the Vancouver Lake – Lake River Area. Clark County, Washington.* U.S. Army Corps of Engineers. Portland, OR.

Eder, Jeanne 2001. Bridge of the Gods. *Frontiers* 22(3).

EPA (U.S. Environmental Protection Agency) 2006. "Willamette River: Fact Sheet." American Heritage Rivers. http://www.epa.gov/rivers/98rivers/fswillam.html. Google. 2007.

Fagan, John L. 2004. *Archaeological Exploration at 35MU4, the Sunken Village Site, A National Historic Landmark in Multnomah County, Oregon.* Archaeological Investigations Northwest, Inc. Report No. 1342. Report submitted to The Portland District, U.S. Army Corps of Engineers, Portland Oregon.

Fedje, Daryl W. and Rolf W. Mathewes (eds) 2005 *Haida Gwaii, Human History and Environment from Time of Loon to the Time of the Iron People*. U.B.C. Press: Vancouver, B.C.

Fenn, Elizabeth A. 2001. *Pox Americana: The Great Smallpox Epidemic of 1775–82*. Hill and Wang. A division of Farrar, Straus and Giroux: New York.

Ferring, C. Reid 1992. Alluvial pedology and geoarchaeological research. In Vance T. Holliday (ed.), *Soils in Archaeology Landscape Evolution and Human Occupation*, 1–40. Smithsonian Institution Press: Washington D.C..

Fiacco, R. Joseph, Jr., Julie M. Palais, Mark S. Germani, Gregory A. Zielinski, and Paul A. Mayewski 1993. Characteristics and possible source of a 1479 A.D. volcanic ash layer in a Greenland ice core. *Quaternary Research* 39(3), 267–273.

Florian, Mary-Lou E., Dale Paul Kronkright and Ruth E. Norton 2002. *The Conservation of Artifacts Made from Plant Materials*. J. Paul Getty Trust.

Foged, N. 1981. *Diatoms in Alaska*. Bibliotheca Phycologica, Band 53: Vaduz, J. Cramer.

Franchére, Gabriel 1954. *A Voyage to the Northwest Coast of America*. Milo Milton Quaife (ed.). Lakeside Press. R. R. Donnelley and Sons Company: Chicago.

Friedman, Janet 1978. *Wood Identification By Microscopic Examination: A Guide for the Archaeologist on the Northwest Coast of North America*. British Columbia Provincial Museum.

Friedman, Janet 2005. Prehistoric Uses of Wood at Ozette Archaeological Site. *OzetteArchaeological Project Research Reports*, 99–212. WSU Department of Anthropology Reports of Investigations 68, National Park Service, Northwest Regional Office.

Gifford, E. W. 1936. California Balanophagy. In Heizer, R. F. and Whipple, M. A. 1971, *The California Indians*. University of California Press: Berkeley.

Gill, Steven J. 2005 [1983]. Ethnobotany of the Makah and Ozette People, Olympic Peninsula, Washington. *Ozette Archaeological Project Research Reports*, 55–94, 339–430. WSU Department of Anthropology Reports of Investigations 68. National Park Service, Northwest Regional Office.

Gleeson, Paul F. 2005. Ozette Woodworking Technology, *Ozette Archaeological Project Research Reports*, 221–332. WSU Department of Anthropology Reports of Investigations 68. National Park Service, Northwest Regional Office.

Goodyear, Albert C. 1974. *The Brand Site: A Techno-Functional Study of Dalton Site in Northeast Arkansas*. Publications on Archaeology, Research Series 7. Fayetteville: Arkansas Archaeological Survey.

Greiser, Sally T. 1977. Micro-analysis of Wear Patterns on Projectile Points and Knifes From the Jurgens Site, Lersey, Colorado. *Plains Anthropologists* 22, 107–16.

Grove, J.M. 1987. Glacier Fluctuations and Hazards. *The Geographic Journal* 153(3), 351–367.

Gumbus, A. 1999. Lithic Attribute Designations. LITHICS-Net. Http://members.aol.com/artgumbus/lithinfo.html. Accessed 1/10/2006

Gunther, Erna 1973[1945]. *Ethnobotany of Western Washington: The Knowledge and Use of Indigenous Plants by Native Americans*. University of Washington Press: Seattle and London.

Hajda, Yvonne P. 1984. *Regional Social Organization in the Greater Lower Columbia, 1792–1830*. Dissertation. Chairperson of the Supervisory Committee: Professor James B. Watson, Department of Anthropology. University of Washington.

Harper, J. Russel, (ed.) 1971. *Paul Kane's Frontier*. University of Toronto Press: Toronto, Canada.

Hawes, Kathleen. 2007. *Wood and Fiber Artifact Identification: Cellular Analysis*. Paper presented at Northwest Anthropological Conference, Washington State University, Pullman, Washington, March 15–17.

Heaton, T. H. and Snavely, P. D. 1985. Possible tsunami along the northwestern coast of the United States inferred from Indian traditions. *Bulletin of the Seismological Society of America* 75, 1,455–1,460.

Hemphill-Haley, E. 1993. *Taxonomy of recent and fossil (Holocene) diatoms (Bacillariophyta) from northern Willapa Bay, Washington.* U.S. Geological Survey, Open-File Report 93–289: 151p.

Hemphill-Haley, E. and R. C. Lewis 1995. *Distribution and taxonomy of diatoms (Bacillariophyta) in surface samples and two-meter core from Winslow Marsh, Bainbridge Island, Washington.* U.S. Geological Survey Open-File Report 59–833pp.

Hibbs, Charles F. 1972. *Archaeological Survey of the Southern Shore of Vancouver Lake, Clark County, Washington.* Ms. on file, Department of Archaeology and Historic Preservation. Olympia, WA.

Hibbs, Charles F. 1987. *Mist to Sauvie Island Pipeline Survey.* Draft of report to Northwest Natural Gas Company. Charles F. Hibbs and Associates: St. Johns, OR.

Hibbs, Charles F., and David V. Ellis 1988. *An Inventory of cultural Resources and an Evaluation of the Effects of the Proposed North Coast Feeder Gas Pipeline, Located Between Deer Island and Sauvie Island, Lower Columbia River Valley, in Oregon.* 3 vols. Charles Hibbs and Associates, Inc.: Portland, Oregon. Submitted to Northwest Natural Gas Company. Portland, OR.

Hitchcock, Leo C. and Arthur Cronquist 1973. *Flora of the Pacific Northwest: an Illustrated Manual.* University of Washington Press.

Homan, Amy 2008. *You say Potato I say Potato: Current Investigations of the Katzie First Nation, Wapato, and Pitt Polder, British Columbia, Canada.* Paper presented at the 61st Annual Northwest Anthropological Conference, Victoria, British Columbia, Canada.

Hunn, Eugene S. 1990. *Nch'I-Wa'na, "The Big River": Mid-Columbia Indians and their land.* Seattle, Washington: University of Washington Press.

Jacobs, M. 1959. *Clackamas Chinook Texts II.* Indiana University Research Center in Anthropology, Folklore, and Linguistics, Publication 11. Bloomington, Indiana.

Jermann, J. V., and J. Hollenbeck 1976. *An Archaeological Assessment of Fifty-two Proposed Disposal Sites on the Lower Columbia River.* University of Washington Office of Public Archaeology: Seattle, Washington.

Jewett, Stanley G., Walter P. Taylor, William T. Shaw and John W. Aldrich 1953. *Birds of Washington State.* University of Washington Press: Seattle.

John, J. 1983. The diatom flora of the Swan River Estuary, Western Australia. *Bibliotheca Phycologica,* Band 64: Vaduz, J. Cramer, 359p.

Jones, Joan M. 1968. *Northwest Coast Basketry and Cultural Change.* Research Report No. 1. The Thomas Burke Memorial Washington State Museum. Seattle, WA.

Jones, Joan M. 1976. *Northwest Coast Indian Basketry, a Stylistic Analysis.* Unpublished doctoral dissertation, University of Washington, Seattle, WA.

Jones, Roy F. 1972. *Wappato Indians.* Privately Published: Vancouver, Washington.

Keeley, Lawrence H. 1980. Experimental Determination of Stone Tool Uses. In *Prehistoric Archeology and Ecology Series.* The University of Chicago Press: Chicago and London.

Kidder, Tristram R. 1997. Sugar Reflotation: An Alternative Method for Sorting Flotation – derived Heavy Fraction Samples. *Journal of Field Archaeology* 24(1), 93–45. Boston University.

Kirk, Ruth and Richard D. Daugherty 2007. *Archaeology in Washington.* University of Washington Press: Seattle, Washington.

Kongas, Lembi 1979. *The Blue Lake Survey Region: A Cultural Resources Approach*. Portland State University: Portland, Oregon.

Kooyman, Brian P. 2000. *Understanding Stone Tools and Archaeological Sites*. University of Calgary Press.

Kramer, K. and H. Lange-Bertalot 1986. *Bacillariophyceae*. 1. Teil: Naviculaceae. In H. Ettl, J. Gerloff, H. Heynig, and D. Mollenhauser (eds.), Süsswasserflora von Mitteleuropa 2/1. Gustav Fischer Verlag, Stuttgart, 876pp.

Kramer, K. and H. Lange-Bertalot 1988. *Bacillariophyceae*. 2. Teil: Bacillariacea, Epithemiaceae, Surirellaceae. In H. Ettl, J. Gerloff, H. Heynig, and D. Mollenhauser (eds), Süsswasserflora von Mitteleuropa 2/2. Gustav Fischer Verlag, Stuttgart, 596pp.

Kramer, K. and H. Lange-Bertalot 1991a. *Bacillariophyceae*. 3. Teil: Centrales, Fragilariaceae, Eunotiaceae. In H. Ettl, J. Gerloff, H. Heynig, and D. Mollenhauser (eds), Süsswasserflora von Mitteleuropa 2/3. Gustav Fischer Verlag, Stuttgart, 437pp.

Kramer, K. and H. Lange-Bertalot 1991b. *Bacillariophyceae*. 4. Teil: Achnanthaceae. Kritische Ergänzungen zu Navicula (Lineolate) und Gomphonema. In H. Ettl, J. Gerloff, H. Heynig, and D. Mollenhauser (eds), Süsswasserflora von Mitteleuropa 2/4. Gustav Fischer Verlag, Stuttgart, 876pp.

Kuykendall, G. 1889. A Graphic Account of the Religions or Mythology of the Indians of the Pacific Northwest, Including a History of Their Superstitions, Marriage Customs, Moral Ideas and Domestic Relations, and Their Conception of a Future State, and the Re-habiliment of the Dead. In Elwood Evans *et al.*, *History of the Pacific Northwest, Oregon and Washington, vol. 2*, 60–95. Portland, Oregon: North Pacific History Co.

Lawrence, D. B. and E. G. Lawrence 1958. Bridge of the Gods Legend, Its Origin, History and Dating. *Mazama* 40(13), 40–41.

Laws, R. A. 1988. Diatoms (Bacillariophyceae) from surface sediments in the San Francisco Bay estuary. *Proceedings of the California Academy of Science* 45, 133–254.

Liberty, Lee M., M. A. Hemphill-Haley, and I. P. Madin 2003. The Portland Hills Fault: uncovering a hidden fault in Portland, Oregon using high-resolution geophysical methods. *Tectonophysics*, 368, 89–103.

Löffler, Germán 2007. *Microscopy Analysis Utilized in the Identification of Cutting, Scraping, Slicing and Whittling Activities on Flake Tools from the Qwu?gwes (45TN240), Hartstene, and the Sunken Village (35MU4) sites in the Central Northwest Coast of North America*. M.A. Thesis, Department of Anthropology, Washington State University, Pullman.

Löffler, Germán 2008 (in prep). Microscopy Analysis in Identifying Whittling, Scraping and Slicing Activities on Blade-like-flake Tools from the Qwu?gwes Site near Olympia, Washington, for Production of Wood and Fiber Artifacts. *Journal of Northwest Anthropology* 42(2).

Losey, R. 2001. Oral Traditions of Earthquakes and Tsunamis on the Central Cascadia Coast: Variation of Accounts and Relations to Historically Observed Patterns across the Northwest Coast. In Younker, Jason, Mark A. Tveskov, and David G. Lewis (eds), *Changing Landscapes: Telling Our Stories*. Proceedings of the 4th Annual Coquille Cultural Preservation Conference, 2000. Coquille Indian Tribe, North Bend, Oregon.

Ludwin, R. 1999. Cascadia Megathrust Earthquakes in Pacific Northwest Indian Myths and Legends. Draft accessed online at: http://www.ess.washington.edu/SEIS/PNSN/HIST_CAT/STORIES/draft1.html

Ludwin, R. S., Dennis, R., Carver, D., McMillan, A. D., Losey, R., Clague, J., Jonientz-Trisler, C., Bowechop, J., Wray, J., and James, K. 2005. Dating the 1700 Cascadia Earthquake: Great

Coastal Earthquakes in Native Stories. *Seismological Research Letters*, 76(2), 140–148.

Lyons, C. P. 1977. *Trees, Shrubs and Flowers to Know in Washington*. J. M. Dent and Sons Ltd.

Mackey, Harold 2004. *The Kalapuyans A Sourcebook on the Indians of the Willamette Valley*. Mission Mill Museum and The Confederated Tribes of Grand Ronde Community of Oregon. Salem, Oregon.

Madin, I. P. 1990. Earthquake hazard geology maps of the Portland Metropolitan area, Oregon – text and map explanation; Oregon Department of Geology and Mineral Industries, Open-File Report 0–90–2.

Major, Jon J. and Kevin M. Scott 1988. Volcaniclastic sedimentation in the Lewis River valley, Mount St. Helens, Washington – Processes, extent, and hazards. *U.S. Geological Survey Bulletin 1383–D*, 1–38.

Mason, Otis T. 1904. *Aboriginal American Basketry: Studies in a Textile Art without Machinery*. Annual Report of the Smithsonian Institution: Washington, D.C.

Mason, S. L. R. 2000. Fire and Mesolithic Subsistence – managing oaks for acorns in Northwest Europe? *Palaeogeography, Palaeoclimatology, Palaeoecology* 164(1), 139–150.

Mathews, Bethany 2007. *The Acorn-Leaching Pits of Sauvie Island: Macroflora Analysis, Comparison of Regional Acorn Use, and Human Population Size Estimate*. Paper presented at the 60th Northwest Anthropology Conference, Washington State University, Pullman, Washington, March 15–17. Washington State University: Pullman, Washington.

McArthur, Lewis A. 1974. *Oregon Geographical Names*. 4th Ed., Oregon Historical Society Press: Portland, OR.

McCarthy, Helen 1993. *A Political Economy of Western Mono Acorn Production*. Ph.D. dissertation, Department of Anthropology, University of California, Berkley.

McClure, Dudley 1983. Sauvies Project Gets Approval of Engineers. *The Oregonian*. March 1983. The Oregonian Publishing Co.: Portland, OR. (from the Oregon Historical Society clip files).

McKenzie, K. 1974. *Ozette prehistory: prelude*. M.A. Thesis, Department of Archaeology, University of Calgary.

McMillan, A. D. and Hutchinson, I. 2002. When the Mountain Dwarfs Danced: Aboriginal Traditions of Paleoseismic Events along the Cascadia Subduction Zone of North America. *Ethnohistory* 49, 41–68.

Miall, Andrew D. 2006. *The Geology of Fluvial Deposits: Sedimentary Facies, Basin Analysis, and Petroleum Geology*. 4th Corrected Printing. Springer Berlin Heidelberg: New York.

Minnis, Paul E. 1981. Seeds in Archaeological Sites: Sources and Some Interpretive Problems. *American Antiquity* 46 (1) 143–152.

Moerman, Daniel E. 2002. *Native American Ethnobotany*. Portland, Oregon: Timber Press, Inc.

Moerman, Daniel E. 2003. *Native American Ethnobotany: A Database of Foods, Drugs, Dyes and Fibers of Native American Peoples, Derived from Plants*. University of Michigan, Dearborn.

Mullineaux, Donal R. 1996. Pre-1980 tephra-fall deposits erupted from Mount St. Helens, Washington. *U.S. Geological Survey Professional Paper 1563*, 1–99. [accessed Feb. 12, 2002 at http://greenwood.cr.usgs.gov/pub/ppapers/p1563/]

Munsell, David A. 1973. *An Archeological Survey of the Clark County Park at Vancouver Lake, Clark County, Washington*. Clark County Parks and Recreation Commission: Vancouver, Washington.

Munsell, David A. 1976a. The Wapato Creek fish weir site 45PI47, Tacoma, Washington. In Dale R. Croes (ed.), The excavation of water-saturated archaeological sites (wet sites) on the Northwest Coast of North America. *National Museum of Man Mercury Series* 50, 45–47.

Munsell, David A. 1976b. Excavation of the Conway wet site 45SK59b, Conway, Washington. In Dale R. Croes (ed.), The excavation of water-saturated archaeological sites (wet sites) on the Northwest Coast of North America. *National Museum of Man Mercury Series* 50:86–121.

Naftz, D. L. *et al.* 1996. Little Ice Age Evidence from a South-Central North Americana Ice Core, U.S.A. *Arctic and Alpine Research* 28(1), 35–41.

Nance, Jack D. 1971. Functional Interpretations From Microscopic Analysis. *American Antiquity* 36, 361–6.

National Oceanic and Atmospheric Administration 2007. National Weather Service Forecast Office, Portland, OR. http://www.wrh.noaa.gov/pqr/pdxclimate/index.php.

National Oceanic and Atmospheric Administration 2008. Port of Portland. Chart 18526, edition 58. Washington D.C.

Nelson, A.R., and K. Kashima 1993. Diatom zonation in southern Oregon tidal marshes relative to vascular plants, foraminifera, and sea level. *Journal of Coastal Research* 9, 673–697.

Ness, Olivia 2007. *Sauvie Basketry, Basketry Waste Materials and Experimental Archaeology* In Dale R. Croes, John L. Fagan and Maureen M. Zehendner (eds),*A U.S. National Historic Landmark Wet Site, the Sunken Village Site (35MU4), Portland, Oregon – the First Explorations*, Report No. 5, Department of Anthropology, South Puget Sound Community College and Archaeological Investigations Northwest, Inc., 129–149. Submitted as 2007 report to the Oregon State Historic Preservation Office.

Newman, Maureen McNassar 1991. *Description and Management Plan for 35MU4, The Sunken Village Archaeological Site At Sauvie Island, Multnomah County, Oregon.* Unpublished M. A. Thesis, Department of Anthropology. Portland State University.

Newman, Thomas M., and Judy Starkey 1977. Blue Lake Park Site. Ms. on file, Archaeological Investigations Northwest, Inc.: Portland, Oregon.

Nordquist, Delmar 1961. Bound net weights from 45SN100. *Washington Archaeologist* 5(1) January.

Nordquist, Delmar 1974. 45SN100 – The Biederbost site, Kidd's Duvall site. In Dale R. Croes (ed.), The excavation of water-saturated archaeological sites (wet sites) on the Northwest Coast of North America. *National Museum of Man Mercury Series* 50, 186–200.

Norton, Helen H. 1979. The Association between Anthropogenic Prairies and Important Food Plants in Western Washington. *Northwest Anthropological Research Notes* 13(2), 175–199.

NRCS 2006 PRISM Climate Mapping Project. Climate Summary, Portland, Oregon. http://www.ocs.orst.edu/page_links/climate_data_zones/info_sheets/mme6751.html.

O'Connor, Jim E. 2004. The Evolving Landscape of the Columbia River Gorge, Lewis and Clark, and Cataclysms on the Columbia. *Oregon Historical Quarterly* 105(3).

Odell, George H. 1981. The Mechanics of Use-Breakage of Stone Tools: Some Testable Hypotheses. *Journal of Field Archaeology* 8(22), 197–209.

Olivier, Adrian 2004. Great Expectations: the English Heritage Approach to the Management of the Historic Environment in England's Wetlands. *Journal of Wetland Archaeology* 4, 155–168.

Orem, Hollis M. 1968. *Discharge in the Lower Columbia River Basin, 1928–1965.* Geological Survey Circular 550. U.S. Department of the Interior.

Ortiz, Bev. 1991. *It Will Live Forever: Traditional Yosemite Indian Acorn Preparation.* Heyday Books: Berkeley, California.

Page, Lawrence and Brooks M. Burr 1991. *A Field Guide to Freshwater fishes, North America North of Mexico*. Houghton Mifflin Co.: Boston.

Pallister, John S., Richard P. Hoblitt, Dwight R. Crandell, and Donal R. Mullineaux 1992. Mount St. Helens a decade after the 1980 eruptions – Magmatic models, chemical cycles, and a revised hazards statement. *Bulletin of Volcanology* 54(2), 126–146.

Palmer, L. A. 1977. Large landslides of the Columbia River gorge, Oregon and Washington. I. Coates, D. R. (ed.), Landslides. Geological Society of America Reviews in *Engineering Geology* III, 69–83.

Pankow, H. 1990. *Ostee-Algenflora*. Jena, Gustav Fischer Verlag, 648.

Patrick, R. and C. W. Reimer 1966 The Diatoms of the United States Exclusive of Alaska and Hawaii. II (1). *Monographs of Academy of Natural Science*. Philadelphia, Pennsylvania. 13, 688.

Patrick, R. and C. W. Reimer 1975. The Diatoms of the United States Exclusive of Alaska and Hawaii. II (1). *Monographs of Academy of Natural Science*. Philadelphia, Pennsylvania. 13, 213.

Percy, Harrison and Gillian Waites 1997. *The Cassell Dictionary of Science*. London, England: Cassell Wellington House.

Personius, S. F., Dart, R. L., Bradley, L., and Haller, K. M. 2003. Map and data for Quaternary faults and folds in Oregon. U. S. Department of the Interior, U. S. Geological Survey, Open-File Report 03–095. Denver, Colorado: U. S. Geological Survey.

Peter, David and Constance Harrington 2002. Site and Tree Factors in Oregon White Oak Acorn Production in Western Washington and Oregon. *Northwest Science* 76(3), 189–201.

Peterkin, Gail L. 1993. Lithic and Organic hunting technology in the French Upper Paleolithic. In Gail Larson Peterkin, Harvey M. Bricker, and Paul Mellars (eds), *Hunting and Animal Exploitation in the Later Paleolithic and Mesolithic of Eurasia*, 49–68. Archeological Papers 4. Arlington, Virginia: American Anthropological Association.

Petersen, Marilyn 1978 *Mobile Stone Sculptures of the Lower Columbia River Valley*. M.A. Thesis. Portland State University. Portland, OR.

Peterson, Curt D., M. Scott Waibel, Daniel Bida, Tim Blazina, Darrick Boschmann, Adriane Bovero, Charles Cannon, Annie Donehey, Erin Dunbar, Kristy Hauver, Adam Jones, Keith Olson, G. Anthony Ordway, Danielle Sitts, T. J. Schepker, Fiona Seifert, and Steve Wilson 2007. *Hydrogeoarchaeology Investigation of Native American Acorn Leach Pits at Sauvie Island, Oregon: Preliminary GPR Profiling of Shallow-Subsurface Stratigraphy And LIDAR Landform Analysis of the Multnomah-Sauvie Island Channel Bank at the Sunken Village Locality*. Portland State University, Department of Geology. Report on file, Sunken Village Project, SPSCC.

Pettigrew, Richard M. 1973. Site form of 35MU4. On file, State Historic Preservation Office, Salem, Oregon.

Pettigrew, Richard M. 1977. *A Prehistoric Culture Sequence in the Portland Basin of the Lower Columbia Valley*. Ph.D. Dissertation, University of Oregon. Eugene, Oregon.

Pettigrew, Richard M. 1981. *A Prehistoric Culture Sequence in the Portland Basin of the Lower Columbia Valley*. C. Melvin (ed.). University of Oregon Anthropological Papers (22).

Pettigrew, Richard M. 1990. Prehistory of the Lower Columbia and Willamette Valley. In Wayne Suttles (ed.), *Handbook of North American Indians. Vol. 7. Northwest Coast*. Smithsonian: Washington D.C.

Pettigrew, Richard M., and Clayton G. Lebow 1987. *Archaeological Investigations at the Sunken Village Site (35MU4), Multnomah County, Oregon*. Infotech Research Incorporation Report

No. PNW87–10. Prepared for Oregon Division of State Lands. Salem, OR.

Pielou, E. C. 1998. *Fresh Water.* University of Chicago Press: Chicago, Il.

Pojar, Jim and Andy MacKinnon (eds) 1994. *Plants of the Pacific Northwest Coast: Washington, Oregon, British Columbia and Alaska.* Lone Pine Publishing: Renton, WA.

Postel, Sandra and Brian Richter 2003. *Rivers for Life: Managing Water for People and Nature.* Island Press: Washington D.C..

Pratt, T. L., J. Odum, W. Stephenson, R. Williams, S. Dadisman, M. Holmes, and B. Haug. 2001. Late Pleistocene and Holocene tectonics of the Portland Basin, Oregon and Washington, from high resolution seismic profiling. *Bulletin of the Seismological Society of America* 91(4), 637–650.

Pringle, Patrick T. 2002 [Revised Edition]. Roadside Geology of Mount St. Helens National Volcanic Monument and Vicinity. *Washington Division of Geology and Earth Resources Information Circular 88.* 1993, 1–122. Washington State Department of Natural Resources.

Pringle, Patrick T., Thomas C. Pierson, and Kenneth A. Cameron 2002. A circa A.D. 1781 eruption and lahars at Mount Hood, Oregon – Evidence from tree-ring dating and from observations of Lewis and Clark in 1805–6 [abstract]. *Geological Society of America Abstracts with Programs* 34(6), 511. [Accessed on May 29, 2007 at http://gsa.confex.com/gsa/2002AM/finalprogram/abstract_46581.htm]

Punke, Michele 2007. Geoarchaeological Investigations. In Dale R. Croes, John L. Fagan and Maureen M. Zehendner (eds), *A U.S. National Historic Landmark Wet Site, the Sunken Village Site (35MU4), Portland, Oregon – the First Explorations,* Report No. 5, Department of Anthropology, South Puget Sound Community College and Archaeological Investigations Northwest, Inc. Submitted as 2007 report to the Oregon State Historic Preservation Office.

Ray, Verne Frederick 1938. *Lower Chinook Ethnographic Notes.* University of Washington: Seattle.

Ray, Verne Frederick 1975. The Chinook Indians in the early 1800's In T. Vaughan (ed.), *The Western Shore: Oregon country essays honoring the American revolution,* 120–149. Portland: Oregon Historical Society. HRAF Publication Information: New Haven, Conn.: HRAF, 2004. Computer File.

Reese, Jo, John L. Fagan, William F. Willingham, and Bonnie Mills. 1990. Report to the Oregon State Historic Preservation Office on Results of the Columbia River Shoreline Archaeological Survey. *The Cultural Heritage Foundation Report* 2(1) Part 1. Portland, Oregon.

Renfrew, Jane M. 1973. *Paleoethnobotany.* Columbia University Press, New York.

Robock, Alan 2000. Volcanic Eruptions and Climate. *Reviews of Geophysics* 38(2) Paper No. 1998RG000054. http://geog-www.sbs.ohio-state.edu/courses/G820.01/volcanic%20eruption%20and%20climate.pdf.

Rockey, Clinton C. D. 2007. *Climate of Portland Oregon.* Climate Narrative. NOAA National Weather Service Forecast Office, Portland, OR. 2007. http://www.wrh.noaa.gov/pdxclimate/PG1TO4.html.

Saleeby, Becky 1983. *Prehistoric Settlement Patterns in the Portland Basin of the Lower Columbia River: Ethnohistoric, Archaeological, and Biogeographic Perspectives.* Ph.D. dissertation. University of Oregon.

Schopmeyer, C. S. 1974. Seeds of Woody Plants In the United States. In *Agriculture Handbook* No. 450. Forest Service, U. S. Department of Agriculture, Washington, D. C.

Shennan Stephen 1997. *Quantifying Archaeology.* 2nd edition. Iowa Press.

Silverstein, Michael 1990. Chinookans of the Lower Columbia. In Wayne Suttles (ed.), *Handbook of North American Indians Vol. 7. Northwest Coast*. Smithsonian Institution: Washington D.C.

Smart, Tristine Lee and Ellen S. Hoffman 1988. Environmental Interpretation of Archaeological Charcoal. In Hastorf C. and Popper, V. (eds), *Current Paleoethnobotany: Analytical Methods and Cultural Interpretation of Archaeological Plant Remains*, 167–205. The University of Chicago Press, Chicago and London.

Spencer, Omar Corwin 1950. *The Story of Sauvies Island*. Binfords and Mort. Portland, Oregon.

Springer, Vera 1976. *Power and the Pacific Northwest: a History of the Bonneville Power Administration 1937–1976*. Paul Alelyunas and Dan Schausten (eds). U.S. Department of the Interior.

Steele, H. 1978. 35MU4 Endangered. *Screenings* 28:2. Portland, Oregon: Oregon Archaeological Society.

Stein, William I. 1990. Quercus garryana Dougl. ex Hook. In *Silvics of North America*, Volume 2, Hardwoods, USDA Forest Service Agriculture Handbook 654. R.M. Bums and B.H. Honkala, technical coordinators, 650–660. Washington, D.C.: USDA Forest Service.

Stenholm, Nancy 1994. "Flotation Results from 45PC101" Appendix 1 in Ray DePuydt (ed.), *Data Recovery Excavations from Site 45PC101 Pacific County, Washington*. Eastern Washington University Reports in Archaeology and History, 100–79. Eastern Washington University Press, Spokane, WA.

Stewart, Hilary 1973. *Artifacts of the Northwest Coast Indians*. Hancock House Publishers, Saanichton, B.C.

Stewart, Hilary 1984. *Cedar*. University of Washington Press, Seattle.

Strong, Emory 1952. Sauvies Island Cooking Pits. *The Sunday Oregonian Magazine*. June 11, 1952. The Oregonian Publishing Company. Portland, OR.

Strong, Emory 1959. *Stone Age on the Columbia River*. Binfords and Mort. Portland, Oregon.

Strong, E. and Galbraith, H. (eds) 1955. Pothunter's Prize Proves Perfect. *Screenings* 4:2. Portland, Oregon: Oregon Archaeological Society.

Suttles, Wayne (ed.) 1990. *Handbook of North American Indians, Vol. 7: Northwest Coast*. Washington, D.C.: Smithsonian Institute.

Swofford, David L. 1998. *PAUP*: Phylogenetic Analysis Using Parsimony (*and other methods). Version 4.0*. Sunderland, MA. Sinauer Associates.

Thwaites, Reuben Gold (ed.) 1969. (1904–1905) Original Journals of the Lewis and Clark Expedition 1804–1806. 8 Vols. Arno Press. New York NY.

Tucker, Libby 2007. "Spokane, Washington Based General Contractor for Sauvie Island Bridge." *Daily Journal of Commerce*, Portland, OR, December 3, 2007.

USACE (US Army Corps of Engineers) Portland District 2003. Reservoir Regulation and Water Quality Section; Graphics/Willamette Project. December 2003. http://www.nwd-wc.usace.army.mil/nwp/graphics/willproj.html.

USACE (US Army Corps of Engineers) 2004. Portland-Vancouver Harbor Information Packet. Second Edition. Reservoir Regulation and Water Quality Section. http://www.nwd-wc.usace.army.mil/nwp/Reports/Portland_Harbor.pdf.

USDA (U.S. Department of Agriculture), Soil Conservation Service 1983. *Soil Survey of Multnomah County, Oregon*. Soil Conservation Service and Oregon Agricultural Experimental Station, Corvalis/Portland.

USDA (U.S. Department of Agriculture), Natural Resource Conservation Service 2008. *Plants Database*. http://plants.usda.gov/index.html

U.S. Environmental Protection Agency (EPA) 1996. To Prepare a Draft Environmental Impact Statement for the Willamette River Basin Review Feasibility Study. *Federal Register Environmental Documents*. 61 (187).

U.S. Environmental Protection Agency (EPA) 2006. Columbia River Basin. *Columbia/ Snake River Maps and Photo Gallery*. http://yosemite.epa.gov/R10/WATER. NSF/ac5dc0447a281f4e882569ed0073521f/5896e9e63772fad288256a31005570b8!- OpenDocument.

U.S. Environmental Protection Agency (EPA) 2006. Willamette River: Fact Sheet. *American Heritage Rivers*. http://www.epa.gov/rivers/98rivers/fswillam.html.

U.S. Geological Survey (USGS) 1999 Volcanic Sulfur Aerosols Affect Global Climate and the Earth's Ozone Layer. *Volcano Hazards Program*. 14 November 1999. VHP WWW Team. U.S. Department of the Interior, U.S. Geological Survey, Menlo Park, CA, USA.2006 Description: Mount Hood Volcano, Oregon. Cascades Volcano Observatory. Vancouver, Washington. http://vulcan.wr.usgs.gov/Volcanoes/Hood/description_hood.html.

Wagner, Gail E. 1982. Testing Flotation Recovery Rates. *American Antiquity* 47(1), 127– 132.

Waibel, M. S., Bida, D., Blazina, T., Boschmann, D., Bovero, A., Cannon, C., Donehey, A., Dunbar, E., Hauver, K., Jones, A., Olson, K., Ordway, G. A., Peterson, C. D., Sitts, D., Schepker, T. J., Seifert, F., Wilson, S. 2007. *Hydrogeoarchaeology Investigation of Native American Acorn Leach Pits at Sauvie Island, Oregon: Preliminary GPR Profiling of Shallow-Subsurface Stratigraphy And LIDAR Landform Analysis of the Multnomah-Sauvie Island Channel Bank at the Sunken Village Locality*. Unpublished Field Report, Portland State University, Oregon.

Walshaw, Sarah 2004. *Flotation Methods for Eastern African Archaeology*. Unpublished paper, Department of Archaeology, Simon Fraser University, Burnaby, B.C.

White, Richard 1980 *Land Use, Environment, and Social Change: the shaping of Island County, Washington*. University of Washington Press: Seattle, Washington.

Wilkins, David E. 2007. *American Indian Politics and American Political System*. Rowman and Littlefield Publishers, Inc: New York, New York.

Wong, I., W. Silva, J. Bott, D. Wright, P. Thomas, N. Gregor, S. Li, M. Mabey, A. Sojourner, Y. Wang. 1999. *Earthquake scenario and probabilistic ground shaking maps for the Portland, Oregon metropolitan area*. Technical report to U.S. Geological Survey, under Contract 1434–HQ–96–GR-02727, 16p., 12pls.

Wray, Jacilee 2009 (in prep.). *From the Hands of a Weaver: Olympic Peninsula Basketry through Time*.

Yamaguchi, David K. 1983. New tree-ring dates for Recent eruptions of Mount St. Helens. *Quaternary Research*. 20(2), 246–250.

Yeats, R. S., Sieh, K., and Allen, C. R. 1997. *The Geology of Earthquakes*. Oxford University Press, Inc.: New York, New York.

Young, James A. and Cheryl G. Young. 1994. [1992] *Seeds of Woody Plants in North America* (revised and enlarged edition). Portland, Oregon: Dioscorides Press

End-piece. Experimental acorn-leaching pit. A half-pit has been constructed in a fish aquarium, lined with hemlock boughs and filled with acorns, to show the equivalent of a section through an ancient acorn-leaching pit (cf. Figure 6.7). Water was pumped through the model for five months, to remove the tannic acid from the acorns. Experiment and aquarium model sponsored as a future exhibit in the Siletz Cultural Center by the Siletz Tribal Charitable Contributions Fund, grant No. 07-969.

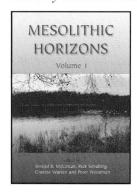

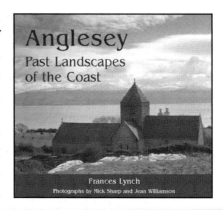